Service Oriented Architecture For Dummies®

Cheat Sheet

D0764648

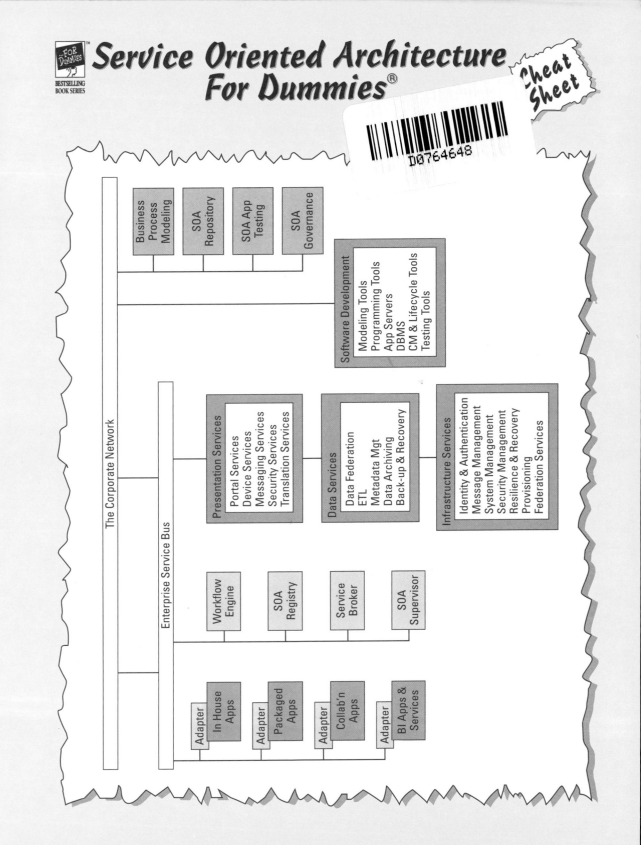

Service Oriented Architecture For Dummies®

Cheat Sheet

Elements of an SOA (Keeping things in the figure straight)

- **Adapter:** A software module added to an application or system that allows access to its capabilities via a standards-compliant services interface.

- **Business Process Modeling:** A procedure for mapping out what the business process does, both in terms of what various applications are expected to do and what the human participants in the business process are expected to do.

- **Enterprise Service Bus:** The enterprise service bus is the communications nerve center for services in a service oriented architecture. It tends to be a jack-of-all-trades, connecting to various types of middleware, repositories of metadata definitions (such as how we define a customer number), registries (how to locate information), and interfaces of every kind (for just about any application).

- **Service Broker:** Software in an SOA framework that brings components together using the rules associated with each component.

- **SOA Governance:** SOA governance is an element of overall IT governance, and as such lays down the law when it comes to policy, process, and metadata management. (Metadata here simply means data that defines the source of the data, the owner of the data, and who can change the data.)

- **SOA Repository:** A database for all SOA software and components, with an emphasis on revision control and configuration management. Where they keep the good stuff, in other words.

- **SOA Supervisor:** Software that orchestrates the entire collection of computers, network resources, and software in an SOA framework so that they can run continuously at an appropriate level of service.

- **SOA Registry:** A single source for all the metadata needed to utilize the Web service of a software component in a SOA environment.

Wiley, the Wiley Publishing logo, For Dummies, the Dummies Man logo, the For Dummies Bestselling Book Series logo and all related trade dress are trademarks or registered trademarks of John Wiley & Sons, Inc. and/or its affiliates. All other trademarks are property of their respective owners.

Copyright © 2007 Wiley Publishing, Inc.
All rights reserved.

Item 5435-2.

For more information about Wiley Publishing,
call 1-800-762-2974.

For Dummies: Bestselling Book Series for Beginners

Service Oriented Architecture

FOR

DUMMIES®

Service Oriented Architecture

FOR DUMMIES®

by Judith Hurwitz, Robin Bloor, Carol Baroudi,
and Marcia Kaufman

Wiley Publishing, Inc.

Service Oriented Architecture For Dummies®

Published by
Wiley Publishing, Inc.
111 River Street
Hoboken, NJ 07030-5774
www.wiley.com

Copyright © 2007 by Wiley Publishing, Inc., Indianapolis, Indiana

Published by Wiley Publishing, Inc., Indianapolis, Indiana

Published simultaneously in Canada

No part of this publication may be reproduced, stored in a retrieval system or transmitted in any form or by any means, electronic, mechanical, photocopying, recording, scanning or otherwise, except as permitted under Sections 107 or 108 of the 1976 United States Copyright Act, without either the prior written permission of the Publisher, or authorization through payment of the appropriate per-copy fee to the Copyright Clearance Center, 222 Rosewood Drive, Danvers, MA 01923, (978) 750-8400, fax (978) 646-8600. Requests to the Publisher for permission should be addressed to the Legal Department, Wiley Publishing, Inc., 10475 Crosspoint Blvd., Indianapolis, IN 46256, (317) 572-3447, fax (317) 572-4355, or online at http://www.wiley.com/go/permissions.

Trademarks: Wiley, the Wiley Publishing logo, For Dummies, the Dummies Man logo, A Reference for the Rest of Us!, The Dummies Way, Dummies Daily, The Fun and Easy Way, Dummies.com, and related trade dress are trademarks or registered trademarks of John Wiley & Sons, Inc. and/or its affiliates in the United States and other countries, and may not be used without written permission. All other trademarks are the property of their respective owners. Wiley Publishing, Inc., is not associated with any product or vendor mentioned in this book.

LIMIT OF LIABILITY/DISCLAIMER OF WARRANTY: THE PUBLISHER AND THE AUTHOR MAKE NO REPRESENTATIONS OR WARRANTIES WITH RESPECT TO THE ACCURACY OR COMPLETENESS OF THE CONTENTS OF THIS WORK AND SPECIFICALLY DISCLAIM ALL WARRANTIES, INCLUDING WITHOUT LIMITATION WARRANTIES OF FITNESS FOR A PARTICULAR PURPOSE. NO WARRANTY MAY BE CREATED OR EXTENDED BY SALES OR PROMOTIONAL MATERIALS. THE ADVICE AND STRATEGIES CONTAINED HEREIN MAY NOT BE SUITABLE FOR EVERY SITUATION. THIS WORK IS SOLD WITH THE UNDERSTANDING THAT THE PUBLISHER IS NOT ENGAGED IN RENDERING LEGAL, ACCOUNTING, OR OTHER PROFESSIONAL SERVICES. IF PROFESSIONAL ASSISTANCE IS REQUIRED, THE SERVICES OF A COMPETENT PROFESSIONAL PERSON SHOULD BE SOUGHT. NEITHER THE PUBLISHER NOR THE AUTHOR SHALL BE LIABLE FOR DAMAGES ARISING HEREFROM. THE FACT THAT AN ORGANIZATION OR WEBSITE IS REFERRED TO IN THIS WORK AS A CITATION AND/OR A POTENTIAL SOURCE OF FURTHER INFORMATION DOES NOT MEAN THAT THE AUTHOR OR THE PUBLISHER ENDORSES THE INFORMATION THE ORGANIZATION OR WEBSITE MAY PROVIDE OR RECOMMENDATIONS IT MAY MAKE. FURTHER, READERS SHOULD BE AWARE THAT INTERNET WEBSITES LISTED IN THIS WORK MAY HAVE CHANGED OR DISAPPEARED BETWEEN WHEN THIS WORK WAS WRITTEN AND WHEN IT IS READ.

For general information on our other products and services, please contact our Customer Care Department within the U.S. at 800-762-2974, outside the U.S. at 317-572-3993, or fax 317-572-4002.

For technical support, please visit www.wiley.com/techsupport.

Wiley also publishes its books in a variety of electronic formats. Some content that appears in print may not be available in electronic books.

Library of Congress Control Number: 2006927652

ISBN-13: 978-0-470-05435-2

ISBN-10: 0-470-05435-2

Manufactured in the United States of America

10 9 8 7 6 5 4 3 2

1B/RV/QS/QX/IN

WILEY

About the Authors

Judith Hurwitz has been a leader in the technology research and strategy consulting fields for more than 20 years. In 1992, she founded the industry-leading research and consulting organization, Hurwitz Group. Currently, she is the President of Hurwitz & Associates, a research and consulting firm with a portfolio of service offerings focused on identifying customer benefit and best practices for buyers and sellers of information technology in the United States and Europe.

Judith has held senior positions at John Hancock and Apollo Computer and is a frequent keynote speaker at industry events. She earned BS and MS degrees from Boston University and was honored by Boston University's College of Arts & Sciences, when it named her a distinguished alumnus in 2005. She is also a recipient of the 2005 Massachusetts Technology Leadership Council award.

Robin Bloor was born in Liverpool, England, in the 1950s, a little too late to become a member of The Beatles and, in any event, completely bereft of musical talent. In his late teens he went to Nottingham University, where he acquired a degree in mathematics, a love for computers, and a number of severe hangovers.

After toiling in the English IT trenches for a number of years, Robin, following in the steps of the Pilgrim Fathers, emigrated to the United States, eventually settling in Texas. In 2003, for reasons beyond his comprehension, he was awarded an honorary PhD in Computer Science by Wolverhampton University in the United Kingdom, in recognition of "Services to the IT Industry." In 2004, he became a partner with Hurwitz & Associates.

Carol Baroudi makes technical concepts understandable to ordinary human beings. She's the primary instigator and eager co-conspirator with Judith, Robin, and Marcia on their first *For Dummies* venture. Clocking more than 30 years in the computer industry, she's been writing *For Dummies* books since 1993. (You might be familiar with *The Internet For Dummies* in one of its ten editions.) Carol's been an industry analyst since 1999 and now leads SOA Research for the Aberdeen Group.

Marcia Kaufman is a founding partner of Hurwitz & Associates. With 20 years of experience in business strategy, industry research, and analytics, her primary research focus is on the business and technology benefit of emerging technologies. She has a special interest in information management, information as a service, and data quality. Marcia received her MBA from Boston University School of Management and her BA in Mathematics and Economics from Connecticut College.

Dedication

Judith dedicates her part of the book to her family — her husband, Warren, her children, Sara and David, and her mother, Elaine. She also dedicates this book in memory of her father, David.

Robin dedicates his part of the book to Judy, for her encouragement, support, and advice.

Carol dedicates her part of the book to Josh, with all her love.

Marcia dedicates her part of the book to her husband, Matthew, her daughters, Sara and Emily, and her parents, Larry and Gloria.

Authors' Acknowledgments

We heartily thank our friends at Wiley, most especially Mary Bednarek, Katie Feltman and Paul Levesque. Thank you to our tech editor, Arnold Reinhold. Our colleagues at Hurwitz & Associates, particularly Carol Caliendo, Fern Halper, and Fran Howarth, deserve our heartfelt thanks. We also thank Hurwitz friends Judy Reiser, Beverly Bruce, Paula Slotkin, Sabrina Horn, Andrew Joseph, Nelson Hsu, Vickie Farrell, and Todd Stone.

Though the entire software industry is espousing SOA, the commitment from Sandy Carter at IBM to help make this book happen was instrumental in its timely release. Thanks to IBMers Steve Mills, Robert LeBlanc, Bob Zurek, Michael Curry, Glen Hintze, John Simonds, John Choi, Shaun Jones, Sarita Torres, and Martha Leversuch.

Thanks to HP's David Gee, Mark Potts, Ann Livermore, Russ Daniels, Mark Perreira, Cheryl Rose Hayden, and Mike Jastrab.

Thanks to Progress Software's John Stewart, Stacey Redden Dore, and Trip Kucera; Jboss's Shaun Connoly; Oracle's Claire Dessaux; Microsoft's Jason Campbell; and SAP's Ramin Hummel.

Thanks to Starwood Hotels' Israel del Rio; Delaware Electric's Gary Cripps; NYSE's Firas Sammen; Whirlpool Corporation's Esat Sezer; ecenter solutions' Didier Beck and Nick Stefania; Helio's Brandon Behrstock and Rick Heineman; Jack Henry & Associates' Kevin Sligar; RLPTechnologies' Norman Marks and Joe Lafeir; Schwarz Communications' Amy Burnis; Waggener Edstrom's Rob Schatz; and Burson-Marsteller's Lisa Newman Lindenbaum.

Publisher's Acknowledgments

We're proud of this book; please send us your comments through our online registration form located at `www.dummies.com/register/`.

Some of the people who helped bring this book to market include the following:

Acquisitions, Editorial, and Media Development

Project Editor: Paul Levesque

Acquisitions Editor: Katie Feltman

Copy Editor: Andy Hollandbeck

Technical Editor: Arnold Reinhold

Editorial Manager: Leah Cameron

Media Development Specialists: Angela Denny, Kate Jenkins, Steven Kudirka, Kit Malone

Media Development Coordinator: Laura Atkinson

Media Project Supervisor: Laura Moss

Media Development Manager: Laura VanWinkle

Editorial Assistant: Amanda Foxworth

Sr. Editorial Assistant: Cherie Case

Cartoons: Rich Tennant (`www.the5thwave.com`)

Composition Services

Project Coordinator: Adrienne Martinez

Layout and Graphics: Claudia Bell, Jonelle Burns, Lavonne Cook, Heather Ryan, Rashell Smith, Alicia South

Proofreaders: Laura Albert, Christine Pingleton, Techbooks

Indexer: Techbooks

Anniversary Logo Design: Richard Pacifico

Publishing and Editorial for Technology Dummies

> **Richard Swadley,** Vice President and Executive Group Publisher
>
> **Andy Cummings,** Vice President and Publisher
>
> **Mary Bednarek,** Executive Acquisitions Director
>
> **Mary C. Corder,** Editorial Director

Publishing for Consumer Dummies

> **Diane Graves Steele,** Vice President and Publisher
>
> **Joyce Pepple,** Acquisitions Director

Composition Services

> **Gerry Fahey,** Vice President of Production Services
>
> **Debbie Stailey,** Director of Composition Services

Contents at a Glance

Table of Contents

Introduction

Welcome to Service Oriented Architecture (SOA) For Dummies. We are very excited by this topic and hope our enthusiasm is contagious. We believe SOA is the most important technology initiative facing businesses today. SOA is game changing, and early SOA successes make it clear that SOA is here to stay. We hope this book is enough to ground you in SOA basics and to whet your appetite for the SOA adventure.

Service oriented architecture is more than a bunch of new software products strung together to allow technology companies to have something else to sell. SOA represents a dramatic change in the relationship between business and IT. SOA makes technology a true business enabler and empowers business and technology leaders alike.

The software industry has been on a journey toward a service oriented approach to software for more than 20 years. Smart people have known for a long time that if software can be created in such a way that it can be reused, life will be a lot better. If software can be designed to reflect the way business operates, business and technology can align themselves for success. Finding good ways to reuse the years of investment in software means money spent wisely. These issues are at the heart of SOA and are among the reasons we think this book is so important.

SOA is not a quick fix, but a very rewarding adventure. It's an approach built on industry standards — with large doses of forethought and planning. It is indeed a journey. We hope this book inspires you and helps you get started.

About This Book

Service oriented architecture is a big new area and requires that a lot of people familiarize themselves with it in a relatively short period of time. That's why we wrote this book. Some people may want to get deeper into the technological details, while others may care only about the business implications.

We recommend that you read the first five chapters, regardless of how deeply or shallowly you want to wander into the SOA pool. They ground you in basic SOA concepts and prepare you for intelligent conversations about the subject. We also recommend that everyone read the case studies in Part V, "Real Life with SOA," because seeing how real people are putting SOA to work is probably the best way to get a handle on what's in it for you.

You can read from cover to cover, if you're that kind of person, but we've tried to adhere to the *For Dummies* style of keeping chapters self-contained so that you can go straight to the topics that interest you most. Wherever you start, we wish you well.

Foolish Assumptions

Try as we might to be all things to all people, when it came to writing this book, we had to pick who we thought would be most interested in *Service Oriented Architecture For Dummies*. Here's who we think you are:

- ✔ **You're smart.** You're no dummy, yet the topic of service oriented architecture gives you an uneasy feeling; you can't quite get your head around it, and if pressed for a definition, you might try to change the subject.
- ✔ **You're a businessperson who wants little or nothing to do with technology,** but you live in the 21st century and find that you can't actually escape it. Everybody around is saying "SOA this" and "SOA that," so you think you better find out what they're talking about.
- ✔ **Alternatively, you're an IT person who knows a heck of a lot about technology,** but this SOA stuff is new, and everybody says it's something different. Once and for all, you want the whole picture.

Whoever you are, welcome. We're here to help.

How This Book Is Organized

We divide our book into six parts for easy consumption of SOA topics. Feel free to skip about.

Part 1: Introducing SOA

In this part, we explain why SOA is such a big deal and why you should care. We also introduce you to the major concepts and components so that you can hold your own in any meaningful conversation about SOA.

Part 11: Nitty-Gritty SOA

Some folks are more technically oriented than others, and in Part II we dive deeper into the actual SOA architecture components. The material in these chapters is groundbreaking. We've done the research and put into print concepts that the software industry has been struggling to articulate for the past few years. At this point, you won't find this material anywhere else in print.

Part III: SOA Sustenance

Creating a SOA is one thing. Keeping it up and running, growing, adapting, and supporting business requires a lot more. This part delves into areas critical to SOA's longevity.

Part IV: Getting Started with SOA

When you've had enough concept and think you're ready to start your journey, we have some pointers on how to get started.

Part V: Real Life with SOA

SOA is real. Real businesses are using it today to great advantage. This part shares stories that come to us from eight companies actively helping organizations put SOA into practice. We interviewed people from each of the projects we describe. You can take their word for it. SOA rules!

Part VI: The Part of Tens

If you're new to the *For Dummies* treasure trove, you're no doubt unfamiliar with "The Part of Tens." In "The Part of Tens," Wiley editors torture *For Dummies* authors into creating useful bits of information easily accessible in lists containing ten (more or less) elucidating elements. We started these chapters kicking and screaming but are ultimately very glad they're here. We think you'll be, too.

Appendixes

The Glossary
We try diligently to define terms as we go along, but we think having a handy-dandy reference is very useful.

Icons Used in This Book

We think this a particularly useful point to pay attention to.

Pay attention. The bother you save may be your own.

You may be sorry if this little tidbit slips your mind.

Tidbits for the more technically inclined that we hope augment their understanding, but those with sensitive stomachs can gleefully avoid that.

Where to Go from Here

We've created an overview of SOA and introduce you to all its significant components. Many chapters here could be expanded into full-length books of their own. Depending on your desires, you can drill down on any particular topic or keep up with general trends by checking out Chapter 27. (Don't forget to check out the book's Web site at www.dummies.com/go/soafordummies for more goodies.) SOA is a big theme for us at Hurwitz & Associates, and we invite you to visit our Web site and sign up for our newsletter at www.hurwitz.com.

Part I
Introducing SOA

The 5th Wave   By Rich Tennant

"That reminds me — I have to sort out the business services on the corporate network."

In this part . . .

SOA's a big deal, but what is it exactly? In this part, we tell you the whys and wherefores of SOA to ground you in essential SOA concepts and prepare you for the journey ahead.

Chapter 1

SOA What?

Service oriented architecture (SOA) is the hottest topic being bandied about by IT vendors across the globe. IBM, HP, BEA, Oracle, SAP, and Microsoft (just to drop a few names) are all singing from the SOA songbook, and hundreds of vendors are adding their tunes as we speak.

"What's SOA?" you ask. We suspect that you've already skimmed a dozen articles and recycled a tree's-worth of junk mail from vendors pushing SOA, but the answers you've gotten so far have been, well, vague and inadequate. The short answer is that SOA is a new approach to building IT systems that allows businesses to leverage existing assets and easily enable the inevitable changes required to support the business.

For you impatient readers out there, know that we expand on this short answer in Chapter 2. However, right now, we think the more important question is, "Why should I care about SOA?" We try to answer this question first.

The promise of service oriented architecture is to liberate business from the constraints of technology and unshackle technologists from the chains they themselves have forged. ("IT workers of the world, unite! You have nothing to lose but your chains!" as it were.) This has major implications both for the business and for the IT that supports the business.

From our perspective, one of the most important aspects of SOA is that it is a *business* approach and methodology as much as it is a *technological* approach and methodology. SOA enables businesses to make business decisions *supported* by technology instead of making business decisions *determined* by or *constrained* by technology. And with SOA, the folks in IT finally get to say "yes" more often than they say "no."

We pronounce *SOA* to rhyme with *boa*. Stretching it out by clearly articulating each letter (S-O-A) is perfectly acceptable, but may leave you stymied when we say things like "SOA what?"

Business Lib

One of the myths that plagues business today is that senior management is in charge. Yes, we know who holds the title, but a management title is a lot like the title to a car. The title is one thing, and the keys are another. And, although no one ever saw it coming, the keys to the business have been slipping, little by little, into the hands of IT. This is not good for business, and what is not good for business is ultimately not good for IT because without the business, IT ceases to exist.

Now, we are not advocating that business should (or can) wrest the keys from the hands of IT. Our businesses are inextricably tied to technology. No sizable business can function without IT — it's as simple as that. However, we are advocating a new world order. We are advocating that business and IT work together to create this new world order. *Together,* business leaders and IT determine how the business should operate and work together to make it a reality by using SOA. *Together,* IT and business leaders determine a strategy that both liberates business from IT and allows IT to create maintainable, extensible, compliant systems.

Tech Lib

Just because business has become constrained by technology, don't think the folks in IT are having a jolly old time basking in their new-found power. On the contrary, the IT staff gets to spend its time in endless meetings accounting for why projects are late, explaining why applications can't easily be adapted to changing business conditions, and pleading for more staff. When some clever marketer presents a new concept for selling more widgets via the Internet or mobile devices or some other new channel, IT management is always the wet blanket, having to explain why, despite the company's investment in all the latest software and hardware, it will take 18 months to implement the new plan.

With SOA, corporate geeks finally get to be part of the business adventure again, developing new ways to use technology to grow the firm, helping to spot new trends and opportunities, and seeing new ideas to fruition. But before you go marching off to save the world, we have some more explaining to do. A story will help.

Once Upon a Time

Once upon a time, there was an insurance company called ABC Insurance Incorporated. When ABC was born, oh, maybe 150 years ago, it began by selling insurance policies to factories and manufacturers. In those days, there were no computers to mess things up. A nice person sent a letter inquiring about a policy. A smart person set a rate, sold a policy, and hoped that nothing caught fire or blew up. ABC thrived for more than a hundred years.

But then, things got complicated. Other companies started stealing their business. Customers were asking for insurance for different kinds of risk. ABC had to change or die.

ABC was an early user of punch-card accounting systems. In the 1960s, ABC bought computers and hired programmers and built software applications to support its business. In the 1980s, it bought software packages from different suppliers to help it continue to compete. It bought or built business applications to solve problems all over the company — one at a time. For example, it bought an application for the corporate finance department, created one to handle customer claims, and procured other applications to manage research information about what type of accidents were most common under what circumstances.

This worked well for many years, until the 1990s, when ABC found itself competing against financial services companies who decided *they* could sell insurance, too. Suddenly, ABC needed to find new ways to make money that didn't cost too much. Its leaders thought up exciting new solutions based on the knowledge of their business and their customers and through new, cool *technology.*

In addition, Management thought ABC could better compete by acquiring some other insurance companies with complementary products. ABC could sell these new products to existing ABC customers and sell ABC's products to the customers of the companies they acquired. These smart guys and gals understood business strategy. Everyone got really excited until . . .

Management talked to IT, and IT said, "This is really, really exciting, but we have a *small* problem."

"What could it be?" cried Management.

"It is this," said IT. "We can no longer simply buy or build more programs to implement our new moneymaking, cost-saving ideas. Everything we want to do has to work in concert with what we already have. The very running of our company depends on all the business applications that we have built and acquired over years working together smoothly — the programs to tally the money coming in, the programs to administer the claims processing going out, to do risk analysis, premium billing, payroll, invoicing, and sales commission calculation. When you come right down to it, our company is the aggregation of all our programs. Everything we need in order to carry out our day-to-day business functions — all our policies and information, including all the information about our customers — is locked inside these programs."

"Well," said Management, "You can just write new programs to tie everything together. We'll *integrate* and we will all be very happy."

And IT said, "Yes, it is possible to *integrate*, but integrating will take *a very, very long time*. Integrating will take at least 18 months, maybe 2 years, and by then you may want more changes that will take another 18 months or 2 years, and by then it may be too late. And," IT continued, "*it will cost lots and lots of money*."

Management and IT were very sad. They knew that ABC would not survive if they couldn't find *a new way of thinking*. So they began asking everyone they knew if there was any way to save ABC. They searched and they studied and they prayed until one day a package arrived from Amazon.com. In that package were several copies of a yellow-and-black book. On the cover of the yellow-and-black books, they read *Service Oriented Architecture For Dummies*.

Both Management and IT took copies of the book and read. They were very excited to discover that they didn't have to throw stuff away and that they could reap benefits in a short time. In the end, they came up with a *new* strategy, one based on four key elements:

1. The IT organization will partner with the line of business managers to create a high-level map of what the business will look like.

2. The IT organization will create a flexible structure that will turn key IT software assets into reusable services that can be used no matter how the business changes. These services will include everything from business processes and best practices to consistent data definitions to code that performs specific business functions.

3. The IT organization will use only accepted industry standards to link these software assets together.

4. The IT organization will use the service oriented architecture concept described in the rest of this book to begin to create business services that are consistent with the way the business operates.

Together, Management and IT began a journey, and, as far as we know, they are living happily ever after . . . In Part V, we give you many real-life case studies from real-life companies you may know that indeed are alive and well and living happily on their *Journey to SOA.*

Better Living through Reuse

One of the biggest deals in the SOA world is the idea that you don't throw things out. You take the stuff (software assets) that you use every day — well, the *best* of the stuff you use every day — and package it in a way that lets you use it, reuse it, and keep on reusing it.

One problem common to many large companies that have been around for a while is that they have lots of similar programs. Every time a department wants something slightly different, the department builds its own version of that something so that, across a particular company, you can find umpteen versions of more or less the same program — with, of course, slight variations. Many IT shops have policies and procedures designed to prevent this sort of thing, but when deadlines loom and budgets are tight, it's often easier and quicker to write something from scratch that fills the need rather than coordinate with other divisions. This sort of duplication also happens a lot when one company acquires another and finds that they have similar (but not identical) programs purporting to do the same thing.

These slight variations are precisely what make systems very complicated and expensive to maintain — if you make a change in business policy that affects the sundry applications, for example, you have to find and change each and every instance in every application that is affected. And even the slightest difference in implementation can result in inconsistencies — not a nice thing to find when those compliance auditors come snooping.

With SOA, these important programs become *business services.* (We talk more about this in Chapter 2.) You end up with one single business service for a given function that gets used everywhere in your organization. With SOA, when you need to change a business policy, you change it in one place and, because the same service is used everywhere, you have consistency throughout your organization.

For example, you know that if you decide to create a new department in your organization, you are not going to create a new Accounting department, new Human Resources department, new Legal department, new Cleaning department, new Training department, and new Travel department to go along with it. We trust that you will use your existing Accounting department (you may have to add staff), your existing HR, and your existing Cleaning, Training, and Travel departments to — note the expression — *service* this new department.

The problem is that, over time, IT — not those nice folks in the IT department today, but IT *over time* — ends up embedding redundant function in individual programs everywhere in the organization. That redundancy, just like having separate Accounting, HR, Legal, Cleaning, Training, and Travel departments for every department, is what SOA will ultimately eliminate — giving you the same obvious benefits of scalability, consistency, and maintainability.

With SOA, business managers work with IT to identify business services. Together, they determine policy and best practices. These policies and best practices become *codified business services,* impervious to the whims and fancies of errant engineers, audacious autocrats, tyrannous technologists, business bigots, and other such unsavory suspects. No more random acts of software. No more self-designated despots. Hail the new world order!

Dancing with Strangers

If you dance any kind of formal dance, from the cha-cha to the waltz, you know that form matters. The *form* is what allows you to dance with someone you've never met. When both partners truly know the form, they move in tandem, are flexible, and navigate with ease and grace.

SOA is form. It enables the business to move, change, partner, and reinvent itself with ease and grace. In the beginning, mastering new steps requires focus and attention. Over time, the steps become second nature.

Implicit in the notion of form is standards. Using industry standard interfaces and creating business services without dependencies (more later, we promise) allows the business vastly more flexibility than it enjoys today to change its business model, to reorchestrate itself, and to partner dynamically.

You feel confident that the appliances that you plug in at home today will plug in equally well at the office or if you move across town. You may also be aware that if you travel abroad, you will likely need adapters. You can plug in anywhere that the standard interfaces agree. Where they are different, you must adapt. Likewise, working with industry standards set forth by standards bodies enables autonomous entities (partners, customers, suppliers, hint, hint) to dance at the ball.

Redundant reiteration again

For any IT old-timers out there who have labored long and hard in the IT trenches, the concept of reuse is not new. You're familiar with the great theme of object orientation, and you extol the virtues of standardization. "What's the big deal with SOA?" you ask. "Aren't we already doing this?" Well, yes and no. Yes, because the world of SOA depends on a good understanding of reuse and on the building of reusable components. No, because SOA extends the idea of reuse not only to *Web services* but also to *business services.* (For definitions of *business services* and *Web services,* look in Chapters 2 and 3.) In the world of SOA, the level of granularity shifts profoundly. No longer are we talking simply about reusable low-level components; we're talking about reusable high-level business services. This shift, and its implementation, is no mean feat either for business managers or for IT, but the rewards for everyone are dramatic.

Hiding the Unsightly

In the next chapter, we talk a lot about architecture. For those of you who already know a lot about systems architecture and want more nuts and bolts, we suggest you skim quickly through the next few "conceptual" chapters to make sure you understand what we mean by the terms we've decided to use. Then dive headlong into Part II, which we promise will put meat on the bones and give you a lot to chew on — metaphorically of course.

One big reason we think business managers are going to like SOA is that, with SOA, business gets to focus more on business and less on technology. Like the plumbing in a well-designed home, SOA technology just works — it's there, but it is mostly invisible at the business layer. We show and tell you all about this in the next chapter, but right here in Chapter 1, we want you to consider what your life would be like if technology was not an obstacle but an aide in making your business act the way you want it to act.

SOA enables business managers and IT to talk in business terms that both sides understand. Without SOA, the IT developer and business manager typically use very different words to describe the process of creating, for example, an invoice. The IT developer is concerned with APIs (application program interfaces) and how to go about creating customer records from ten different Oracle database tables. The business manager describes the actual *business* process used to create an invoice. With SOA, a business service is a business service is a business service. How that business service is implemented in the technology layer is the purview of IT, and business managers need not worry about it or its associated technical jargon. Really. Trust us.

Why Is This Story Different from Every Other Story?

Perhaps you're skeptical. Perhaps, for as long as you can remember, the software industry has been promising yet another silver bullet to rid you of all business woes. We think now's a good time to repeat that SOA is not about "out with the old, in with the new." SOA is about *reuse*. SOA is about taking what you have and structuring it in a way that allows you not only to continue to use it, but to use it secure in the knowledge that future change will be simple, straightforward, safe, and fast. SOA is indeed a journey — it can't be built overnight. But organizations can begin SOA now and can benefit now. Ultimately, SOA renders a business more flexible — and IT more reliable, sustainable, extensible, manageable, and accountable.

We think SOA is the most important mandate facing business and IT today. And because SOA is a joint venture between business managers and IT, we present the basics necessary for everyone to come to the table with a good grounding from a conceptual level.

Chapter 2

Noah's Architecture

We're about to define service oriented architecture. If you find our definition fraught with terms we haven't yet defined, you're right. Hold tight, we'll get there — we promise. Ready? Take a deep breath. . . .

We define a *service oriented architecture* as a software architecture for building applications that implement business processes or services by using a set of loosely coupled black-box components orchestrated to deliver a well-defined level of service.

Okay, now we're going to explain that definition.

What's an Architecture?

Before we go jumping off into explaining *service oriented architecture*, we're going to start with just plain old *architecture* (from an information technology point of view) to make sure we're all on the same page.

In the beginning, there were programs, and programs were good, and programs didn't need no stinking architectures. And then there was business, and the business grew, and the programs grew, and chaos was on the face of the business. And so, in an effort to create order, programmers adopted systematic structures to organize the programs and help the business. And any structure, be it a strip mall or the Taj Mahal, or even Noah's Ark, has some underlying design, however haphazard, known as an *architecture*. When we describe software structures, we call the underlying design principles, well, *software architectures*.

Every building has a structure of some sort. The idea of architecture implies thoughtful planning according to a set of guidelines or rules. In a building, for example, the steelwork has to support both the current floor loading and future additions. Some architectures are better than others; the same thing applies to software architectures. A good software architecture specifies how data is stored, how users interact, how programs communicate, and much, much more.

Business applications, the programs that make corporations run (from accounts receivable to order processing to warehouse management), need to access information from many different places. In the Good Old Days, a business unit would ask the IT department to create an application to solve a specific business problem. To accomplish this goal, the IT department would write a set of customized programs. These programs included all sorts of assumptions related to the problem being solved, the data being used, and even the hardware the newly created programs would run on. New problems to solve meant new programs to write, and everyone lived happily ever after. Sort of.

Whatever structure the IT department used in creating programs was the *architecture* of the systems they developed, and for the most part they were self-contained structures created to serve a particular function. They were not originally built to be connected to each other; in fact, they were more like two multistory buildings built next to one another, each with different heights per story. And, like many an eclectic mix cobbled together over time, these disparate architectures make running the information technology of a contemporary company, well, uh, tough.

SOA to the rescue

Businesses keep changing, and requests for new programs keep coming. What's new and different is the idea that businesses don't have to keep reinventing the wheel; that they can organize programs for easy reuse, for easy maintenance and support, for coherent, consistent results across their organizations, and for easily sharing their data and resources. And that, in a nutshell, is the idea behind a service oriented architecture.

In a service oriented architecture world, business applications are assembled by using a set of building blocks known as *components* — some of which may be available "off the shelf," and some of which may have to be built from scratch. (We talk a lot more about components in Chapter 3, so if you feel compelled to find out more about components at this very instant, you can jump there. However, if you have a vague notion of what components are, we suggest you keep reading.)

Software architecture

In computer science, the term *architecture* describes the overall design and structure of a computer system. Software architecture diagrams depict the components of a computer system, providing some indication of how they connect and interact. Such diagrams are frequently produced by software designers and IT vendors to explain the workings of some system or software product. At this level, designers tend not to use any formal scheme to create such diagrams — the idea here is just to provide some helpful illustrations. However, when software design is taken to a more detailed level, designers do turn to formal schemes in order to accurately capture the functional details of the design diagrammatically.

In years gone by designers used flow charts to illustrate and describe the flow of a process. These were superseded by more detailed methodologies called *graphical modeling languages*. Nowadays, the most commonly used formal scheme in software design is the *Unified Modeling Language* (UML). If you'd like to know more about it, you can obtain the official documents that define it from www.omg.org, the Object Management Group's Web site. However, we think you'll find it easier going if you consult *UML 2 For Dummies,* by Michael Chonoles and James Schardt (Wiley).

The software architecture defines which software components to use and how those components interact with each other. Sounds pretty simple when we put it that way, but we're not going to hide the ugly truth from you: Creating a service oriented architecture takes thought, patience, planning, and time. We call it a journey, and depending on the size and scope of an organization, it may be a journey of years or even a decade. But you can start seeing returns on your SOA investment very quickly, without having to rewrite all your software.

Basic architecture

We start with a very simple example of a software architecture. (Don't worry. You'll get a look at more complex structures before the chapter's through.)

Figure 2-1 shows the underlying software architecture for an order-processing application that allows customers to place orders through the Internet. It has the following five components:

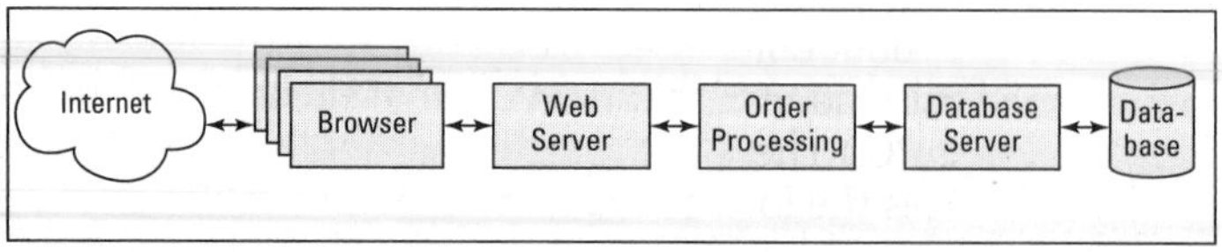

Figure 2-1:
A simple
software
architecture.

✔ **The Browser** is a program located on a user's device (PC, laptop, PDA, or cellphone) that accesses the business application through a Web site. Many users can access the application at the same time, so many browsers will typically link to the Web server. The primary job of the browser is to display information and accept input from the user.

✔ **The Web Server** manages when and how the many Web pages are sent to the browsers of the users who access the business application. (Web servers may do other things as well, but we are concentrating on its primary service.)

✔ **The Order-Processing Application** carries out the business process that is being executed, which in this case means carrying out the necessary steps to accept the order and fulfill the customer's request, if possible. This component embodies the company's business practices for interacting with customers.

✔ **The Database Server** is computer software that reads data from a database and sends the data where it is needed.

✔ **The Database** is where the definitions of the business data and the data itself are stored.

Information passes from the browser to the Web server to the order-processing application, which decides what to do next. The order-processing application might pass data to the database server to write to disk, or it may request data from the database, or it may simply send information back to the browser through the Web server. What the order-processing application does depends upon the information and commands passed to it by the user via the browser.

Basic service

We all know what a service is — we pay for services all the time. We pay for electrical service, telephone service, and service at a restaurant. Using the restaurant example, we sit down at a table, consult a menu, give our order to the waiter, and the meal is delivered as soon as it is prepared. We pass a simple set of information to the waiter (what we want to eat and drink), and somehow, magically, the restaurant provides it. Usually, we don't see the food cooked or participate in its preparation or serving. The meal is the service that we pay for.

We can talk about the restaurant in terms of *components* and how they interact. (We say more about components in Chapter 3.) We order food from the server. (No, not that kind of server; it's a "PC" term for *waiter or waitress* — no, not *that* kind of PC.) The server sends or takes the order to the kitchen. The kitchen prepares the food and alerts the server, who then, we hope, brings us what we asked for. We are a component, the server is a component, and the kitchen is a component. The service oriented architecture of the restaurant comprises these components and more — a cleaning component and a supply-ordering component, for example.

Business services

We can also talk about the restaurant in terms of *services*. In the complicated, convoluted, controversial contrivance called a corporation, services abound. It is no mean feat to discover and identify them all, but ultimately a business needs to. For now, we are going to introduce a formal definition of a business service.

We define a *business service* as "the logical encapsulation of business function." In simple terms, we mean that you wrap up everything you have to do to make a particular business function happen and give that rolled-up something a name and call it a business service.

So, in our restaurant example, everything the kitchen has to do to prepare the meal, from chopping vegetables to cooking to plating, could be called the *meal-preparation service*. Everything the server does to extract the order from us (elucidate menu items, tell us what isn't available right now, suggest appetizers and side dishes, write down our order) could be rolled up into the *order-taking service*.

Elementary service oriented architecture

In a *service oriented architecture*, business services interact with each other in ways similar to how the various services of the restaurant interact.

Now, you can think of the restaurant from two levels — from the business services level, which describes the functions and how they interact, and from an "implementation" point of view, that is, how the food actually gets prepared, how it actually gets onto the plate, and so on. The various services pass information, ask for tasks to be performed, and serve up the results. We can illustrate this division of function by adding a new credit-checking component to our previous architecture diagram.

In Figure 2-2, we add a credit-checking component. Its service is called on when new customers place an order to determine whether they are credit-worthy. In the figure, we don't show or even care about how the credit check-ing is done. For the sake of simplicity, say that the credit-checking software component is run by an external company and simply provides a service. The company using this credit-checking software is confident that the service conducts a credit check in the right way.

Figure 2-2:
Adding a
service
oriented
component.

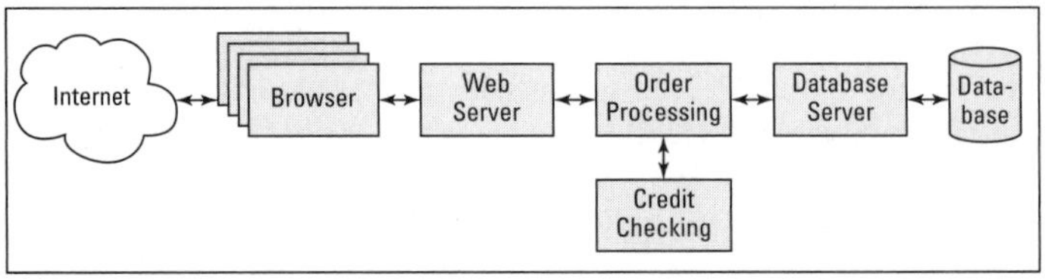

The order-processing application simply requests the credit-checking service and passes along the necessary information (a person's name and Social Security number). The credit-checking component consults its information sources, does some calculations, and passes back a credit rating. The credit-checking component may connect to many computers, consult many differ-ent data sources, and use a very sophisticated algorithm to calculate the credit rating, but this is of no concern to the order-processing application. As far as the order-processing application is concerned, credit checking is just a *black box*.

Also, we need to emphasize that the credit-checking component *does only credit checking*. It doesn't offer a wide range of services. It is precisely because the components have a narrowly defined scope — that is, they do "just one thing" — that they can be used and reused as building blocks.

SOA's use and reuse of components makes it easier to build new applications as well as change existing applications. Using well-proven, tested compo-nents makes testing new applications more efficient.

It's So Simple; It Has Taken Only 40 Years. . . .

You may be thinking, "Well, of course software should work this way. Isn't it always built to work this way?" The answer is no. It may surprise folks not involved with IT, but the software industry has spent more than 40 years trying to get to the point where it can build *modular* software applications.

In the following sections, we explain why life in the world of corporate IT hasn't always worked the way we want it to work. We introduce four major complications and do our best to not only elucidate the complications but to also show you how service oriented architecture resolves these complications.

Complication #1: Business logic and plumbing

To build a software application, you have to tell the computer how to do what you want, both in human terms — which we call *the business logic* — and in computer terms — the stuff we call *the plumbing*. (We will try to avoid getting scatological.)

Business applications comprise lines of instructions (program code) that tell computers what actions to take. Some of these instructions are written as business logic ("add an item line to the order," for example), and some are simply plumbing (computer-level directives such as "check that the printer is available"). Both are necessary. If you don't describe the application's activity in simple business logic (purchase orders, products, customers, accounts, and so on), you quickly lose sight of what you're trying to achieve. If you don't describe in computer terms exactly how the computer should carry out its task, the software simply won't work.

One of the biggest problems in programming is that it is very difficult to keep the business logic separate from the plumbing because you need to control both at the same time. Though the tasks are related, they can be separated. It's work, and it requires both the use of appropriate software tools and programmer discipline to ensure that the business logic is kept separate from the technology that makes it happen.

For example, if you want to change the order in which particular business functions happen, and you've kept your business logic separate from your plumbing, making these changes is no big deal in a SOA. But if your business logic and your plumbing are one giant application, changes are costly and complicated, take time, require extensive testing, and are a very big deal indeed.

Many software components deal only with managing a specific aspect of computer plumbing. For example, Web servers manage the presentation of information to Web browsers, and database software manages how information is stored and retrieved. These components involve no business logic. Business logic needs to be as free of plumbing dependencies as possible.

With this in mind, we can now redraw our architecture diagram to be both a little bit more service oriented *and* a little bit more general.

The separation of concerns

The separation of business logic (what an application does) from computer logic (how the computer is directed to do it) is known as the *separation of concerns* and is a software engineering best practice that should be applied in the design of all technology systems intended for business users. Unfortunately, this best practice has been observed more in theory than in practice. If you discuss this issue with software engineers, you may hear many excuses. The separation of concerns is often ignored simply because it takes effort to abide by it, and the costs of ignoring it are all in the future — in other words, too often, "quick and dirty" wins out over "slow and sure." Another pernicious factor thwarting the separation of concerns is the perennial desire of *some* IT vendors to lock your business logic into their proprietary technology. (Never underestimate the greed factor.)

Creating a reusable architecture takes discipline. And discipline inevitably takes more time than you'd ever expect to establish itself. Management may need to be educated. The upfront costs of establishing and requiring discipline pay manifold dividends over time.

In Figure 2-3, we introduce the idea of a business layer and a plumbing layer, and in doing so, we introduce the idea of specific services. (For simplicity's sake, we've left out the Web server and the browser.) It works like this:

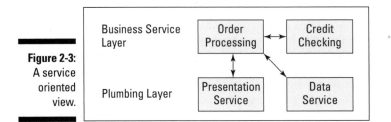

Figure 2-3:
A service oriented view.

▶ **The Business Service Layer** consists of software components that provide and carry out specific business functions. Another way to say this is that they *deliver specific business services*.

▶ **The Plumbing Layer** consists of components that support the above-mentioned business services by marshalling and managing actual computer resources. Here are two such components:

   • *Presentation Service:* The Web server called by a different name

   • *Data Service:* The database server called by a different name

By splitting the architecture diagram into two layers, we divide the software that is of direct relevance to the business — because it carries out business functions — from the software that supports the use and management of computer resources. With our SOA-based approach, we have, to some degree, divided business logic from plumbing.

If you're not a techie, don't panic. As we mention in the beginning of the chapter, SOA is a _journey._ Now's a good time to take another deep breath. If you are a techie, we hope you're beginning to see some possibilities.

"All is well and good," you're saying, "in a hypothetical world. But we have real systems that have been in place for years, and in some cases decades. We can't exactly throw everything out and start from scratch." We know. We have a solution. Trust us.

Complication #2: The not-so-green field

Complication #2 is that businesses don't live in a perfect world. They cannot start from scratch, which means they depend on legacy systems that are in place and operational right now — and, besides, they certainly don't have the time or budget to start from scratch. The good news is that SOA is a journey (remember that part?) that takes place over time, and best of all, _it reuses what already exists_. SOA is not "out with the old, in with the new"; it is about separating the wheat from the chaff so that you can have your cake and eat it, too. (We like mixing metaphors.)

With SOA, you can use almost all your existing business applications. True, you may need to change them a little in order to include them in a SOA, but it is possible, and it is not all that hard. For example, you can treat an entire application as a service, or you can take some code out of an application and make just that code into a service.

In Figure 2-4, you'll notice that we've added an existing application. Now, our Internet order-processing system uses both a credit-checking component and an invoicing component. It interacts with the existing Invoicing system to send out an invoice. To make it possible for the Invoicing system to work in this way, we create a simple "adapter."

Now, the "simple adapter" may not be so simple for IT folks to create, but the idea is simple enough to understand. A SOA uses very specific, industry-agreed-upon standards to create interfaces that make it possible for various components of the SOA to talk to each other. In Chapter 7, we get very explicit about these adapters and how they manage to talk to each other. For now, leave the creating to us and assume that when the time comes, you (or someone near and dear to you) will be able to create all the adapters you need.

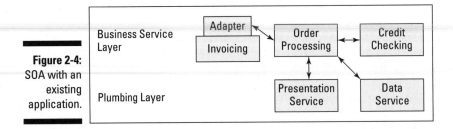

Figure 2-4:
SOA with an
existing
application.

After you have all the required elements of a SOA in place, you can include an existing application or piece of an application within the SOA framework. Sounds great, but before you go out and start plugging everything lying about the office into your planned SOA — coffee machine included — you should know that we still have quite a few SOA components to discuss. Before we can do that, however, we still need to talk about Complications #3 and #4.

Complication #3: Application archaeology

Despite doing your best to split the architecture between a business layer and a plumbing layer, you'll likely find that almost all the business layer components will still include some "plumbing" activities. This is because many of the business layer components come from existing applications, and existing business applications were likely built in very different ways, at different times, by different people, and for different reasons, maybe even using different computers.

Unlike a PC that you might hold onto for three or four years, application software tends to hang around a company for decades. Therefore, one company could have hundreds of applications that are all designed in different ways. Programs that are still in use from prior eras of technology are fondly referred to as *legacy code* and include mainframe applications, client/server applications, and just about everything that is functional that existed before you started your job. These applications contain a lot of company knowledge. Many of these systems are the foundation for how business is done. They are used to bill customers, pay sales commissions, and transfer funds. Even if you consider these applications to be ugly, they perform essential work.

Digging in the dirt

Consider the layers of applications on which your current business runs as archaeological layers. If you had to understand in detail how each layer works, how each is connected to various components, and how the thing is managed, it would take years and, because business and its applications are continually changing, you would never be done. Fortunately, you don't have to scrounge around playing archaeologist. You can wallow in blissful igno-rance and ignore layers of code. Just as builders hide wiring and plumbing behind the walls — out of sight except where absolutely necessary — soft-ware engineers hide a lot of complicated, messy code in convenient "black boxes."

The magical black box

We use the term *black box* in the traditional sense to mean a component or device whose workings are not understood or accessible by the user. Many programmers, for example, do not know how a CPU works but understand how to use it to execute programs. Similarly, a regional sales manager may not know how a spreadsheet is designed but understands how to use it to create a sales forecast.

Intelligent black-boxing is an important aspect of SOA. With a SOA, you can build a whole new computing environment by using all the resources that you already have by treating many components as black boxes. Particularly, you need to treat existing application components as black boxes, making them accessible by adding adapters. For example, you should use a black box to include older plumbing components that still work. The black box pre-vents you from spending money to replace something that works just fine. Or, as the sages say, "If it ain't broke, don't fix it.

Complication #4: Who's in charge?

So far so good. You are wrapping your ugly code into nice black boxes, making services out of existing applications, and life is wonderful. Right? Uh, not exactly. How exactly are components strung together to ensure the end-to-end service you expect? For example, how do you know that, when you place your restaurant order, food (specifically the food you ordered) will be prepared and delivered to you in a timely fashion?

Because any SOA you can think of is orders of magnitude more complex than our restaurant example — many more components, for starters — it behooves you to ask, "Who's running the show?" You have every good reason to be concerned about this because you don't want to have to worry about whether all the components have compatible plumbing. If the plumbing for one component doesn't work with the plumbing for several other compo-nents, how will an end-to-end process work? If it fails, how will you know?

Stymied? As an example of black-boxing a problem — that is, wrapping it up so you don't have to contend with intricacies that don't interest you — we're now going to let you know that any and all problems associated with the end-to-end processing of components are dealt with by a little something called the *SOA supervisor*. So, no need to worry, because the SOA supervisor will take care of things. The SOA supervisor acts something like a traffic cop and helps prevent SOA accidents. If you want to know exactly how it does it, we refer you to Chapter 10.

Figure 2-5 adds our own little graphical depiction of the SOA supervisor to our overall SOA model. Notice that we have also made the computer network and the Internet visible, for two reasons:

✓ Doing so more accurately depicts how software components actually connect with each other across a computer network. In most cases, applications run on separate server machines that connect via the network or possibly over the Internet.

✓ The SOA supervisor needs to connect to every other component within the SOA in order to do its job. If we drew each of the connections in, the diagram would get very busy very quickly.

Taking a look at Figure 2-5, you can see that the SOA supervisor manages the end-to-end computer process created by connecting all the other software components together. In our depiction, applications are divided between *external* components (components outside the corporate network) and *internal* components (components inside the corporate network). The credit-checking component, for example, is an external component that is connected through the Internet.

One of the SOA supervisor's responsibilities is to monitor the various components within the SOA. The SOA supervisor directly monitors only things in its purview. However it can also monitor results and responses from services provided from the outside.

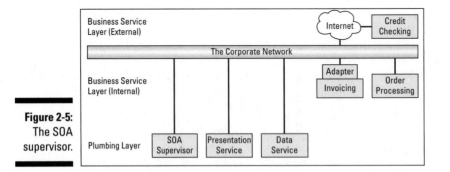

Figure 2-5:
The SOA
supervisor.

You certainly will not be able to do much if an external service suddenly fails or goes very slowly. However, with internal components, the SOA supervisor not only monitors the whole service that a component provides but may also initiate corrective activity if things start to go wrong.

Now, with regard to the corporate computer network depicted in Figure 2-5, we do have to admit that an actual network can be a complex arrangement of networking hardware (switches, routers, hubs, and so on) and connections (copper wires, fiber optic wires, and wireless connections), with computers of various kinds attached at various points. However, in line with our black-box approach to hiding complexity, you can think of the corporate computer network as a kind of pipe. The thing to be concerned about, more than anything else, is whether the pipe can accommodate the flow of data that is required.

Service Oriented Architecture — Reprise

It has taken us only a dozen or so pages to expand on our definition of a service oriented architecture. Just to refresh your memory, a service oriented architecture is *an architecture for building business applications as a set of loosely coupled black-box components orchestrated to deliver a well-defined level of service by linking together business processes.*

Admittedly, this definition doesn't yet flow trippingly from the tongue. However, from it springs a sustainable, reusable, extensible approach to business and technology that is already providing huge competitive advantage to organizations around the globe. Here's a little elucidation:

- ✔ **SOA is for building *business applications.*** Many legitimate approaches to software architecture exist, and SOA is not intended for building every kind of software. It is intended explicitly for building *business* applications.

- ✔ **SOA is a *black-box component architecture.*** SOA deliberately hides complexity wherever possible, and the idea of the black box is integral to SOA. The black box enables the reuse of existing business applications by adding a fairly simple adapter to them, no matter how they were built.

- ✔ **SOA components are *loosely coupled.*** The term "loosely coupled" refers to how two components interact within a SOA. One component passes data to another component and makes a request. The second component carries out the request and, if necessary, passes data back to the first. The emphasis is on simplicity and autonomy. Each component offers a small range of simple services to other components.

A set of loosely coupled components does the same work that used to be done inside tightly structured applications, but the components can be combined and recombined in myriad ways. This makes the overall IT infrastructure much more flexible. We talk a lot more about loose coupling in Chapter 5.

✔ **SOA components are orchestrated to link together through business processes to deliver a well-defined level of service.** SOA creates a simple arrangement of components that can, collectively, deliver a very complex business service. Simultaneously, SOA must provide acceptable service levels. To that end, the architecture embodies components that ensure a dependable service level. Service level is directly tied into the best practices of conducting business — commonly referred to as *business process management.* We have a lot more to say about business process management, but not until Chapter 4.

Why SOA? Better Business and Better IT

SOA can make it easier and faster to build and deploy IT systems that directly serve the goals of a business. Contemporary business is completely reliant on its IT, and never have business and IT needed to be more aligned. The very survival of a business hinges on its ability to adapt its IT to meet ever-changing business challenges. SOA integrates business and IT into a framework that simultaneously leverages existing systems and enables business change. A SOA enables the business to keep its focus on business and allows IT to evolve and keep pace in a dynamically changing world.

We divide the world of SOA into the business services layer and the plumbing layer. Imagine a diagram that shows all the software that your organization runs. Divide it into the business services layer and into the plumbing layer. The business services layer contains your business logic. Your plumbing deals with your computing resources.

Business managers need not understand the intricacies of the plumbing layer and everything it contains. If you cover up the plumbing layer, you are left with a diagram that shows all the business services that software applications provide, both inside your organization and to others that interact (technologically speaking) from outside, like your customers, business partners, and suppliers. Looking at your organization's software resources in this way, you may be able to think about ways to improve or better exploit the software assets you have.

Likewise, if you cover up all the business functionality in your SOA diagram, you are left with a set of plumbing services that your IT department is responsible for providing. We know that many of your "legacy" applications also have a good deal of plumbing in them, and the plumbing layer does not replace that. However, SOA enables an IT department to choose how it will evolve toward providing a "service oriented architecture" and in time may obviate a good deal of lousy plumbing.

SOA doesn't guarantee a happier, healthier life, free from business concerns. However, movement toward SOA is usually a movement toward technical freedom and business flexibility and bodes well for the performance and profitability of an organization and for the sanity of the people managing the business.

Chapter 3

Not So Simple SOA

"*O*kay, if SOA's so wonderful, what's the catch?" you shrewdly ask. Like a lot of things worth having, SOA takes work and time — *and* it's really worth it. SOA represents a new world order in which business leadership and technology leadership together navigate the business challenges of the "All Technology, All the Time" era we inhabit.

If you want to be a part of this new world order, you have to have some fluency in the basic concepts. That's why we're here — to help you with those basic concepts. If you can remember back 10 or 15 years, you might not have known what e-mail was, and you had never surfed the Web — we know, some of us were writing *The Internet For Dummies* back then. For businesses everywhere, the concepts we're introducing now are every bit as revolutionary and important as the Internet was ten years ago, and we have confidence that when you're through with us (or vice versa), you'll be no dummy.

Components and Component Wannabes

Traditional software applications aren't very flexible. It's the sad truth. To be flexible — meaning to move and bend (change) and not break — requires malice aforethought (well, at least forethought) and some hard work. Flexible software is best built from reusable pieces of software code known as *components*. Well-written components can be used over and over again in different ways to form different applications.

The difference between inflexible and flexible code is a lot like the difference between a boombox and a *component* stereo system. In a fancy boombox, you might find a tape deck or two, a CD changer, an AM/FM radio, an amplifier, and speakers. When you go to the beach, it's all or nothing — you take the whole boombox, not just the CD player. With your extensible, flexible component stereo system, you can swap out your old tape deck or other components and plug in new ones whenever you want.

If you've had your boombox for five years, you know it's obsolete. It may play your CDs and your cassettes, but it certainly won't play your MP3 files. If you want to play your MP3 files on your boombox, you have to get radical and buy another boombox. (And just try to find one that plays your MP3 files and still plays your old cassettes!) And Heaven help you if you're stuck in pre-boombox land with one of those all-in-one systems that includes a turntable — because you can't imagine ever ditching your vinyl collection — but still want to play the newest tunes you downloaded from an online music service.

Talk about wanting it all. It's tough enough trying to manage one's music collection, but just imagine the different kinds of systems at play in a corporate environment. In that world, you could think of your LPs and cassettes as legacy code, and, if they are important enough to you, you have to maintain the systems that support them. Some companies have the equivalent of eight-track cassettes. Such is the state of most corporate IT, but more about that later. Meanwhile, back to components. . .

In software, as in stereo systems, the component model yields flexibility and reuse. And those great software architects on high have been talking about component architectures for more than a decade and have been expanding the concepts of reuse for more than half a century — subroutines, structured programs, data that is stored in centralized databases and object-orientation are all milestones in the advance of reusability — but they never seem to get it quite right.

Making sure your components play nicely together

If one person sets about making components for his or her own personal use, he or she will undoubtedly get better at it over time and will eventually find precisely those components that help make the creation of new and different programs faster and easier — for himself or herself. However, as soon as that individual has to make things usable by other people or has to use other people's components, the need for agreement on how components should talk to each other takes center stage. Beyond that, the effort involved in letting other people know that you have great components, finding useful components other people have already built so you don't have to make them yourself, making sure everything really works as advertised, and all that piddling little stuff is enough to drive sane people away.

Fortunately for you, the software industry has recognized this issue, and many hardworking folks have been solving these problems so that you don't have to. The important point for you to remember is that not all components are reusable components. For components to be reusable, they *must* be constructed with standard interfaces — they must be created to talk to other components according to established and agreed-upon rules for talking to other components.

Standards are a big deal, by the way. Without standards, you can't be sure that a light bulb will work with your lamp, that your toaster will work at your home as well as at your school, that the new telephone you just plugged into your telephone outlet will actually accept calls, and that the batteries from the corner store will work in your flashlight. When it comes to computer systems, making the interfaces — the places where one thing meets another — standards helps ensure that they'll work together reliably and predictably.

Software components

The idea of a software component is deceptively simple. Consider your music collection. It consists of a number of musical tracks. If you digitize the collection, the music is stored somewhere on a disk along with some useful pieces of data like the track name, track length, artist, album, genre, date recorded (to the disk), and perhaps more. Lots of programs play music. What they do may be complex in terms of translating the digital recording into sound that comes out of the speakers, but the information you provide the program is quite simple. It only needs a command (the action you want) and some data (what the action applies to). (The song you want played and its location is enough.) All software components work like that and inevitably must work like that whether they are written in Java, C#, COBOL, or any other programming language. You pass a command and some data and they go off and do something. When you are working on your PC, either typing information or clicking with the mouse, you are giving commands of some kind and passing data to some software component.

It gets confusing because software components are called by many different names: Applications, programs, functions, modules, dynamic link libraries, subroutines, and classes are all software components. These different names have cropped up over many years based on the specifics of different software languages and protocols. However, they all refer to basically the same thing — a software component is a set of program logic. Software is riddled with components and components within components, but they all work in the same way. They all respond to commands and data.

The entire personal computer industry is built on standards. The QWERTY keyboard has been used since the late 19th century. The RS-232 serial port and ASCII character set date back to the 1960s. Floppy disks, computer buses, SCS, VGA, and USB ports all have become standardized, some after a deliberative committee process, some based on the initial success of a new product. (The Centronics port long outlived the printer company that named it.)

Of course, all this makes sense to most thinking individuals these days. But before the Internet became a significant influence in the software industry, software vendors did not necessarily want their components talking to other people's components. Competitive business practice encouraged the development of "proprietary" systems — systems that didn't talk to other people's systems — all in the name of "locking in" customers so they didn't get it into their heads to "mix and match" software from different companies.

With the Internet, however, users everywhere were suddenly using common software — namely, the browser. Although Web surfers still use various browsers today, all browsers do pretty much the same thing — they help navigate to different sites, they display the contents of the Web pages, and then they allow interaction with the site. This is possible only because industrious, indefatigable, farsighted individuals worked to create *standard* ways to tag information for display and *standard* ways to display tagged information. This standard is known as HTML (HyperText Markup Language).

You don't need to know more about HTML, but the concept of a standard interface is critical to your understanding of service oriented architecture. For example, the browser interface has become a de facto standard user interface to all software. Even software that doesn't use the Internet is now being designed with the assumption that you know how to point and click, you know what a link is, and you know how to "navigate," even if the place you're navigating to is another part of the software application. Without standardization, we would have no Web.

Building in reusability

Building reusable components means creating a specific function or set of functions and supplying the standard interfaces that allow them to be used over and over again by generations yet unknown. To show you what we mean, we're going to extend our order-processing example from Chapter 2.

Our pumped-up example (see Figure 3-1) shows the order-processing application as comprising three sets of functions:

✔ The **Orders functions** let you add new orders, alter orders, delete orders, and inquire about orders.

✔ The **Customers functions** let you add new customers, change customer details, delete customers, and make inquiries about customers.

✔ The **Payments functions** let you accept payments by credit card or by customer account and to inquire about payments or accounts.

All business applications have the same basic structure when looked at from the user perspective. They are made up of a set of functions that the user actually uses. Real-world order-processing applications may be a little more sophisticated than our example, including stuff like discount routines (that follow specific rules) or a customer-loyalty rewards scheme (like air miles). No matter how complicated the application is, it always consists of a set of functions.

If you put this order-processing application on the Internet, customers can use their browsers as the standard user interface to place an order, make a payment, and enter other needed information such as name, billing address, shipping address, and so on.

To "put" the order-processing application on the Web just requires the use of standard Web services interfaces. After that's done, browsers can talk to the order-processing application, and everyone can live happily ever after.

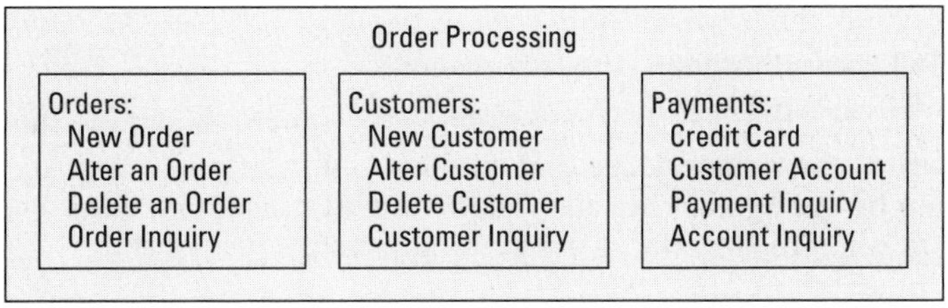

Figure 3-1:
Order
processing
as a set of
functions.

Order Processing		
Orders: New Order Alter an Order Delete an Order Order Inquiry	Customers: New Customer Alter Customer Delete Customer Customer Inquiry	Payments: Credit Card Customer Account Payment Inquiry Account Inquiry

Web Services: The Early Days

In 1993, the first year *The Internet For Dummies* appeared in print, there were 130 Web sites and no browsers as we know them. (Our technical editor reminds us that by standing on your head and whispering secret incantations, you could telnet to a computer that had a browser on it.) The World Wide Web was covered in just one chapter toward the back of that first edition. We called early Web sites *brochureware* because the first attempts to use the Web for business often consisted of companies taking what they normally put into printed brochures and putting it up on the Web for the world to see. The sites were not interactive — they were just there.

It didn't take long (relatively speaking) for clever programmers to start offering services from the Web — Amazon.com, eBay, and Travelocity were among the first companies to demonstrate that the world was changing and that no one could ignore the Internet. The Web became a ubiquitous vehicle for the delivery of services — weather, news, real estate listings, tax forms, movie listings, distance learning, maps, directions. You name it; it's available on the Web.

At the same time, smart companies used the same technologies that delivered services to ordinary people to deliver services to other businesses or to other software applications. For example, IBM used a site that provided foreign currency exchange rates to help process staff expense reports. If the expense report included expenses submitted in a foreign currency, the program that captured the expenses went to the Web to get the appropriate foreign exchange rate for the same date as the expense item.

Strangely enough, the technologies that performed these services on the Web became known as Web services. We define a *Web service* as any piece of software that uses standard Web interfaces to communicate with other software containing Web service interfaces. (We could get a lot more technical, but we think that's enough for right now.) The big point here is that Web services use *standard interfaces;* in fact, it is precisely *because* the interfaces are standard that Web services can

- ✔ Talk to each other in the first place.
- ✔ Provide a framework where different people from all over the globe can write new Web services that could potentially talk to Web services written by strangers. They use a common interface. Just like a plug and a socket, if the interfaces are standard, things just work.

Web services are fundamentally more useful than plain old application functions because all sorts of other programs can use them over and over again. This is possible because Web service interfaces use standards that have been agreed upon across the industry. Because everyone uses the standardized interfaces, like a socket and a plug, they just work. (Yes, we are repeating ourselves — but it's really, really important.)

Earlier efforts to promote software reuse required everyone to use the same computer language or operating system or foundation classes, but the entire industry could never be pinned down like that. Web services piggybacked on the universal acceptance of the underlying standards of the Internet. After every browser could talk to any Web site, it became possible for any computer program to talk to any other program, as long as they both had some path to the Internet.

If every function of the order-processing application is a Web service, other programs can use those functions instead of reinventing the wheel. Figure 3-2 gives you an idea of what we mean. Here you can see the various order-processing applications broken down into reusable Web services. Using the very same Web service for the same function in every application that needs that function ensures that you get the same results everywhere the service is used. This can radically reduce errors, make change easier, and make the folks responsible for regulatory compliance a lot happier. Web services are good.

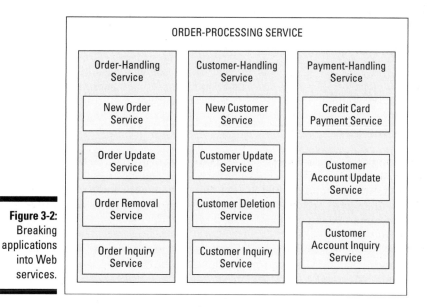

Figure 3-2:
Breaking
applications
into Web
services.

When Web Services Grow Up

Much to our frustration, a lot of folks think a service oriented architecture is "Web services on steroids." Though critical to a service oriented architecture, Web services are not the same thing as a service oriented architecture, and here's why:

In order for business to free itself from technology, the business logic must be separated from the plumbing, as we describe in Chapter 2. Web services technology is what allows us to make this separation, creating business service components from business applications. The business logic sits above the plumbing in the business services layer. These business service components bring to the business the same efficiencies of reuse, ease of change, and consistency of results as Web services do on the programming level. And

Web services standards

The key standards with Web services are XML, WSDL, and SOAP. XML (eXtensible Markup Language) is a special language that enables programmers to define data in a way that any program can understand. It can also be used to standardize the commands that programs send each other. Now, you may remember — if you've dutifully read the beginning of this chapter — that software components work by processing a command and some data that is sent to it. WSDL (Web Services Description Language) is a special language that describes all the commands — and the data that must be associated with them — that a software component will accept from another software component. SOAP (Simple Object Access Protocol) is a standard language that enables software components to talk to each other.

It was no small achievement for the industry to find a way to standardize these three things: a common definition language (XML), a common format for defining interfaces (WSDL), and a common format for messages between software components (SOAP).

this is a big deal. The business services layer ensures that the business can respond quickly to new opportunities by making changes to business services without having to change the plumbing. Business can change without rewriting the world because business components, like stereo components, can be swapped in and out as needed.

The creation of a service oriented architecture involves identifying the key *business services* and working top-down, versus bottom-up. Figure 3-3 shows order processing and credit checking as business services.

Identifying key business services is a major, major deal. Key business services are different for different companies. Making key business services into black boxes (as we talk about in Chapter 2) means that business can reorganize itself as needed. Services critical to the business become codified best practices, ensuring that business is conducted under the explicit policies and principles defined by the business, instead of by the ad hoc practices that typically emerge and vary from one part of a company to another.

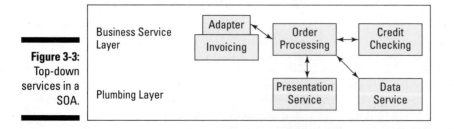

Figure 3-3:
Top-down services in a SOA.

Defining Business Processes

Imagine for a moment that you have identified and created several key business services. You have converted all your business applications into a set of modular components with supporting Web service interfaces. Now that you have them, what do you want to do with them? Well, you probably want to string them together in ways that are useful to you. One way to string business services together is to create a business process.

We define a *business process* as the codification of rules and practices (hopefully best practices) that constitute the business. Simply stated, a business process is what has to happen for anything to get done. From a SOA perspective, a business process includes people, business services (which in turn comprise software applications that are collections of business functions), adapters (when needed to convert business functions into Web services), and some sort of process management activity that manages the flow of work between all the parts we just listed.

Business processes vary from business to business. In an insurance company, "claims handling" is a business process. In a hospital, "admitting a patient" is a business process. In a furniture store, "selling a cabinet" is a business process. Note that a business process is *not* by definition automated. It may indeed require manual participation or intervention. Great gains in efficiency come when a process is automated "from end to end," but this is not always possible.

The handy example

Figure 3-4 depicts a business process that embraces all the end-to-end activities that occur from the time a customer places an order to when goods are dispatched to the customer. Here's a summary of what actually happens:

1. A clerk uses the order-processing software to record an order, perhaps checking on stock before accepting it. This process automatically links to the inventory control process, which is part of the warehouse system. This checks to see if any stock reordering is necessary and places orders for new stock.

2. The order itself is converted to a picking list, ordered by aisle and location, and passed, via the order assembly application, to an assembler who gets every item on the order from a warehouse.

3. The assembler packages these items and sends them to the dispatch application.

4. The dispatch application prints a delivery note that lists all the items assembled.

5. The dispatcher packages and ships the order.

Rented software

Nearly all businesses use packaged applications that they license from software vendors. Indeed, most businesses rely heavily on this kind of software. Some packaged software vendors, like SAP and Oracle, are large and have thousands of customers; others are small with just a handful of customers. Regardless of whose software you license, you, as a business, do not own the software — you rent it.

In an ideal world, you may want to take the applications that you use and chop them up into component parts and then add Web services interfaces, giving you incredible flexibility and maybe even making you happy. The problem is that you don't own that software, so you don't have the legal right to change anything about that code.

Don't get discouraged. The movement to SOA is changing everything in the commercial applications world. In time, software vendors will have to change their applications to come into line with the industry movement or risk their own extinction. They will also have to change their licenses to cover the use of their applications as a set of modular components that can be linked together with Web services.

Meanwhile, you have plenty of work to do to focus on identifying business services. With luck, smart vendors will make their software available to you as a service sooner rather than later.

The process management activity here involves linking together every manual activity and business function and passing data and instructions to the person or the business function when necessary. You can think of the people represented in the diagram as carrying out business functions that have not yet been automated or that cannot be automated (packing boxes, making phone calls, or any place human involvement is required).

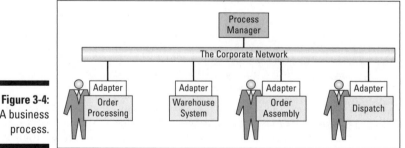

Figure 3-4:
A business
process.

Business processes are production lines

Business processes typically have other business processes nested inside them like Russian dolls. "Taking and fulfilling an order" is a broad business process that consists of a collection of narrower business processes, such as recording the order, assembling the order, updating inventory, dispatching the order and posting to the general ledger. And exactly what is done and how it is done, for each such process, may vary.

If we model such *subprocesses* from a SOA perspective, the models consist of manual activities linked to application functions or to other manual activities, and the process management component takes care of the flow from one activity to the next.

The flow of activity in business processes, as they are currently implemented by most organizations, is rarely fully automated and is often completely manual. Because process management is relatively new, applications running in quite a number of organizations lack formal process management.

You can think of a business process as a production line. The process follows a set path or, more likely, one of several possible paths, until it completes. The process manager determines the path the process follows. In following the path, various business functions are executed, and various manual tasks are carried out. The process can be repeated indefinitely. All the standard issues in production lines come into play: average capacity, surge capacity, bottlenecks, single points of failure, and so on.

New Applications from Old — Composite Applications

Another way to put your newly harvested Web services to use is to create new applications from them. *Composite applications* are applications built from the business functions of existing applications, with perhaps one or two new components added.

Figure 3-5 shows a composite application. In this example, a business sets up a call center to sell directly to customers over the phone. It uses new SOA-enabled call center software to manage the calls. This application consists of six business functions (C1, C2, . . .). The call center must be able to enter orders and process payments, so it requires all the order-processing functions (O1, O2, . . .). The telephone sales staff needs to be able to check on stock, so they need, for example, function W4 from the warehouse system. Hiring the telephone sales staff requires all the functions (H1, H2, . . .) of the human resources and payroll systems. The call history module logs all the calls to the call center. To pay the sales staff, a specially calculated commission may require writing a function (or module). A function to link call records to customer records must also be written.

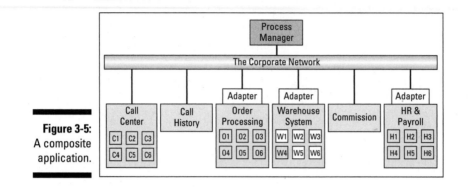

Figure 3-5:
A composite
application.

Thread all these things together and add the process manager and, presto, you have a composite application that takes care of the call center operation. The composite application is built by the SOA sewing all the components together.

The telephone sales operation now naturally feeds into the rest of the company's operation. There is no need to change the workflow because the telephone sales personnel also fulfill the function of order-processing staff.

A composite application capability usually delivers benefits in two significant areas. The first — the one we illustrate here — involves situations in which existing applications are extended to incorporate their use in a slightly different way (such as through a call center). The second area involves integrating existing business applications that heretofore have interacted directly with one another. The reality of most business applications is that they automate a specific set of tasks well, but they don't integrate well with the applications "on each side" of them. Usually, a set of manual tasks compensate for the fact that applications are poorly integrated. For that reason, integrating business applications typically pays dividends.

Toward end-to-end process

When you start thinking in terms of end-to-end processes, you have to sacrifice a view of the world that is fundamentally based on application silos. If you've ever crossed grain-growing fields, you probably remember the tall, autonomous structures that store grain. These structures are independent and free standing — and, most important, are not designed to have any connection with silos found anywhere else. In contemporary business IT parlance, *siloed applications* are those applications built specifically for immediate and exclusive use by one specific set of users with no intention or preparation for their use by others. Application silos, often harboring mission-critical code, blight the landscape of most organizations.

Siloed applications were built to satisfy the needs of one specific department or section of a company. It happened partly because of the way companies were organized and partly because of the way applications were built. Each department did what it could to ensure that it had the applications that served its specific needs. When these applications were built, no global standards for application integration or data integration existed, so the problems that arise today are not really anybody's fault. Those early analysts and coders probably did the best job they could with the knowledge of their time, and they probably did a pretty good job if their programs are still in use today — both the good news and the bad in one sentence.

The inability to easily integrate the pieces was no secret. Everyone knew there was an integration problem. To some extent, Enterprise Resource Planning (ERP) software vendors such as SAP and Oracle addressed this problem by pre-integrating a set of the most commonly used components, such as human resources (HR) and financial accounting. But such solutions went only so far and were of no help in specialized areas or when anomalies emerged.

Siloed applications generate the following two (very specific) problems:

- ✔ **Inconsistent data definitions:** Simply stated, applications built at different times or by different people often define the same set of data differently. A good example is the data that defines the customer. Almost all large organizations have, buried in their business applications, several differing definitions of *customer*. Is the customer the General Motors financial department that processes the invoices sent by your accounts system? A Chevrolet assembly plant that orders parts through your order processing system? A particular engineer in the design shop who collaborates with your designers on the custom tools you provide? They are inconsistent because each was created for a specific application and there was no master definition to use, so a new definition was invented for each new application.

- ✔ **Duplication of software processes:** Companies often have many applications that include individualized code representing the same business processes. Similar to inconsistent data definitions, duplicated software processes result in wasted time and effort. For example, we know a company that has two methods of calculating a discount. The quotations and order-processing application calculate the discount one way, and the accounting department created its own routine to calculate the discount. Because of inconsistent data definitions, the routines don't always agree and can't be made to agree. In this case, the company set up a manual activity to reconcile the difference between the two calculations. We wish this scenario were unusual, but it isn't. It's so common that companies regularly write reconciliation programs to deal with disparities.

The problems of siloed applications are frequently masked by flexible staff who compensate for computer systems that don't work well. While the immediate problem appears to be solved, the consequences of this ad hoc approach may prove dire. In a world that demands accountability in the form of regulatory compliance and audit, these behaviors are certainly suspect. SOA is very good for cleaning up these kinds of discrepancies — with SOA, the exact same function is performed the exact same way every time.

Adopting business processes and composite applications

SOA is conceptually different from traditional software architectures and requires you to think in new ways. We suggest you start integrating your application silos together to create end-to-end business processes and threading their components into composite applications. Why? Because application silos contain a wealth of reusable resources, and with SOA, they need not be hostile to change, difficult to maintain, inefficient, and intransigent. SOA makes them more supple, extensible, and responsive to change.

As you well know, you can't change everything at once. One nice thing about SOA is that you can change things gradually, over time, knowing all the while that the changes you are making make future changes easier. Previous IT investments usually "ripped and replaced" still earlier investments with brand-new somethings. With SOA, you don't rip down a silo and start from scratch. You gently transform it into a well structured collection of reusable components. SOA allows you to harvest those early investments and plant them in renewable, reusable, fertile soil. Gosh, we're getting downright agrarian here.

The two-headed desk

On more than one consulting assignment we have come across a worker with two computers on his or her desk. More often than not, we find the employee is responsible for coordinating two siloed computer systems, taking data from some report screen on one system and entering it into the other. Often, the screens are festooned with sticky notes around the borders: "Account numbers on System A in the 80 series must be entered with the 537 prefix on System B" or "We get an extra 5% discount through March" or "Call Sandy in receivables if the check doesn't come on time." SOA is designed to eliminate two-headed desks and let siloed applications talk to each other, with easy ways to add and maintain the necessary business rules for handling exceptions.

Chapter 4

SOA Sophistication

*I*f you've been dutifully following along, reading all about Web services and business processes and composite applications, you may have already noticed that (so far) we do a pretty good job of hiding the gnarly bits of intricate technology that make all this possible. We think, however, that you may still need to know the critical components that make SOA SOA, so we carry on.

In this chapter, we introduce the major components of a service oriented architecture. This is the appetizer chapter. Many components are so important that they (later) get entire chapters of their own, but we introduce them here to show them in relationship to each other and to help you with "the big picture."

Making SOA Happen

We show major components of a service oriented architecture in Figure 4-1. The enterprise service bus (ESB), the SOA registry, workflow engine, service broker, SOA supervisor each have a role to play, both independently and with each other. The ESB makes sure that messages get passed back and forth between the components of a SOA implementation. The SOA registry contains important *reference* information about where the components of a SOA are located. The workflow engine provides the technology to connect people to people, to connect people to processes and processes to processes; while the service broker connects services to services, which in the end enables the flow of business process.

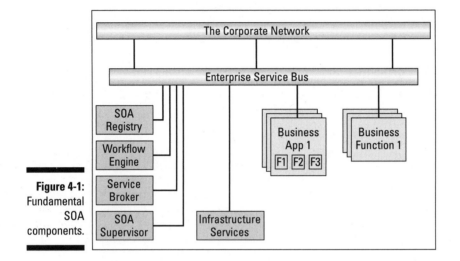

Figure 4-1:
Fundamental
SOA
components.

The role of the SOA supervisor is to make sure that the platform underneath the SOA environment works in a consistent and predictable way. The goal is to create an environment where all these components work together to improve the flow of business process. All these services are required to link unrelated technology components together as though they were *designed* to work together. Later in this chapter, we provide additional information on business process management (BPM) as it relates to SOA.

When all these component parts work together and sing the same tune, the result is improved service levels The finely tuned SOA is what guarantees service levels.

Catching the Enterprise Service Bus

In service oriented architectures, all the different pieces of software talk to each other by sending each other messages, a lot of messages. The messages are critical to delivering end-to-end service. They must be delivered quickly, and their arrival must be guaranteed. If that doesn't happen, "end-to-end" service quickly becomes "lack of service."

To transport the messages between software components, SOAs typically use an enterprise service bus (ESB). The ESB is so important to SOA that some people think that you can't have a SOA without one, and still others think that if you have an ESB, you have a SOA. Neither statement is accurate. You don't need to have an ESB to have a SOA, but you do need to have something that plays the ESB role. And an ESB does not a SOA make. If it did, we would have told you so in Chapter 1. However, the ESB is so important that it has it's own chapter — Chapter 9.

The ESB is a bit like a phone system. You can think of it as a special layer that runs on top of the network that provides a guaranteed messaging service for the most important messages on the network, including the messages that the components of SOA continuously send to each other.

Usually, in architecture diagrams, the ESB is represented as a separate pipe through which information and instructions flow. (Refer to Figure 4-1 to see what we mean.) In reality, it is not. It is a collection of software components that manage messaging from one software component to another. A software component connects to the ESB and passes it a message by using a specified format along with the address of the software component that needs to receive the message. The ESB completes the job of getting the message from the sending component to the receiving component.

Although you could conceivably build your own ESB, it is the kind of sophisticated software component that most companies are more than happy to buy. We are strongly in favor of companies "buying" rather than "building" an ESB. Many vendors offer ESBs, including IBM, Cape Clear, Iona, Progress Software, BEA, Software AG, Oracle, and others.

Welcome to the SOA Registry

It may have occurred to you that somebody or something must have to keep track of all the available pieces — you know, all those services that have been garnered from your old business applications? All those reusable components have to be recorded somewhere, and that somewhere is the *SOA registry*.

The SOA registry is a kind of electronic catalog where you store information describing what each component does. It has two roles: one rooted in the operational environment and one rooted in the world of programmers and business analysts. In the operational environment, the SOA registry provides reference information about software components that are running or available for use — information that is particularly important to the service broker. (We talk a lot more about the service broker in Chapter 8.)

For programmers and business analysts, on the other hand, the SOA registry acts as a reference that helps them select components and connect them together to create composite applications and build processes. It also stores information about *how* each component connects to other components. In other words, the SOA registry documents the rules and descriptions associated with every given component.

Some SOA implementers build their own registry — that is, they develop their own software to provide this capability. Many others purchase registry software. (Systinet Registry is an example here, or Infravio's X-Registry.)

The SOA registry is extremely important because it acts as the central reference point within a service oriented architecture. The SOA registry contains information (metadata) about all the components that the SOA supports. For that reason, it defines the "domain" of the architecture.

The SOA registry isn't just a place where you store definitions of your software components for developers and business analysts to use. The SOA registry is also where you *publish* components for more "public" entities — potentially, your customers and business partners — to use.

The idea of *publishing* Web services is critical to SOA. You can only reuse services that are available for reuse.

The SOA registry is so important that, later on in the book, we devote several chapters to the topic. (In Chapter 8 we talk about the SOA registry and the SOA broker and, as an added bonus, we also talk about repositories and how they relate to registries in Chapter 15.)

I never metadata I didn't like

The term *metadata* means "data about data" — data that defines, for example, what a set of data items contains. The metadata for a database of books might, for example, be *author, title, publisher,* and *classification*. When it comes to SOA registries, the term *metadata* encompasses a lot more information — a full definition of each software component, for example, as well as the data that can be passed to it with each particular message it will accept and the data that it will provide with each response it can give. The metadata effectively defines all the possibilities of the software component; it is all the information that any other software component needs to communicate with it.

Introducing the workflow engine

The workflow engine is a software component designed to connect a whole business process from end to end, flowing work from one individual or process to another until the entire business process is carried out. Workflow development technologies provide a modeling capability that allows you to model a business process to produce a *workflow pattern.* The workflow pattern is, in effect, the set of instructions that the workflow engine runs.

Workflow development products existed long before SOA; thus, there are many products in this category, often with different emphases on their main area of usage. About ten years ago, many workflow development products were associated with document management systems. More recently, they have tended to be associated with business process management (BPM) tools and many have even repositioned themselves as BPM tools. Their functionality is part of the offerings available from most major SOA vendors.

Every business has workflow, be it casual or formal, efficient or disastrous. Formalizing the workflow goes a long way toward codifying business process — which is a good thing, in case you're curious. Using business process management, you can monitor and codify the way your business actually works. We say more about BPM later in this chapter.

Your friendly neighborhood service broker

Your components are registered in the SOA registry. The workflow engine strings processes together to make things happen. What more could you need? You need a *service broker.* You have probably come across some sort of broker in your life — a real estate broker, a mortgage broker, a stock broker. The broker is the deal maker, and the service broker brokers the deals between components. It listens very carefully to all the constraints and concerns on both sides of the equation and makes everyone happy.

The service broker is the component that actually makes all the connections between components work. It acts like a needle threading one component to the next in a business process. It uses information about the components it finds in the SOA registry and threads the components together for the workflow engine. The service broker gets things started. After it does its job of threading all the components of one business process together, it wanders off looking for another one to start.

Service brokers are middleware products. Some of the products in this category evolved from object request brokers associated with the object oriented software trend. Some were direct Enterprise Application Integration (EAI) products, such as those from BEA, Sun Microsystems' SeeBeyond offering, and Microsoft. Some grew from Enterprise Information Integration products, such as those from Cape Clear or Attunity. Some of these are gradually evolving to become ESBs, as has happened for example with Cape Clear. Most ESBs can also act as service brokers.

The SOA supervisor, again

Way back when you could barely spell SOA, we put a black box in a picture and called it the SOA supervisor (back in Chapter 2.) By now, you probably understand that there's a ton to supervise, so this SOA supervisor thing better be good stuff. The SOA supervisor is the master conductor, the grand choreographer, the traffic cop and all-around central point of control responsible for all SOA orchestration.

Just to get a sense of who's talking to whom, think about business function components passing data and instructions to each other. At the same time, the workflow engine is passing instructions and data around. The SOA supervisor's agents are sending information to the SOA supervisor, which in turn may be communicating with plumbing services. There's a whole lot of talking going on. (We describe this in greater detail in Chapter 10.)

The SOA supervisor interacts with the infrastructure services. If any of the components in the end-to-end service have any performance problems, the SOA supervisor sends the details to the appropriate infrastructure services, and the infrastructure services try to fix the problem. Aren't you glad that plumbing is invisible to the business?

The SOA supervisor is responsible for many things, but it is above all responsible for ensuring service levels. It uses reports from monitoring agents (initiated by the service broker) to keep track of exactly what's happening. The monitoring agents report on the service level being achieved at each point in the process. The SOA supervisor is then in a position to know when the service gets bad or when any part of it fails.

Software products that offer SOA supervisor capability include Hewlett-Packard's OpenView SOA Manager, Amberpoint's SOA Management System, and Looking Glass from Progress Software. Incidentally, this is a technology area where we expect to see a much greater level of sophistication emerge in the future. Most of the software products here are "first generation," meaning "hot off the shelf," "not entirely broken in," you know, "new."

Managing Business Process under SOA

With all this discussion of registries and buses, we want to remind you that the whole point of SOA is to make a business more manageable, more flexible, and more responsive to change. The primary culprit when it comes to instigating change is business process — how businesses do things. Businesses are constantly changing *how* they do things — not necessarily changing *what* they do. For example, an insurance company might change the methods it uses to introduce new products or how it handles insurance claims — but, when all is said and done, it still sells insurance. SOA enables businesspeople to change business processes without having to focus on the underlying technological plumbing. You can concentrate on designing and improving business processes by threading together business services. IT can build composite applications from existing business functions, adding other functions or making changes where necessary. Together, business and IT can determine the flow of work from one person to another (or from a person to a process or from a process to a person) within the larger business process.

"But how do they do that exactly?" you may wonder. Thanks for asking. With all these business processes to manage, the somewhat obvious solution is *business process management* (BPM). BPM is the modern approach to designing and managing business processes, and many business managers and business analysts receive BPM training. All by itself, BPM has contributed significantly to the liberation of business from technology. Coupled with SOA, BPM is even more powerful.

In addition to the BPM methodologies and approaches being bandied about by sharply dressed consultants in countless corporate conference rooms, you'll find software tools out there that have been created specifically to help automate business process management. They are called, oddly enough, *BPM tools*. BPM tools organize workflows, thread together existing business functions, and create new functions.

With SOA, you want to harvest existing business functions by taking them out of their existing application homes — applications that have provided the "connective tissue" necessary to keep them functioning smoothly. The new connective tissue you need to house the harvested business functions comes in the form either of the business process itself or of a composite application. BPM tools are critical here because they help you design and manage just such business processes.

From the Orient

What we call BPM today is the result of a western adaptation of management best practices that evolved primarily from Japanese manufacturing. The closest equivalent Japanese term is *Kaizen*, which can be defined as "continuous improvement," or perhaps more aptly, "to take apart and put back together in a better way." Beyond continuous improvement, BPM embraces other management methods, such as Total Quality Management and Six Sigma.

Business processes actually codify how a business works, and this very codification of business processes is a critical step for any organization subject to any kind of regulatory compliance, such as the Sarbanes-Oxley Act, the Health Insurance Portability and Accountability Act (HIPAA), and a host of others.

BPM enables businesses to monitor business processes, which can lead to continuous improvement by identifying possible changes in a process that could result in better efficiency. Over time, more and more business processes are tied to software. When supported by SOA, continuous business improvement becomes a lot easier because the underlying software is "loosely coupled," meaning that it can be modified more easily when required. When business needs to change in order to address strategic opportunities and threats, the flexible service oriented architecture facilitates the change.

BPM tools

Here's how a BPM tool uses the components of process management to make SOA sing:

- ✔ **It enables the creation of new business functions.** A developer may add whole new business functions or may simply add logic to run before or after an existing business function. In order to do this, the BPM tool includes some way of specifying a software process. When a new business function is created, the BPM tool adds the function's details to the SOA registry, including information about how it links to other components.

- ✔ **It links together business functions from existing applications.** The BPM tool refers to the SOA registry to identify business functions that are published there. It enables a developer to link them together to make composite applications or slot them in at the appropriate point in the overall workflow. The BPM tool stores this information in the SOA registry.

✔ **It programs the workflow engine to carry out the business process.**
Using the BPM tool, business analysts design process flows and specify
the movement of work from one person to another within a business
process, linking in the applications that they need to use for the tasks
that they have to carry out.

Figure 4-2 gives you a nice graphical representation of how a BPM tool
accomplishes these three tasks.

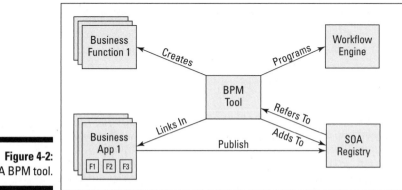

Figure 4-2:
A BPM tool.

The BPM lay of the land

All the major infrastructure vendors with a SOA offering — folks like IBM, HP,
BEA, Oracle, and SAP — are also very interested in business process management. (You can read about all these vendors in Part V.) In fact, BPM is so
closely tied into SOA that many of the SOA software vendors have been
investing heavily in new software development or strengthening partnerships
to build their BPM solutions. For example, one of the long-standing leaders in
BPM, IDS Scheer, entered into two new significant licensing agreements in
2006, one with Oracle and one with Lombardi Software, a BPM software
vendor. IDS Scheer's BPM product is called the ARIS platform. It is a portfolio
of tools that provide customers with an integrated way to model, implement,
and control their business processes. Oracle will call the product the Oracle
Business Process Analysis (BPA) Suite and it will combine with Oracle's BPL
Process Manager. As for Lombardi Software, they've integrated their
TeamWorks product with the IDS Scheer ARIS platform.

These agreements are just the most recent of IDS Scheer's partnership
arrangements with software vendors in the area of business process management. IDS Scheer also partners with Software AG for their BPM solution and

the company has a deep partnership arrangement with SAP going back many years. IDS Scheer and SAP jointly provide SAP NetWeaver and ARIS for SAP NetWeaver. This solution allows customers to model their business processes, ensure the quality of those processes, and describe the configuration of business process models based on their SAP application. The various partnership arrangements give customers the flexibility to use the ARIS platform to manage the business process life cycle and execute the business process model by using the engine provided by the vendor of their choice.

Intalio is an Open Source BPM vendor and has a growing list of customers and partners. Other software vendors focused on BPM include MetaStorm, Savion, and PegaSystems.

Guaranteeing Service

Now that you've been exposed to some of the critical components of a service oriented architecture, it's a good time to dredge up the definition of a service oriented architecture from Chapter 2 — hopeful that it now makes more sense than it did a few chapters ago. Doing so will give focus to the vital last phrase of the definition, which we have so skillfully avoided until now.

If you read Chapter 2, you may remember that we define a *service oriented architecture* as a software *architecture* for building applications that implement business processes or *services* by using a set of loosely coupled black-box components orchestrated to deliver a well-defined level of service.

The "well-defined level of service" piece comes front and center now. Service *levels,* as the name implies, means that service is not so black and white. By way of illustration, think about service in a restaurant (as we did in Chapter 2): You could have great service or lousy service or so-so service. Or it may have started out great but when it came to getting your check, your waiter couldn't be found.

Service levels in IT have become critically important in the last decade because business has become more and more dependent on IT. Furthermore, IT itself has transitioned from using autonomous software packages serving a well-defined, limited set of users to using software delivered as a service over a network to huge numbers of users (just like telephone service and electricity). And just as you know if you've ever been caught in a power outage or experienced downed telephone lines, the lack of IT service, depending on when it happens and how long it lasts, ranges from somewhat inconvenient to ruinous. For many organizations, an hour of IT downtime costs millions of dollars.

99.999%

Perhaps you are perplexed by why the last percent of reliability and availability is so very expensive, and why 99.999% should cost so much more than plain old 99%. We'll try to explain. (99.999, by the way, is sometimes referred to as "Five Nines" and is said with a great deal of awe and respect.)

Say, for example, that you have a server that's up most of the time — it rarely crashes. Maybe it's down three days a year. That's roughly 99% available. Now if you really truly need 100% availability (or as close as you can get), you have to do more than just buy another server. You may have to buy multiple servers, invest in failover capabilities, and guarantee that you have no single point of failure, such as the power supply. You may need a generator. Do you begin to see the cost of being "always on?" The bigger and more complicated your system, the greater the number of vulnerabilities or points of failure. Ensuring availability (and extra capacity for peak loads) is not small change.

Businesses whose very livelihoods depend on their being available 24/7 go to great lengths to ensure that availability. Many businesses calculate one hour of downtime as costing millions of dollars, so three days of downtime could cost over $200,000,000.

Thus, businesses that depend on services often enter into agreements with their service providers that guarantee a specific level of service, focused primarily on the availability and speed of service. For example, 100 percent uptime means that systems are available 100 percent of the time (absolutely no downtime — virtually impossible).

The ability to guarantee high levels of availability and high speeds of service usually implies higher levels of investment in computer systems — including having redundant systems in place in case of an emergency as well as having extra capacity should the need arise. The higher the level of service, the more it costs. So guaranteeing service availability at the 99.999% level is significantly more costly than guaranteeing availability at a 99% level. See the sidebar, "99.999%," to find out why.

And perhaps you have gleaned, being the astute reader that you are, that a *service* oriented architecture, being, as it were, all about service, has the potential to deliver variable levels of service. Will your SOA deliver good service, bad service, so-so service, intermittent service, or unpredictable service? Obviously, anything less than good service (or maybe even great service) will put your entire business at risk.

Service oriented architectures must make composite applications and business processes available, reliable, and predictable. Although the responsibility of all the choreography needed to make and keep service levels high falls squarely on IT, we think everybody should know the basic principles. And understanding the basic principles can go a long way toward bettering the communication flow between business and IT, which are jointly responsible in the new world order.

Application failures — Let us count the ways

Understanding service levels as they apply to application availability means understanding how and why applications fail and the consequences of the failure.

Applications can fail because the hardware they are running on fails or because the network connecting the users to the application fails. Or the application itself can fail, or the operating system running the application can fail, or some of the management software managing the application can fail . . . and on and on.

When software components fail, it takes time to find the cause of the failure and to get the system back into action. If this can be done automatically, so much the better; but even if it can, it could take more than a minute or two. If it isn't automatic, it's likely to take hours.

Not all problems cause outright failure. Some may simply slow the application down. Just as applications can fail for many reasons, they can also slow down for many reasons.

Measuring service levels

The only way to know that an application is delivering the service that the business users require is to define the service level the business needs and to measure the application's activity to see whether it is achieving that level. Because application interruptions are sporadic, you need to measure service constantly and average it out over a period of a month (and/or a year) to arrive at a meaningful number.

A detailed definition of a service level for an order-processing application might be as follows:

- ✔ Application to be available 99.9% of the time every weekday from 6 a.m. to 10 p.m. EST.
- ✔ In the event of a failure, the application should recover within 20 minutes.

✔ The response time for order inquiries, changes to orders, and entering new orders should average 1 second and should never be worse than 2 seconds, 99.9% of the time.

✔ In the event of degraded service occurring and response times slowing, normal service should be restored within 1 hour.

Defining the service level this way serves both business and IT well. Compliance with this service level agreement would mean that the order-processing application would be unavailable for, at worst, 4 hours 10 minutes during the whole year — little more than half a day. The response time could be poor for as much as 4 hours 10 minutes in the year. In the worst-case scenario, the application is unavailable for 20 minutes when it does fail. And when service degrades, it is always back to normal within an hour.

IT needs the right set of computer equipment and supporting software to deliver a service level of this kind for the application, including the appropriate failover capability as necessary. And if the application gets more users, IT needs to upgrade the computers to keep pace with the resource requirements.

End-to-end service

Delivering high levels of service for a stand-alone application isn't so tough — you have relatively few people to make happy. However, when you involve a network and begin to deliver services across that network, life ceases to be simple.

With SOA, you might (and probably will) link together components from different applications. But the service level that you want to deliver in the new application you create this way is not necessarily the same service level delivered by each of the different applications you're taking components from. In fact, they could differ from each other, and your new application could have a service level different from any of its components.

Do you have a headache yet? Consider the development of a new order-processing application that is very similar to an old one but that is written specifically to work on the Internet. You build a few new software components and use most of the components from your old order-processing system. The service levels for the old system might be acceptable, except for one thing: Because this is an *Internet* application, it needs to run 24/7.

So why not just leave the old application running all the time? Simply put, the old application wasn't designed to run all the time. It was designed to allow data backups to occur at night and for data to be extracted from the database at night when the application wasn't running.

Of course, this isn't an unmitigated disaster. You could just change the old application in some way. However, changing the old application takes time, and it will have to change again whenever your business needs change again. The reality of most businesses is that change is the only thing that is predictable. To support continuous change, linking software components together makes much more sense than recoding applications.

When you consider linking together many software components from many applications, a bigger issue emerges. The applications that were built to deliver specific service levels linked together end to end must deliver service end to-end. To deliver dependable service levels means controlling the end-to-end process, which means you need the SOA supervisor.

Just one more look

To round this chapter off, we can take another look at the component we simply referred to as the Process Manager back in Chapter 3. We were making life easy for you by representing it as a single component. In reality, the activity of process management is carried out by three components: the SOA registry, the workflow engine, and the service broker. (See Figure 4-3.)

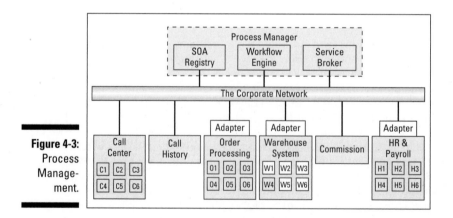

Figure 4-3:
Process
Manage-
ment.

This diagram ought to look suspiciously like Figure 3-5 in Chapter 3, because it is. The difference is that in this version, we break the component we called the Process Manager into three separate components:

✔ The SOA registry stores information describing what each SOA component does so that business analysts or programmers can select components and connect components together to create composite applications. The registry also stores information about how one component connects to another.

✔ The workflow engine connects together a whole business process in an end-to-end manner, flowing work from one individual or process to another as the business process is carried out.

✔ The service broker actually makes all the connections between components work. The service broker is a needle that threads together all the software components of a business process by using information it gleans from the registry.

For SOA to achieve the sophistication that we predict it can, we need to pull the pieces of hardware, software, services, infrastructure, process, and even people together so they act like a single system. The greatest benefit of SOA is that you can change the piece parts and still have a well-oiled machine.

Chapter 5

Playing Fast and Loose: Loose Coupling and Federation

*B*oth traditional packaged software applications (the kind you buy from some company somewhere) and extensive homegrown software systems (created specifically to solve particular problems for a particular set of people) share a common difficulty: They were not designed for substantive change. One pervasive characteristic that makes both kinds of applications especially brittle is just how *intertwined* the various programs that constitute the software applications are. The various programs are dependent on each other for little bits of code — without such bits, they cannot run. These dependencies were often created in the name of efficiency, especially in the days when hardware and memory were expensive.

Why Am I So Dependent?

Have you ever seen the children's toy that has pictures of animals on cards, but the cards are divided into thirds — the top third of each card has the head of the animal; the second third, the middle; and the bottom third, the bottom of the animal? Mixing them up can keep some people entertained for hours. However, if you tried the same stunt with written stories, taking the first part of the story from, say, *Little Red Riding Hood*, the middle from *Goldilocks and the Three Bears*, and the ending from *Hansel and Gretel*, the story you'd end up with probably wouldn't be too amusing — in fact, such a story probably wouldn't make any sense at all because a coherent story is *dependent* upon the characters, settings, and storyline remaining consistent "from end to end."

Why are we telling you this? Because traditional software applications bear a striking resemblance to stories that have a beginning, a middle, and an end. In the world of service oriented architecture, however, the rules change. Old applications are broken down into reusable services — components that can then be used to build even more new and glorious applications.

Sounds great in theory, but the devil's in the details when it comes to putting said theory into practice. In making such components, you must take great care to eliminate *dependencies* — those nasty artifacts of traditional software design that can tie your wonderful new application into unsightly knots. What you are trying to do is ensure that each component carries out a single, easily understood function and does nothing else. Your goal is to be able to create flexible composite applications that can be easily changed when change is necessary. That's not possible if your component parts have dependencies.

In the SOA world, you hear as much about deconstruction as you used to hear about integration. Not only must you deconstruct applications, but businesses must also deconstruct their business processes by breaking them down into fundamental components. Then in the same way that the software components can be reused, the business components can be reused in lots of different business situations. This is a big change for software development, and one that requires cultural changes not just from the information technology group but from the whole of the business.

Avoiding dependencies applies when writing completely new applications as well. Initially, it takes more discipline and more time to write software without dependencies, but eventually it will be just as fast. It's natural for developers to write applications that do what the user has asked for. And it's natural for users to ask for things that specifically fit the way that they want to carry out a particular task. That's how dependencies get created — with the best of intentions. Applications built this way may work extremely well when they are first built; however, if the same functionality is required by some other system, trying to reuse the original application is either impossible or requires a great deal of work. In effect, you have to deconstruct it. In the long run, the reality of dependencies in traditional applications *slows* development and *thwarts* easy business change.

On the business side, business professionals are often impatient to solve their problems quickly, so the initial effort and time required to create software services without dependencies may appear to take far too long. But if they want to be in a position to reuse the software they're investing in, they need to invest in "doing things right."

Loose Coupling

After you have dependency-free software services, you can think about linking them together to create a composite application — that is, an application composed of autonomous services. Even if each of these services had been built and used in older applications that had nothing to do with each other, they can be joined together if you can find a reason to do so. If these component services come together and come apart easily, they are said to be "loosely coupled" — that is, they are not intertwined in the way traditional applications are. They are not dependent on each other and can be mixed and matched with other component services as needed.

An important aspect of loose coupling is that the component services and the plumbing (the basic instructions for how the pieces interact with each other) are deliberately separated so that the service itself has no code related to managing the computing environment. Because of this separation, components can be bound together dynamically in real time and will behave as if they were a single, tightly coupled application.

Not all component services are the same size. In some cases, a software service might be an entire application that offers many individual but similar functions. For example, a quotations application in a life insurance company might be a component service, even though it calculates premiums for many types of policies with many nuances, such as joint life policies and group life policies. If Web service interfaces were added to such an application, it could be used automatically in many contexts.

While this quotations component can now be loosely coupled with other software components, the internals of this particular component are themselves *tightly* coupled — meaning there is one component that determines the price of a term life insurance policy and another component that calculates the risk factor based on health and age. These two components have not been separated out as discrete services. For the use mentioned here, these two components act as a single tightly coupled component. In other situations, these same components can be used individually or together. The relevant aspects of each component get used without re-creating something special, and the consistency of doing the same function exactly the same way yields lots of benefits.

Loose coupling is possible because of all the support provided by various service oriented architecture components, such as the enterprise service bus, the SOA repository, the SOA registry, SOA plumbing, and Web service interfaces such as XML, SOAP, and WSDL. We tell you about all these pieces in greater detail in the next part of this book.

Loose coupling may sound like a new idea to the world of software development, but it's taken for granted in many other industries. Automobile manufacturers long ago understood that they had to make interchangeable parts for automobiles if they were to survive financially.

For example, the same steering column is used in many different car models. Some models may modify it (for example, add a different steering wheel with a leather cover or music system controls), but the basic steering column doesn't change. In addition, the steering column has been designed so that it can be used in a number of different car models, so power steering columns can be substituted for manual columns without alteration to the rest of the car. Most car manufacturers don't view the basic steering mechanism as a significant differentiator or source of innovation.

Loose coupling allows you to do a lot of things more quickly and more efficiently. The following list spells out some of the more significant benefits:

- ✔ **Create new applications quickly by using existing services:** Loose coupling enables you to quickly create new and different applications from existing software services, in effect creating new services only when what you need to do really isn't being done anywhere else.

- ✔ **Replace one service with another without rewriting the whole application:** One of the biggest problems companies face with their software is that it's not easy to change code in the middle of an application without affecting other aspects of the application. In a world in which dependencies often pervade the structure of an application, one small change can lead to another followed by another.

  It can be a lot like pulling a thread out of a sweater. You think getting rid of that single thread will solve your problem. In fact, that one thread is connected to threads throughout the sweater. By the time you are done pulling that "single" thread, you've completely unraveled the sweater.

  With a loosely coupled implementation, each service is independent of the next, so when one service needs to be replaced, it doesn't impact the rest of the services. For example, if you have a credit-checking service and the laws change, you simply replace the old credit-checking service with the new without touching any of the other applications that use the service.

- ✔ **Create secure business applications quickly:** Most organizations don't have end-to-end IT security for their applications. In a traditional software architecture, each application has to include its own code to protect it from security breaches. With a loose coupling approach, security can be designed as a set of services that are independent of any one application. In this way, security policy can be implemented once as a service and linked to each application that it applies to. This means that businesses can have better ways to ensure control over security across their own systems as well as the systems of their closest partners.

We think security is so important that we devote a whole chapter to it. For more on security, see Chapter 12.

✔ **Isolate problems easily:** In traditional applications, finding the cause of bugs can be difficult — especially when systems have been changed significantly over time. A set of dependencies can trigger a huge number of problems in the application that are hard to identify. On the other hand, if each software service is a) built without dependencies and b) tested before deployment, the process of testing the functionality of the new composite application is a lot easier. In essence, each service lives in its own world and doesn't interfere with the next service.

This is important in situations in which a business wants to make part of an old application into a software service. If the dependencies are successfully removed, the service can stand on its own two feet. In the long run, your applications will be more stable.

✔ **Turn software services into cash:** Having created loosely coupled software services, businesses are now finding innovative ways to use these services. For example, a health insurance company we talked to was able to create a software service that manages the processing of insurance claims. After the company figured out how to do this for itself, it was able to sell the claims processing service it had developed to other health insurance companies. What was initially a development cost became a new source of revenue.

Software As a Service

Loose coupling is enabling what may come to be a whole new sector of the software industry, which goes by the name of *software as a service*. The health insurance company we talk about in the preceding section provides an example of software as a service, but many examples have emerged in recent years. With software as a service, the provider hosts the software for you so you don't need to manage it or buy hardware for it. All you have to do is connect to it and use it.

In the long run, the delivery of a great deal of application functionality via software as a service will likely be the norm. Ironically, the computer industry started out with this model. Until the mid-1970s, most companies that computerized their businesses subscribed to time-sharing services. In those days, computers were simply too expensive for one company to own.

Although hardware costs have plummeted dramatically, running software applications and maintaining data centers still cost companies plenty.

When the pioneers in software as a service, such as Salesforce.com, first entered the market, many CIOs were skeptical. The requirements for software as a service were driven largely by business unit management who were attracted by the prospect of not having the overhead of running systems. One of the earliest successes for software as a service came from the Customer Relationship Management (CRM) market. While a lot of companies — large and small — needed to manage customers and prospects, traditional CRM software packages were complex software systems that were hard to implement and even harder to use. They required a lot of work just to implement them properly. Out of desperation, many companies decided they had nothing to lose by experimenting with CRM as a service. Smaller companies, who couldn't afford a big IT organization but still wanted the CRM capabilities, were the first to experiment with this.

Many IT organizations reluctantly went along with the software-as-a-service experiment, with many of them harboring the expectation that when these applications became "mission critical," IT would need to move to a traditional software licensing model. It didn't happen. Salesforce.com, for example, was able to persuade management that the cost to license its software would be prohibitively expensive (if it were even an option) — especially when adding in the costs for hardware, systems management, backup, and the like. By running the same application for many different companies, Salesforce.com achieved powerful economies of scale.

Licensing models and service

An important aspect of this idea of software as a service is that it introduces a completely different license model to the computer world, a model that departs radically from the way customers traditionally acquire software. Basically, the way things have worked for years in the software world is that acquiring software meant signing on to a perpetual license for that software. For example, when you bought a shrink-wrapped software package for your very own computer, you got the manual and CD(s) inside, and you also got lots of legalese and seals that, when broken, indicated your implicit agreement to the software's license agreement that, if violated, meant your children and your children's children would become indentured subjects of the software's manufacturer in perpetuity. When you bought the software, you got a "perpetual license" — you can use the software as long as you have it without having to pay to use it again. The only "gotcha" is that you have to pay if you want the new bells and whistles or if you want the company to fix problems — the money they collect they call *maintenance*.

Software as a service is sold on a subscription basis. If you've had a magazine or newspaper subscription, you know the drill. You pay a certain amount every month or quarter or whatever, and as long as you pay, you get what you paid for. If you stop paying, you stop getting whatever it is you subscribed to. You're already used to paying for other kinds of services — gas, electric, phone service, and Internet access, for example. The new move toward selling software as a service means that software vendors are selling subscriptions rather than perpetual licenses.

Typically, software-as-a-service customers shell out what they need to shell out based on the number of users. There may be variations in this flat-rate plan if an application requires huge volumes of storage. For example, one customer might want to store a terabyte of data, and for that there would most likely be an extra charge.

A major appeal of software as a service lies in the fact that many customers like the idea of being able to try an application before they invest in implementation and training. They also like the ability to use an application they need perhaps only twice a year without having to buy a license. They also like the idea that someone else worries about the hardware, maintenance, and software backup.

With software as a service, excellent service levels are paramount. When customers rely upon the software as an essential aspect of their operation, they get mighty upset when it fails. For example, Salesforce.com was severely criticized by customers when it suffered a number of service outages. This was a tough lesson for this pioneer. Other issues surfaced as well. Customers want to be able to retrieve their data if the company that offers service suddenly goes out of business. They also need tools and/or services to make sure that the data stored in the service is accurate. To answer this customer requirement, SalesForce.com, for example, established a partner network called AppExchange to allow third-party software companies to sell software services related to the SalesForce.com offering.

Software as a service and SOA

If software-as-a-service providers add Web service interfaces and provide all the associated interface information to their customers, software as a service can be integrated within a service oriented architecture.

As companies implementing SOA discover that they've developed some applications that they can offer as services, they'll quickly find out that — without much additional effort — they may have a new revenue source on their hands.

Talkin' 'bout My Federation . . .

Now that you have a basic sense of what loose coupling is all about, we're going to talk about it in a bigger context. In large, distributed organizations — companies that are spread out, aren't centralized, and have branches in different sites (like most bigger businesses, in other words) — the potential for software reuse is likely to be great. However, because there will always be subtle (and sometimes not-so-subtle) differences in how things are done from one place to another, you need to make allowances for local differences while still protecting the integrity of the whole. Remember that the integrity of the whole is premised on processing the same things the same way and keeping consistency all down the line.

When it comes to software services, rules, and policies, you need to allow for local variances while simultaneously implementing organization-wide rules and policies designed to keep everyone on the same page. It's a management issue, a political issue, and a practical issue. To address these issues, you need to implement a *federation*.

By insisting on the federation model, you put your business in a position where it can effectively distribute processing, power, decision making, and knowledge as a way of fostering independent action. The federation model so familiar to us from high-school civics class is still the best model for distributed organizational structures like governments and global corporations.

In the United States, the government has a structure that defines how laws are created and the way disputes are resolved. The federal government has its own set of powers and distributes some powers to the state governments. State governments in turn distribute certain authority to the cities and towns. In this way, the United States has a *federated* government.

For companies, federation is similar. For a very small company, keeping all the decision making under one central authority makes sense. However, when a company becomes complex — with lots of products and functions and lots of offices and divisions — this approach may cease to work. If you insist on absolute centralized authority, you'll soon find yourself with one giant department forced to handle everything from accounting to human resources to product development. We think this makes no sense. We hope you agree.

Most normal companies have separate departments for each of these functions — accounting, HR, whatever. Managers within each department make decisions related to their own local issues — doing performance reviews, allocating budgets, executing projects based on business objectives, and so on. In our experience, corporate management has two vital roles:

✔ First, management needs to view the workings of each department based on the overall goals of the company (financial, strategic partnerships, and so on).

✔ Second, management needs to take action if a department needs help solving an internal problem.

Fine and dandy, you say, but what does federation have to do with a service oriented architecture? Pretty much everything, as the next sections make clear.

SOA and federation

Loosely linking software services together must be both efficient and practical. To avoid chaos, you need rules and governance that determine how the system works overall. A software environment must have a framework or structure that dictates how things operate.

The problem that most organizations face is that, over time, (for some, years; for others, decades) the technical IT infrastructure has become, well, eclectic. You may find some IBM mainframes running a set of applications, a set of Unix servers from Hewlett-Packard or Sun running another set of applications, some Windows servers running yet another bunch of applications, and Linux servers running applications of their own. Such variety is really common. And that's just the beginning. In addition, the same systems that are running different operating systems are also running different databases, different development tools, different management software, different you name it . . .

The idea that you could embrace all of this within a single service oriented architecture — one architecture that works in approximately the same way across the whole corporate network — is very attractive. But it's probably not going to happen. What's far more likely is that you'll end up with a federation of several SOA domains; that is, several separate spheres of SOA influence that in turn can find how to interoperate. This is fine, by the way. Breaking a large whole into more manageable domains doesn't diminish the benefits that a service oriented architecture delivers in any way. Indeed, the fact that SOA can be implemented in domains is one of its benefits. It makes it far less likely that you'll have to tear up and replace parts of your infrastructure.

Figure 5-1 gives you a sense of what we're getting at by illustrating the principle of service oriented architecture domains. Each SOA registry registers a whole set of applications that are broken up into reusable component services. These are shown as connected to the registries in the illustration. The registry also contains rules and policies that specifically apply to these applications. However, it also has a set of policies that apply to all applications. For example, IT security policies are very likely global across all the SOA domains. Conceptually you can think of there being a database of global policies that all the SOA registries access and implement — just like what you see in Figure 5-1. Technically, it's more likely that there will be no separate policy database as such. One of the registries will be designated as the master, and the others will copy the global policies from it.

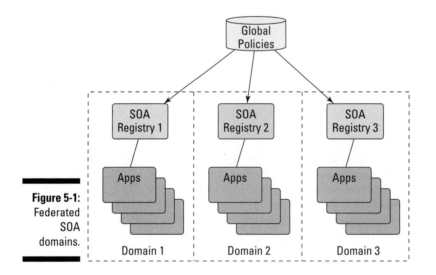

Figure 5-1:
Federated
SOA
domains.

What we are describing here is a *true* federation. The registries implement all the governance rules, each providing local governance, but all obeying a single set of federal governance rules. This structure doesn't limit which components can be connected to which components. Just as a company can start in any one of the United States and set up other offices in other states as long as it abides by local and federal rules, so a composite application could start in one service oriented architecture domain and connect to components in other domains.

If you're wondering whether you need to have three different enterprise service buses if you have three different service oriented architecture domains, the answer is no. You can have as many or as few as you want. You can have multiple workflow engines or just a single one. What defines a SOA domain is the registry and the broker. (Chapter 8 is all about the registry and the broker.) All the other SOA components can be shared with other domains if it makes good technical sense.

Federation is a way to deal with other integration problems in IT. Quite often, when a company wants to provide a global capability, it discovers that it already has some solutions implemented in some areas. If there is no compelling need to rip out these existing solutions, it may be possible to federate them — that is, make the same solution available to other parts of the company.

A couple of specific areas in which some IT vendors are now focusing on federated solutions are federated identity management and federated information management, discussed in the following sections.

Federated identity management

Security is an overarching issue for computing in general. When computing is highly distributed, securing the way software is protected becomes more complicated. When an individual has to interact with lots of software components, it's ridiculous — not to mention impractical — to make that individual sign on and interact with each software component individually. Rather, you need a way to establish rules within software that allow that individual to automatically get access to all software components that they are allowed to access without having to deal with each component separately from a security perspective.

To facilitate this, organizations use software to federate the identity of the individual, passing critical information to the appropriate software parties under strict policies and procedures. And thus, federated identity management is born . . .

Federated information management

The software industry is moving away from the idea that a database belongs to one business application. Within a service oriented architecture, data is being transformed into a service that ends up being used by many different applications. (We talk a lot about information as a service in Chapter 13.) In order to achieve this goal, the data has to be made available based on common definitions of what each data item means and how it's allowed to be used within the corporation. Federating common definitions allows the data to be used by more than one application. For example, if you have consistent definitions for all of your company's products, you can create new applications without worrying about the accuracy of the data. We talk a lot more about information as a service in Chapter 13.

The Industrialization of Software

SOA represents the latest evolutionary step in the industrialization of software. You of course remember the Industrial Revolution. You know, the steam engine, interchangeable rifle parts, the Ford Motor Company? Well, the software industry is growing up to follow in the same footsteps as the manufacture of goods. Software industrialization began to happen with the creation of standard ways to link one piece of code to another. Standard interfaces hide the details of what is inside a piece of software code and make "assembling" new programs easy.

The industrialization of software is possible because of standard Web services interfaces, XML, and messaging buses that enable IT organizations to stop writing everything from scratch. With the industrialization of software, organizations can take existing pieces and put them into common frameworks. Following other industrial models, the software industry has begun to move from the artisan phase, in which each programmer is a craftsperson, to a phase where the developer picks up premanufactured pieces and puts them together. We see important parallels between the industrialization of manufacturing and the industrialization of software. Here are three key elements:

- ✒ The distribution of electrical power parallels the distribution of computer power through PCs and networking.

- ✒ The building of manufactured products from standard components parallels the building of software applications from standard components.

- ✒ The linking together of manufacturing processes via an assembly line parallels the linking together of software components via Web services.

These parallels are remarkably precise. With the advent of the assembly line, manufacturing productivity improved dramatically, and products could be manufactured much more quickly. When distributed computing, software components, and Web services combine, software development productivity increases, and new enterprise business applications can be developed far more quickly. This is the promise of SOA.

Part II
Nitty-Gritty SOA

The 5th Wave   By Rich Tennant

"Great goulash, Stan. That reminds me, are you still in charge of our system architecture?"

In this part . . .

Technologists demand the details, so in this part, we dive headlong into the vast and varied ocean we call *service oriented architecture,* pointing out the myriad elements that make up a SOA along the way — from XML to enterprise service buses to the SOA registry and SOA supervisor. Enjoy the swim!

Chapter 6

Xplicating XML

*A*ccording to the biblical story, early humanity was once united as one people and, in its overweening pride, started to build a tower to reach the heavens. God decided to stop the project and did so without resorting to fire or brimstone. He simply confused the languages of the participants. Pretty soon, work on the project stopped, and humanity never spoke with a single tongue again. The place was called Babel as a result.

Today, humanity — or rather, the computer industry — dissatisfied with the mere 6,000-odd human languages, has created some 8,000 computer languages. The number of human languages is on the decline, by the way, while the number of computer languages persists in climbing. In a world where everybody claims to want to be able to talk to everybody else, such a multiplicity of languages indicates that there's definitely a fly in the IT ointment.

My Computer Is a Lousy Linguist

So here's the problem: The world of computing is awash with programming languages. Even though there is a tendency for many computer users to try to agree on one programming language or another, this attempt to standardize always seems to fail. And even if the attempt succeeded, the world would still be left with millions of applications written in older languages — applications that are still needed by millions of users. Think we're exaggerating? Well, we could tell you of applications that have been around for 30 or 40 years and are still going strong. When Carol wrote *Mastering COBOL* in 1998, there were billions of lines of COBOL code in use, and we're sure we can still find plenty of COBOL squirreled away in countless nooks and crannies of the IT world.

Just in case there's any confusion about this; technically, programming languages are "human language neutral." They consist of standard keywords that are directives to the computer, usually interspersed with comments written in the human language of the programmer (Thai, French, Hindi, Chinese, . . .). The keywords can be in any language. In the Fjölnir programming language, for example, the keywords are Icelandic. The programming language var'aq is based on the Klingon language of Star Trek, and Ook!, our personal favorite, is based on the Orangutan language from Terry Pratchett's Discworld novels.

When programming languages are created, they are built with two fairly important goals in mind:

- ✔ A computer should be able to understand exactly what it is being told to do without any ambiguity.
- ✔ The language should facilitate the efficient creation of reliable programs that can be read and understood by other programmers.

There have been many arguments about how well any programming language fulfills these criteria, but until recently, nobody really thought in terms of there being a third criterion. But, because of the Internet, Web services, and SOA, we now have a third criterion:

- ✔ A program should be able to talk to and interact with other programs.

Given the number of programming languages, teaching them all to understand each other directly is not exactly a viable way to address the third criterion. A far better strategy would be to teach them all to speak one common language — say, French.

The IT industry could have gone in that direction, but it didn't. Instead it invented yet another language — one that really does make it possible for programs to talk to programs. This new language is perhaps the most important computer language that has ever come into existence. You would think, then, that it would be given a very memorable name that highlights its importance, reflects the benefits it delivers, and inspires the world to adopt it everywhere.

But someone had a far more clever idea. Why not call it XML? This would stand for eXtensible Markup Language, and anyone with hours on their hands, a talent for surfing the Web, and a deep love for engineering protocols would eventually be able to find out what the name meant. XML it is.

XML is an agreed-upon standard and is used by many different industries. Even the U.S. government got into the act (literally) with the Administrative Simplification provisions of the Health Insurance Portability and Accountability Act of 1996 (HIPAA, Title II), which requires the Department of Health and Human Services (HHS) to work to establish national standards for electronic healthcare transactions and national identifiers for providers, health plans, and employers. (The act also addresses the security and privacy of health data, an ongoing concern for many U.S. citizens.) In adopting these standards, the government took a major step in improving the efficiency and effectiveness of the U.S. healthcare system by encouraging the widespread use of electronic data interchange in healthcare. The only way that this can be achieved is to use XML as the *lingua franca*.

So what is XML exactly?

Perhaps you find the description "extensible markup language" less than enlightening. We'll try to help. A *markup language* is a set of instructions that you add to a collection of words, pictures, tables, and other stuff that defines precisely how this collection of words, pictures, tables, and other stuff should be laid out on a piece of paper or on a computer screen or wherever you intend it to have it laid out. *Extensible* here really means extendable, as in "extending capabilities, possibilities, and interoperabilities." Over time, smart people will add new and clever instructions to this very clever language.

In XML (and HTML too, by the way) the markup instructions take the form of a set of tags, which are identified by having angled brackets round them, like this: `<tag>`. The tags are embedded with all the content.

If you want to see what a large amount of HTML looks like, you can get a screen full of it by going to www.dummies.com on the Internet with your browser and then choosing View⇨Source from the Internet Explorer menu bar or View⇨Page Source from the menu bar in Firefox. (Most other browsers have similar commands.) The majority of Web pages provide a similar picture, although some also contain Javascript.

Looking at all this unadorned HTML may alarm you because, for most Web pages, you see a great deal more tag information than written words. But fear not. Programmers don't actually have to write all that stuff on their own. Some slick software tool generates most of it automatically.

Browsers are not the only software that needs a markup language to present information. Every piece of software that prints a document on paper or displays it on a screen uses some kind of markup protocol. Adobe PDF files, which are used extensively on the Internet, use a set of markup instructions that were invented by Adobe. Similarly, Microsoft Word .doc files include Microsoft's markup directions. The IT industry has used markup languages for quite a long time.

So you may be wondering why, when HTML already existed, did the IT industry go to the trouble of inventing XML, yet another whole new markup language for the Internet. One reason is that when the need for a standard markup language arose, Netscape and Microsoft were playing tug of war with HTML, each inventing its own version. It was by no means certain at the time that something stable would emerge.

Historically, HTML was derived from the Standard Generalized Markup Language (SGML), which was created in 1986 for defining documents, but it just wasn't suitable for use over the Internet. XML was based on SGML and first saw the light of day in 1998.

One subtle motivation on the part of the IT industry's inventing a whole new markup language is that nobody could predict all the different tags that might be needed in the future to mark up new kinds of content or varied mixtures of content. What was needed was a language that was *extensible* — one that could be easily augmented to support anything new that might happen.

XML's extensibility

When XML was created, everyone was thinking about the different kinds of content that would eventually be made available on the Internet. They really didn't have any idea that it would be used for anything other than describing documents, video, and sound. XML was designed to be extensible with those particular targets in mind. However the IT industry has made the mistake of being too specific many, many times, so XML was designed to be as extensible as possible.

If you find this mysterious, try thinking about how the distribution of music has changed over the last 50 years. If the creators of early stereo systems were thinking the way the designers of XML were thinking, their systems would easily have accommodated first vinyl, and then 8-track tapes, and then cassettes, and then CDs, and now MP3 files. Most important they would accommodate what has yet to be invented.

Rather than thinking up a load of HTML-type tags for displaying stuff, like these tags:

```
<TITLE> - This is the title of the page
</TITLE> - The title ends here.
<BR> - This is a line break.
<YADA YADA YADA> - Enough is enough.
```

XML allows you to invent your own tags. In XML, the following is entirely valid:

```
<Hint>
<To> You, dear reader </To>
<From> The authors </From>
<Heading>USEFUL HINT</Heading>
<Hint_Text> It helps to remember that XML has no fixed
            tags. But you can invent all the ones you need.
            That's why people say it is extensible. And
            they are correct.
</Hint_Text>
</Hint>
```

XML uses some of the same conventions as HTML, such as angled brackets (<>) for tags and a slash (/) to mark the ending member of a tag pair. But it doesn't have any fixed tags, so you can use XML to define a host of other (HTML-like) languages. In fact, after XML had been invented, one of its first uses was to define WML (Wireless Markup Language), a markup language for wireless devices.

Pretty quickly, smart folks figured out that, with its extensibility, XML could be used to describe data itself, not just describe how to display it. This is astoundingly useful to computer programs because the only thing a computer program does is process data. Yet in the history of computing, nobody had dreamed up a foolproof way for programs to send data to other programs and tell them exactly what it was they were sending. Computer programs can talk to other computer programs by using XML; before XML existed, they couldn't. One spoke Chinese and the other spoke Urdu, and no conversation could happen unless a translator could be found. XML is the beginning of a solution to the "too many computer languages" problem.

How does XML work?

The secret to XML is actually pretty simple. Imagine that you have an e-mail program that sends out e-mail for you. You send it the following bit of XML code:

```
<Message>
<To> You, dear reader </To>
<From> The authors </From>
<Heading>USEFUL HINT</Heading>
<Message_Text> It helps to remember that XML tags can be
            used to define data items. And you can invent
            all the ones you need. People say XML is
            extensible. And they are not wrong.
</Message_Text>
</Message>
```

The program reads this and knows at once that it is a <Message>. The <To> tells it where to send it, so it looks up the e-mail address of "You, dear reader." It looks up the e-mail address of "The authors" so it can insert the e-mail addresses of those who are sending it. It fills in the e-mail subject as USEFUL HINT. Then it adds the message and sends it out.

You may be wondering how it knows the meaning of <Message>, <To>, <From> and all the other tags. It actually *doesn't* know until you define your markup tags for e-mail. But with XML, you first define your tags and then write programs that agree on how data is defined for e-mails. You can even agree on standards that everyone throughout the whole world can then use.

If you want to know more about XML, check out *XML For Dummies*, by Lucinda Dykes and Ed Tittel (Wiley).

Acronym-phomania

One aspect of SOA that alienates some people is the profusion of TLAs (three-letter abbreviations) and ETLAs (*extended* three-letter abbreviations — that is, four-letter abbreviations). If you start reading about Web services and SOA, you will undoubtedly run into the common acronyms shown in Table 6-1. These are all names of standards that relate to SOA in one way or another.

Table 6-1	Your Guide to Really Dumb Acronyms	
Acronym	*What It Stands For*	*What It Is and What It's Used For*
HTTP	HyperText Transfer Protocol	The standard for addressing Web pages. For example: http://www.google.com/alerts In addition to defining an address, HTTP can also identify a Web service, such as the news alerts service that Google provides.

Acronym	What It Stands For	What It Is and What It's Used For
XML	eXtensible Markup Language	The definition language that can accompany information. It tells a computer program what that information actually is.
SOAP	Simple Object Access Protocol	SOAP is a standard that uses XML to describe messages that are sent from one program to another. A program uses SOAP to request a service from another program and then pass it related data.
WSDL	Web Services Description Language	WSDL is a standard based on XML. Programmers use WSDL to create an XML document that describes a Web service and how to access it.
UDDI	Universal Description, Discovery, and Integration	UDDI is a framework for doing what it suggests: describing, discovering, and integrating (business) services via the Internet. The UDDI framework uses SOAP to communicate with programs that access it.

If reading the entries in the above table doesn't baffle you, you're not playing fair. It *should* baffle you. We could have made it easier by saying this:

✔ HTTP is the address.

✔ XML is for decoding messages.

✔ SOAP is for writing messages.

✔ WSDL is for describing interfaces.

✔ UDDI is a directory for finding services — just like a telephone directory.

Figure 6-1 shows what they look like when they all work together.

Figure 6-1 gives the full picture. Consider the situation in which a business provides a credit-checking service. The business wants customers anywhere to be able to find this service, so it publishes information about it in a UDDI Registry. This is a little more complicated than publishing a telephone number in a telephone directory; what is being published here is the address of the service (that is, the HTTP address) as well as a description of the service according to a common industry standard. The business publishes a Web services description of its credit-checking service in the UDDI Registry.

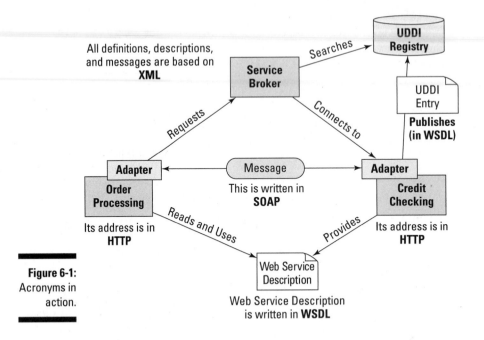

All definitions, descriptions, and messages are based on **XML**

Its address is in **HTTP**

Message — This is written in **SOAP**

Its address is in **HTTP**

UDDI Entry — **Publishes (in WSDL)**

Web Service Description — Web Service Description is written in **WSDL**

Figure 6-1: Acronyms in action.

Now consider an order-processing system that needs to use a credit-checking service. It sends a request to its service broker to search through the UDDI registries it is aware of to find such a service, as indicated in Figure 6-1. It may find many such services, in which case it has to select the one it prefers according to some kind of criteria (such as cost).

Having selected an appropriate service, the service broker can now connect the order-processing application to the credit-checking application. It does this by passing the description of the credit-checking Web service in the UDDI registry to the order-processing application, which then uses it to make a direct connection over the Internet.

After the order-processing and credit-checking applications are connected to each other, they send each other messages by using SOAP.

That might be the end of the story, but it might not be. The idea of having Web services conform to a common industry standard is fine for the situation in which you make such services available on the Web to all comers. However, within the business that provides the credit-checking service, it is quite likely that a much more detailed Web service description of the credit-checking service will be created, which offers extra services or provides a priority service or varies the service in some other way. This Web service description might be available only to users within the business or to special customers.

Whatever the circumstances, the two applications are able to communicate because the requesting service has read a Web service description and knows how to talk to the providing service. After they are connected, they talk to each other in SOAP.

A little bit of SOAP and WSDL

We have no desire to teach you XML beyond giving you some idea of what it is. We'd rather not try to teach you about SOAP or WSDL in any detail, either. But we think you have a right to understand how, together, they pull off the (very difficult) trick of allowing one program to talk to another.

The difficulty in enabling such conversation comes from the fact that a simple data name like, say, START_DATE, doesn't tell a program much. If Program A says to Program B; "Here's a START_DATE, 11/10/2005," Program B is not going to be able to use the information.

That's because this message has no context. Program B isn't even going to know if START_DATE is a date. It looks like a date, and it has a name that indicates that it's a date, but there's nothing here that says for sure that it's a date. Even if it is a date, Program B cannot be sure whether it's in the American form of month, and then day, and then year (mm/dd/yyyy) or the European form of day, and then month, and then year (dd/mm/yyyy).

Even if Program B had asked Program A, "send me the START_DATE," Program B could not be sure about the message it just received. What these two programs need are some definitions that they can share.

Luckily, we have XML, the world-champion definition language. The first step in solving the problem is to use XML to define a data definition language. This language is called XSD (XML Schema Definition), and that gives us YADA (Yet Another Dumb Acronym).

Schema is an IT term that describes the structure and organization of a set of data — usually the data held in a database. So, XSD is a language for comprehensively describing the structure and organization of data. It can be used to describe any kind of data: numbers, dates, text, lists, records, whole databases, indeed anything a program would ever be interested in.

Name spaces

Here's how to pull off the trick of having two programs understand each other:

Use XSD to define all the data that either program might send to the other and define all the labels that will be used to identify the data — START_DATE, for example. Now, if you had to do this for every two programs that wanted to talk to each other, it would take forever and achieve very little. However, that isn't what you do. What you do is define a whole name space for a large number of programs.

Name space refers to the context within which the name of a data item is used. Think about a family. Every new child that is born into a family is given a different name — Washington, Petrov, Simone, Susan, and so on. Those names are unique within the "name space" of the family. When the children go to school, they may meet other children named Washington, Petrov, Simone, Susan, and so on. The names are no longer unique as they are now being used outside the name space.

In case you're wondering — and we're convinced you are — the name space itself also has a name, just as a family might be named Lopez.

So imagine that you use XSD to create a name space for your whole company. When you define START_DATE, you call it START_DATE, and every program running on your company's computers can refer to the name space to know its meaning. The meaning is fixed within the name space, and if one program within the name space sends a message that contains START_DATE to another program, it can be understood. Now, if your programs want to talk to other programs outside the company, they have to agree on the meaning of START_DATE with the programs they talk to.

SOAP comes in envelopes

SOAP (Simple Object Access Protocol) is the message protocol that Web services use to talk to each other, although it isn't confined to use by Web services. It was invented by Microsoft to make it easier for software built with Microsoft's development tools to interact with other software. It is simple and flexible and can be used by any two programs that want to exchange messages.

A SOAP message has up to four components, as follows:

- ✔ **The Envelope** surrounds the content of the message and identifies it as being a SOAP message rather than any other kind of message.

- ✔ **The Header** holds user-defined extensions to SOAP. These can involve additional activities, such as authentication for security purposes, that go beyond the services that one program might be able to provide for another. Quite often there is no Header section in a SOAP message.

✔ **The Body** contains the message, which is likely to be a request for a service or a response, and it is likely to include data.

✔ **The Fault.** Rather bluntly named, this is a response to a SOAP message that generated an error, informing the sender of what the error was. In most messages, there will be no Fault section.

Each of these parts of a SOAP message mentions the name space that its contents use. In fact, the Envelope and the Fault may both refer to the name space _HYPERLINK `"http://schemas.xmlsoap.org/soap/envelope/"`. If you visit this Web page, `http://schemas.xmlsoap.org/soap/envelope/`, you'll see a long list of XSD statements, but be warned, it's not a pretty sight. Nevertheless, that's what a name space looks like in the raw.

The Header and the Body most likely refer to local name spaces defined for local usage.

WSDL

WSDL — the Web Services Description Language — is yet another language that was built by using XML. It is used to define a Web service. Like a SOAP message, a WSDL document is divided into four parts:

✔ **Definition of ports:** We don't really like the use of the word *port* here, but we're stuck with it. A port is a connection point. The WSDL port defines a Web service, the operations that can be requested, and the messages that can be used. In other words, the WSDL description defines what you can do and how you do it after you connect to the port. Another way of describing it is that it is an XML definition of a program function.

✔ **Definition of messages:** Here you see the definitions of the data items for each of the operations that are defined under the specification of the port. These definitions act as templates for the requesting program to make requests and for it to understand the responses it receives. In reality, these definitions are what a programmer thinks of as *function calls*. And as you may expect, they relate to a name space.

✔ **Definition of types:** This defines the data types that are used by the Web service. These relate to a name space as well.

✔ **Definition of binding:** This is technical stuff for the programs involved. It defines exactly how the two programs can connect to each other.

Here's how the whole WSDL shebang works:

1. The service broker goes out looking for a specific service on behalf of Program A. It consults various registries to try to find the service, possibly including a public UDDI registry.

2. It discovers that there is a Web service that Program A wants to use and that Program B provides.

3. The service broker then directs Program A to connect to Program B.

4. Program A refers to Program B's WSDL description of its Web service so that Program A can make requests of Program B that Program B knows how to respond to.

5. Program A sends Program B a request by using a SOAP message.

6. Program B responds to this request by using a SOAP message. They can make sense of all of this, even if these two programs have never met each other before, because every part of every SOAP message — and the WSDL descriptions, too — refers to the name spaces that define all the data and the data types.

7. Programs A and B keep talking until they are done.

Oh, and of course, there's one fact that makes the whole of this set of protocols, languages, and technical gobbledygook very important. They solve the Babel Problem. This scheme works anywhere for any software written in any program language running on any computer. Insofar as anything *can* be, it is technology independent.

Chapter 7

Dealing with Adapters

*A*dapters make SOA possible. No adapters, no SOA — it's as simple as that. More than anything else, SOA is about being able to reuse the business applications that you already have. In order to do that, you need to add interfaces to these applications that allow you to directly invoke — from any other program, mind you — the functions these applications contain. The SOA adapters provide these interfaces.

The easiest way to understand adapters is to realize that all software of any kind has an interface of one kind or another. It doesn't matter what the software does. And not just business software, but any kind of software — word processors, games, PC calculators, Web sites, and programs run by NASA to calculate the correct trajectory for a space probe as it passes Jupiter on its way to Saturn — they all have interfaces. Gobs of them.

All software does something — you would hope — but it does what it does only when some user (or possibly another program) tells it to. The way that the user or the other program gives the software the command is through its interface. And the way the software presents information back to the user or a computer program is also through its interface. That, in fact, is precisely what an interface is — it's the connection point that a program has with a user or some other program. For example, a person might connect with a software application through a multicolored visual display that uses graphics and text to highlight important information.

All programs have interfaces. If they didn't, they could never run because there would be no way to tell them to fire up.

Making Connections

In earlier chapters (Chapter 3 is a good example), we spend some time talking about Web services — those useful thingamajigs that connect services together by using Internet protocols. We spell out how such services work, but we also mention in passing that there are other equally valid ways for a program to connect to another program. Now is the time for us to explore how SOA allows for all such possibilities.

Software has been connecting to other software for decades, and no matter how it is done, it always involves an interface for passing messages and data from one piece of software to another. With early client/server applications, the interface was between an application running on a PC and a database. The messages passed were requests for data that used a specific language (SQL), and typically, the responses were sets of data.

Hundreds of widely used software interfaces that are currently in use inside real-life business applications can be used, in the right circumstances, to enable one software component to get a service of some kind from another. The important question is how to make use of all these potential interfaces. To understand this, you first need to understand adapters and how they implement program interfaces. Take a look at the following example.

Figure 7-1 illustrates the adapter of an order-processing component requesting the services of a credit-checking component. It makes its request through the service broker, which reads information from the registry about the credit-checking service so that it can connect the two components.

An important point to understand here is that the interface details of the credit-checking component are published in the registry, and the service broker is thus able to inform the order-processing adapter about which commands to use and what data to attach when it makes requests of the credit-checking service. To be clear, the order-processing adapter doesn't just sit there wondering what commands to give, look down the list of possibilities in the interface description, and then pick one for fun. It already knows the commands it wants to give. How does it know?

A programmer has written some custom code in the adapter to enable the order-processing component to talk to the credit-checking component. In order to do so, the programmer read the *interface description* that the credit-checking component provides and then wrote the appropriate requests according to the standard specified.

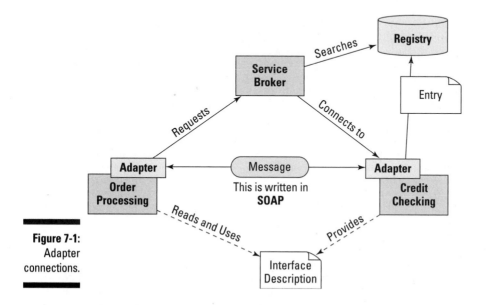

Figure 7-1:
Adapter
connections.

Some of you astute readers may start to wonder "If components have interface descriptions and programmers have to figure all this stuff out to get things to work, why bother at all with a SOA registry and SOA broker?"

Intelligent questions demand intelligent answers, so here goes. The thing about the registry is that it not only knows where everything is and how to get there, it knows it in *real time*. In dynamic environments, things may be moving all the time. By keeping the information about the location of the component in the registry and, therefore, independent from the component itself, you gain flexibility. The order-processing component may have all the rules down pat for talking to the credit-checking component, but it may not necessarily know where the credit-checking component is or exactly how to connect to it. The service broker searches the SOA registry for this information and uses it to make the connection.

Keep in mind that computers can fail, and if they do, the software they are running is normally started up somewhere else. The registry holds the up-to-date address information that allows one component to bind directly to another. (We talk about binding in a few paragraphs, so jump ahead for a moment if you feel compelled. Otherwise, hold tight; we're getting there.)

Another reason why a SOA needs registries and brokers is that any of the components it uses can be radically modified. Imagine that the credit-checking component is changed completely. For example, imagine that it was running on a Microsoft Windows server and now it has been rewritten to run in a completely different environment (IBM mainframe, say) in a completely different programming language using a completely different database and even fundamentally different data encoding. As long as the credit-checking component sticks with the same interface commands, it doesn't matter. You can still pass it a person's name and Social Security number and get a credit rating from it.

The SOA registry knows the new location of the component, and it also knows the translation rules that need to be applied to the requests from the order-processing component in order for them to make sense to the new credit-checking component. The SOA service broker can thus ensure that these rules are executed when messages pass. The upshot is that the order-processing adapter doesn't need to be changed.

In a Bind

We slipped the word *bind* into the previous section without any reasonable warning, didn't we? We were hoping you wouldn't notice, but you did. So now we have to explain what we mean when we say a software component binds to another one. What does *bind* mean?

We apologize, because *bind* is a technical term, but the sad truth is that you probably need to know it. An easy way to think of it is in simple human terms. When you need to make a phone call to someone, you look up her number, dial the number, and wait while the phone rings. The person you are calling may not pick up immediately, but assuming that she does pick up, you go through some niceties to say who you are and why you are calling, and after these pleasantries are done with, you get down to the business of the call.

Well, when an adapter of one software component wants to have a conversation with another, the same kind of thing happens. The process is called *binding,* and it's the service broker that establishes the connection. We could explain it all with complicated words and with references to various protocols, but really it's the same kind of thing as when two people call each other on the phone. The only difference is that when one software component binds to another, they may bind to each other for hours, days, or even months on end, and lots of transactions take place while they are bound to each other.

TECHNICAL STUFF

What kind of bind?

A bind is the act of connecting two software components that want to interact. One binds to the other by issuing a call — in effect naming the object and its location according to some protocol. When two pieces of software bind, each allocates resources to enable the message passing that will take place between the two. If the two pieces of software are on different computers, the whole communications connection between the two components needs to be set up as well. No matter how the bind is achieved, some activity must take place to make it happen.

Technically, there are two types of binding: early binding and late binding. *Early binding* is when most of the program code required to do the binding is created when the program is compiled. *Late binding* is when some of the work is delayed until the point when the connection is made.

In general, early binding can be viewed as faster and late binding as more flexible. In reality, it is a little more complicated than that. How early and late binding work depends on the computing environment and, more important on the computer language. With some computer languages (for example C), the code that executes as the result of a function call needs to be known at compile time; the language requires early binding. By contrast, Java is a late binding language. It works in an entirely different way, running interpretively (or via a Just-In-Time compiler) within a virtual machine. In Java, a set of Java classes (that is, functions) is loaded at run time and calls to them can be and frequently are overridden by a subclass. In effect, Java binds to the class dynamically as it is running; it always binds late.

As regards SOA, whether binding is early or late at the program language level is pretty much irrelevant. Most large computing environments include both early and late binding.

The process of binding takes time. It may not seem like a long time to you if you have to wait several seconds while your e-mail program binds to the e-mail server in order to download some new e-mails. It doesn't seem like a long time at all because the new e-mails start to pop into your inbox in seconds. But you are not a computer. Computers are fast, and they don't wait in seconds, they wait in microseconds — which are millionths of a second.

If a software component is going to talk to another software component for hours, it doesn't have time to bind each time it wants to say something. Binding takes too much time. It binds once and then clings on until the conversation is over. Because of this it may be possible, for example, for hundreds of credit checks to be done every second.

Your Adapter Options

A program's interface is the means by which a user or another program issues a command to a program. If you have that bit of knowledge firmly tucked away in the back of your mind and then ask yourself the question, "what kinds of adapters are out there?," the answer turns out to be that you could write an adapter for every standard kind of program interface that the IT industry has ever produced.

Here's a list of the kinds of adapters that could be written:

- ✓ **Web services adapters:** The adapters that are written to Web services standards and that imitate the connection to an application via a Web page.

- ✓ **Terminal emulation adapters:** In the old days, before PCs became ubiquitous, users of mainframes and minicomputers had *terminals* — keyboards and displays (screens or typewriter-style devices that printed output on paper) that displayed forms and allowed users to enter data. Applications were written to interact with information gathered from terminals. It is possible to write adapters that directly access old applications that date back to this time by having the adapter pretend to be a terminal. (Clever, isn't it?)

- ✓ **Document-based adapters:** A series of standards have been created over time for passing electronic documents from one application to another. This area of software technology went by the name of Electronic Data Interchange (EDI), and a variety of standards emerged that were used to some degree (ANSI X.12 EDI, OAG BOD, to name a few). Now it is possible to write adapters that use such EDI interfaces.

- ✓ **Package application-based adapters:** Commonly used package applications, such as those from SAP, Oracle, and other software companies, have well-documented standard interfaces that allow other programs to connect to them directly. It is possible to write adapters to these specifications. (Packaged applications are business applications that carry out common business functions, such as accounting, order processing, HR, and so on.)

- ✓ **Adapters based on other standards:** Three connection standards in particular are worth mentioning because they have seen significant use. They are Microsoft's .NET standard; CORBA, the object-oriented software standard; and JCA, the Java Connection Architecture. Adapters can be written around these and other connection standards.

- ✓ **Middleware adapters:** One can build adapters that are based on various middleware connectivity products, such as IBM's MQSeries or BEA MessageQ, or even around an enterprise service bus.

✔ **Transaction engine adapters:** Specific adapters for high-volume transaction processing can be written for the various IT transaction engines, such as IBM's CICS or BEA's Tuxedo.

✔ **Data adapters:** Just about every kind of database ever invented has a standard interface that can be used for retrieving data. Additionally, adapters can be built around common data access standards based on SQL — particularly ODBC and JDBC — in order to access data from various databases.

✔ **Technology-specific adapters:** Adapters can also be written for any specific technology, such as specific e-mail systems or geographical information systems.

We sincerely hope that reading through that list didn't give you heartburn. The bad news appears to be that there is a plethora of different standard interfaces that have been used in different ways over decades to connect software to software. But the good news is that XML really did solve the Tower of Babel problem by providing a means by which any standard interface can be translated into any other standard interface.

It's possible to use any standard program interface that was ever created and deployed as the basis of an adapter. And this shouldn't surprise you too much — even if the names of all those standards and products make your head spin — because all anyone ever wants to do to a program is give it some data and tell it to go do something with that data.

So How Do You Build an Adapter?

Technically, building an adapter isn't too difficult. That's one of the big payoffs of XML. The SOA registry contains the XML definitions of all the messages that a given software component can accept. To write a program that issues these messages for Web services interfaces, the WSDL description is the specification that the adapter needs to implement. If the component you want to talk to has some other kind of interface, it too will be defined in the SOA registry in a similar way using XML. Logically, all the adapter needs to do is to issue messages in these formats when prompted.

Consider the situation illustrated previously in the diagram in which the order-processing component connects to the credit-checking component. The situation could be very simple, with only one message being sent — to request a credit rating. The request that the credit-checking component expects might have the form:

```
Get_Rating, name, SSN.
```

When it gets such a request it replies in the form:

```
Rating, name, rating_value.
```

The order-processing component may want to get such information at several different points in its business logic — say, when an order exceeds $3,000, or when a customer's total of all orders placed exceeds $3,000, or when a new customer places an order greater than $1,000. At these points, the adapter is called and passed the necessary information: a name (Jane) and Social Security number. The adapter sends the message in the required form, and when it gets an answer, it passes the answer back.

For standard messages where nothing goes wrong, the adapter has nothing to do but put the message in the right form and send it. If the credit-checking component responds by declaring some kind of error ("name doesn't match SSN," or "SSN doesn't exist," or even "I couldn't read what you sent me"), the adapter has to deal with it according to the standard error-handling procedures that need to be programmed in.

Additionally depending on how you implement the SOA, you may also want to include other standard logic in all adapters. You may want to call a software agent that measures performance. You may also want to include a standard call to a security procedure that checks security credentials. You can include many things in an adapter.

Building adapters sounds like it might be complex, time consuming, and fraught with challenges, but we have good news for you. If you make the right choices, it isn't as hard as you may think. The trick is to let software vendors do most of the work for you.

In all probability, your company uses many different software packages. You can't write the adapters for these packages unless you have the source code of the programs, which is unlikely, and anyway you don't want to. Tell the software vendor that you want them to provide you with adapters.

This isn't an unreasonable request. Most software package vendors are already exposing the various business functions of their software as Web services; indeed, it has become an area of pride and competition. If you have a package supplier who isn't planning to do that, it may be time to consider a different supplier.

Your supplier may well charge you for these adapters, but that's okay because they increase the value of the software package to you.

Adapter math

In the bad old days, before the widespread adoption of SOA (which would be now), those siloed applications sometimes did talk to each other. The HR application might be able to send salary changes to the payroll program, for example. But these interfaces were generally custom designed for the pair of applications that had to talk to each other. If an IT department had 20 applications, you would need 20 x 19 = 380 possible interface pairs for each application to be able to communicate with each other application. The number gets even bigger when you consider that different vendors of the same type of application might support different, proprietary interfaces. By making adapters that follow standards, you need only one adapter per application. When it's in place, any other services-enabled application can talk to it. Twenty adapters are a lot easier to build than 380 paired interfaces, and in today's enterprises, you'd be creating thousands, if not tens of thousands of pairs — like, yuck.

It shouldn't be too long before all software packages come with all their business functions exposed as Web services and available for reuse. In addition, some software companies specialize in providing adapters that give you access to all the various interface standards that have been used over the years. Indeed, there is a wealth of adapter products that you can buy, such as those from IBM, iWay, and Pervasive, for example.

It is also important to understand that business process management software tools write adapters for you when you build new software components or create composite applications. They can do this precisely because the interfaces of software components are accurately specified and held in a SOA registry.

Chapter 8

The Registry and the Broker

In This Chapter
▶ Working with the SOA registry
▶ Breaking things down with the service broker

*O*ne of the most significant benefits of a service oriented architecture is the ability to share existing business services in lots of different situations. (Keep in mind that a business service is a business process that has been codified according to company policies that govern the operations of the business.) So, now you may want to ask the following questions:

✔ How do I go about finding the business services that are available so they can be used to create new composite applications?

✔ After I find a business service, how do I know it is the right one?

✔ How do I keep the service itself current with changing business practices?

If you're asking these three questions, you're heading in the right direction. In this chapter, we explain the mechanisms that let you keep track of services, locate the services you need, and loosely couple services in a flexible way. The mechanism for tracking and finding services is called a *SOA registry;* the mechanism for connecting these services is called a *service broker.* The SOA registry connects to a SOA repository that includes all the important information about the details of every service. (Read all about the SOA repository in Chapter 15.)

Call On the SOA Registry

A SOA registry is a central reference designed to enable the discovery of business services as well as provide descriptions of said services. The SOA registry stores information about each business service that has been approved for use by the various business managers and has passed IT governance rules.

It also includes information about the history of each service (who created it, who can change it, how it can be used, and who is allowed to access the information). After a service has been approved — ensuring that it can be trusted by everyone in the organization — it is published to the SOA registry.

The SOA registry is not a passive directory. It is a real-time registry. It is constantly being changed as the rules of the business change.

The registry has three key functions:

- ✔ Publish and enable the discovery of business services
- ✔ Collect and manage business service metadata
- ✔ Govern the use of business services

The next few sections delve into each of these three key functions in greater detail.

Getting the dirt on business services

The SOA registry provides business users with a view into the organization's collection of sharable business services. In some cases, business services can be useful to users outside the organization, such as your customers and business partners. So, in addition to storing definitions of your software components for your developers and business analysts to use, the SOA registry is the place where you *publish* business services for the benefit of business partners and customers who may also have an interest in directly linking to these services.

Managing your metadata

The SOA registry manages the business service *metadata* — all the data used to describe the business services, the business rules about the services, and the rules governing the use of the services. (For more about metadata, check out Chapter 13.) The metadata includes the technical descriptions of how one business service component connects to another. The SOA registry describes all this information about business services as a way to bring together service consumers and service producers so that everyone can get access to the services they need within a controlled environment.

Keeping business services on track

The business needs to feel confident that business services that are published to the SOA registry follow business rules, including government and industry standards and regulations as well as all the policies of the individual business unit and the enterprise. If a business service has been published in a SOA registry, it will have been through a governance process, either one that the registry itself enforces or one that is enforced by the development components of SOA. (See Chapter 11.) This makes the compliance process more straightforward for company auditors. The techniques, rules, and procedures followed by the company are standardized, categorized, and, when they are recorded in the registry, they are available for discovery.

Ready with a SOA registry

The easiest way to explain when you need a SOA registry is to talk about when you *don't* need one. If you use only six services to build new composite applications, life is pretty easy. You can pick up the phone and say, "Fred, where can I find the claims processing service?" Fred sends it to you, you put it in your composite application, and life is good. When things get more complicated, a manual process simply won't be efficient, accurate, or manageable. Fred cannot possibly remember hundreds of services, nor will he want to take calls from hundreds of different people. Fred will not be able to remember who's allowed to do what to which service. You will not be a happy camper.

Two distinct components together satisfy the need for a central reference. The first, the SOA registry, allows the business services to dynamically connect to each other in real time because all the information about them and how they relate is included in the registry. The second, the SOA repository, allows SOA developers to build and change business services and their rules and processes in a centralized location. (We talk about the SOA repository in Chapter 15.)

Brokering a Deal

The SOA registry holds the pointers to where everything is located. The service broker, aptly enough, *brokers* the deal between two components; it brings them together because it knows everything anybody would ever need to know to make the connection.

The service broker reads information from the registry so that it can make the right connection. In a loosely coupled world — one where business services are designed and built as distinct components rather than bound together in independent applications — the service broker is what links business services to each other, a very important function. The service broker orchestrates the connections between components and, in fact, orchestrates the connections for the complete business process. The registry acts as its source of information and contains the full details of every request you can make to the software component and how the component will respond.

Figure 8-1 shows how the broker does its job working with the registry. The figure illustrates an Order Processing business service requesting the services of a Credit Checking service. The order-processing business service makes its request through the service broker, which reads information from the SOA registry about the credit-checking service so that it can connect these two services together to complete a business function. The service broker uses the registry to get information not only about how to find these two specific services but also how to put the rules that govern how each can be used into effect. The rules are shown in this diagram as being implemented by a policy engine, which can be thought of as a component of the registry. The information about the credit-checking interface has been published in the registry, as shown.

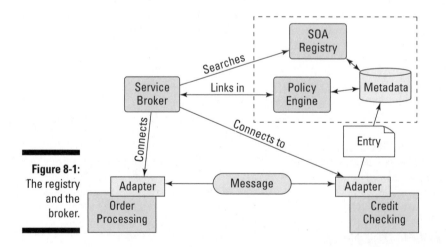

Figure 8-1:
The registry and the broker.

The SOA registry has occasionally been compared to a yellow pages directory that contains, under various headings, telephone numbers of businesses (and hence services) that you can call. You can certainly use the registry to get information about (and the address of) a software component you want to connect to, in the same way that you can use the yellow pages to get the phone number of a tire-changing service. But the SOA registry contains much more background information about the history and appropriate use of a software component than any yellow pages directory holds about a business.

Sign the Registry, Please

Before we describe the exact contents of the SOA registry, we would like to point out that the SOA registry itself is the SOA component that is most likely to change in the future. It is evolving as we speak. What we describe here is what we believe the SOA registry will contain when it is fully evolved. We have formed our opinion by speaking with a variety of software vendors actively working to solve this problem and from our own decades of experience in the software industry.

All the details held by the registry have two things in common: They are all a form of metadata, and they all concern themselves with rules about the management of services in a SOA environment. Having said that, here's a list of what you'll find if you open up a SOA registry:

- ✔ **Web services component interface descriptions:** XML is used very cleverly to provide standards for describing data and services. The overall standard for describing Web services in a SOA registry is called UDDI, Universal Description, Discovery, and Integration. All SOA registries support this standard for describing Web services.

- ✔ **Other types of component interface descriptions:** In addition to XML-based interfaces, it is possible to include interfaces written with existing interface approaches. If you have a lot of legacy interfaces, you don't have to throw them away. In addition, some software vendors publish their program interfaces. Details of any interface of any type can be held in the registry as long as the service broker knows how to handle them.

- ✔ **Business process definitions:** We talk a lot about components linking to other components. However, remember that SOA is all about business processes. It aims to implement the automation or semiautomation of business processes and therefore needs a map of all business processes taken together so that it can orchestrate every component. For that reason, the registry doesn't just store a set of interfaces and translation rules for the various components that fall within its domain; it also holds full definitions of each whole business process. When a business process is initiated, the service broker must immediately connect all the components involved in the whole business process.

found in En SOA registry

✔ **Business process rules:** Businesses create policies and apply rules as to how their business processes are carried out. In traditional packaged applications, these policies and rules are buried inside an application. For SOA flexibility and reuse, you need to be able to find these rules and policies easily.

For example, consider the idea of a sales discount scheme that applies to all customers. You might include this as part of the sales order processing system, but you might also want to make the same scheme available for other applications, such as a sales quotation application. With SOA, you would most likely write this once and then make it available as a component to any other application that wants to use it.

Consider a simple but important business rule, such as, *When you connect to any software anywhere outside the company network, you must apply a standard set of IT security procedures.* This rule doesn't just apply to one business process. It applies to every business process, including those that don't currently connect to any external computer systems (because they may in the future). This is another kind of reusable business component. It is a universal business policy rather than a software component.

If you want to impose specific business rules that apply to multiple business processes, it will be easier to manage and maintain them if they are all specified in one place. This also makes them easier to implement. The logical place for such rules is the SOA registry.

✔ **Service level descriptions:** Each business service stored in the registry needs to have a detailed service level associated with it — one that sets the level of availability and performance that the computer network must try to deliver. This can be thought of as a set of performance rules that the business service needs to abide by if it can. Both the service broker and the SOA supervisor use the service level descriptions. If a component is already running, the service broker checks that the service levels are not being violated at the outset, and the SOA supervisor monitors these service levels while the service is running.

✔ **Governance rules:** The contents of the registry itself must be subject to a set of rules of management. The registry contains a good deal of critical information that ensures that a business service runs correctly. Consequently, any change to this information must be closely controlled so that no errors are made if and when such information is changed. In practice, this means stringent security involving authentication, formal authorization for changes, and a full audit of all changes.

These governance rules will most likely link directly to the change management system that controls the implementation of changes to live computer software and most probably to the identity management security system that the organization has implemented.

You Need a Broker

The service broker functions to connect services together. It gets all the information it needs to do this from the registry. The registry and the service broker must work together. Aside from the rules of governance that the registry itself imposes when there is any attempt to update it, the rules held in the registry are rules that the service broker needs to know and needs to implement when the business service to which the rules refer starts up. The registry holds many kinds of rules: translation rules, service level rules, security rules, and business rules of any kind.

Metadata is information about services and data structures. That information exists so that the service broker, which orchestrates the whole business process, can connect one component to another and the connected components understand each other. For example, when one process says "customer" to the other, they both mean the same thing.

Figure 8-2 shows the service broker orchestrating an end-to-end order-processing and fulfillment service. We have made it simple so that it involves only five components and a rules engine. The dotted lines represent the action of the service broker in orchestrating the implementation of the business service, and the solid lines represent the whole business service when it is running.

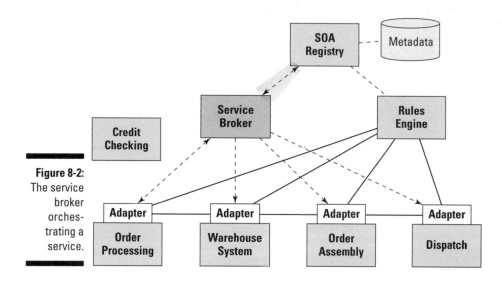

Figure 8-2:
The service broker orchestrating a service.

The service broker proceeds in the following manner:

1. One user logs in and requests the Order Processing and Fulfillment application. As this is not currently running, the service broker is notified and goes into action.

2. The service broker consults the SOA registry to find out what it needs to do in order to run Order Processing and Fulfillment. It first consults the service level rules to see if this business process is allowed to run at this time.

3. The service broker checks to see whether any of the four main components (Order Processing, Warehouse System, Order Assembly, Dispatch) are currently running. (They might be running as part of other business services.) If they are not running, it starts them going.

4. Getting information from the SOA registry, it checks the interfaces between all the components that need to be connected to each other. Because these components have been connected together before, they already have the interface information they need in their adapters. All that the SOA broker needs to do is indicate which set of interface information to use. The components can then bind to each other directly, as indicated by the solid line connecting adapter to adapter in Figure 8-2.

5. The service broker also notes that at each connection between components, the SOA registry indicates that there are additional rules that need to be implemented. For example, if any customer places an order for more than $5,000, a business rule indicates that an automated credit check must be done for that customer. That means connecting to an external automated Credit Checking service. However, the rules also indicate that connection to this service is to be made only when needed, so the service broker doesn't make this connection. If and when the connection to Credit Checking is needed, the Order Processing component notifies the service broker to make the connection.

6. The service broker provides the four components with the information they need to connect to the Rules Engine so that it can execute the rules that are stored there. The four components then bind to the rules engine, and the whole business process executes.

The service broker has finished its act of orchestration and can now take rest.

Chapter 9

The Enterprise Service Bus

*Y*ou or someone you know probably has had the experience of taking a bus — maybe to school or to work. The thing about buses is that no matter how old you are or how smart you are or what clothes you wear or how much stuff you schlep with you, you get on the bus the same way, and the bus takes you where you want to go regardless. After you set foot on the bus, you also know approximately how long it will take to arrive at your destination (barring any accidents). If traffic is backed up, the drivers will take alternative routes to get you where you're going. Believe it or not, if you understand this, you're on your way to understanding an enterprise service bus (ESB).

ESB Basics

The enterprise service bus is *the* communications nerve center for services in a service oriented architecture. As you can see in Figure 9-1, ESBs are designed to act as intermediaries between the SOA components, infrastructure services, and business processes. Admittedly, ESBs were not designed specifically to act as *SOA* intermediaries, but because a service oriented architecture needs a devoted intermediary in order to scale up for large numbers of users, an ESB ended up being just what the doctor ordered for SOA environments.

Why a bus

The word *bus* comes from the Latin *omnibus,* which means "for all." Horse-drawn omnibuses were one of the earliest forms of public transportation. The term jumped from the public transportation field to industrial usage back in the early days of electricity, when power was distributed in factories over long, fat, parallel strips of copper called *busbars.* Machinery in the factory could be easily hooked up anywhere along the busbar. Computers use similar parallel strips of copper for data signals, though these are usually only a few thousandths of an inch wide and etched on printed circuit boards. They are called buses as well.

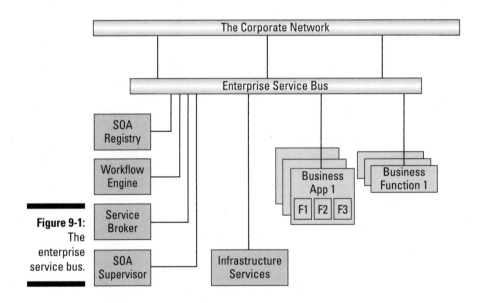

Figure 9-1:
The enterprise service bus.

ESBs are designed to be versatile. They can connect to various types of middleware, repositories of metadata definitions (such as how you define a customer number), registries (how to locate information), and interfaces of every kind (for just about any application).

You may have caught our earlier mention of the ESB back in Chapter 4. There, we concentrate on describing the ESB only in its role within a SOA, showing all the possible SOA components attached to it. We tell you to think of an ESB as a kind of pipe, warning you that in reality, it is not a pipe at all but rather a collection of software components. In our earlier discussion, we focus only on its role as a message transporter. Now it's time to show you that an ESB can, in fact, do much more, as the next section makes clear.

ESB: The Sequel

There are many ESB products out there, and they differ in their capabilities. They all provide an "abstraction layer" with the responsibility of managing the messaging — allowing software components to connect and send messages to each other consistently and efficiently. Some ESBs are highly versatile and work with most kinds of data traffic, from e-mail to SOAP messages. Some even implement encryption and provide comprehensive security. But a point worth understanding is that an ESB is also a *service broker of a kind.* It isn't the kind of service broker that can search SOA registries to discover new services, but you can't have everything. The ESB does most of the simple work of a service broker by making connections between processes.

In this world of possibilities, you also discover that an ESB may have a registry of its own. Now, it won't be a full-fledged SOA registry, but it will contain at least some of the information you would normally find in a SOA registry. To top it all off, an ESB can even take on some of the work of the SOA supervisor, in effect managing the performance and robustness of the service it provides.

If you're wondering why an ESB comes so pumped up, here's why. Over time, developers of ESBs added more and more capability so that they could be used in many different contexts. They created ESBs to manage the transport of data between databases, and ESBs to manage the passing of data to various applications that needed to be connected to a multitude of data feeds. In such circumstances, the ESB is the versatile intermediary that makes many connections between processes work effectively.

ESBs developed independently of SOA. Their capabilities expanded to include the ability to connect Web services components and other kinds of components. So you can have an ESB without having SOA, because you might just use it for some of its connectivity capabilities. But you can also start down the road to SOA by implementing an ESB. With the right ESB product in the right context, this may be a good place to start.

As strange as it may seem to have an ESB without a SOA, it turns out that — Oh! topsy-turvy world! — you can build a SOA without an ESB. Admittedly, you'd have to channel all your connections between SOA components through a pretty robust, high-performance cluster of servers containing the SOA registry, SOA service broker, and SOA supervisor. This works fine on a small scale; indeed, it is the route that many early implementations of SOA took. But (as you may suspect) if your system grows and becomes more complex, you'll be happy if you implement an ESB.

The evolution of software connectivity

Humankind — well, at least the IT industry — has connected applications together for almost as long as there have been applications. To understand the elegance and value of an ESB, it helps to understand earlier efforts at connecting applications.

In the really ancient times — the 1960s — before Software Giants had ever created *packaged* applications, developers (then known as "programmers") wrote complex programs to handle everything from counting numbers to sending information to be printed. Every piece of technology — from computer memory (some of us remember "core") to disks to the computer processors themselves — cost many thousands of dollars. Software had to be written in a very compact way. (In many circumstances, you told the computer both what to do and how to do it and it couldn't look anywhere else for more information because to do so was expensive and complicated.) Abstraction is something we can now afford because computers and their components are relatively cheap in the IT world of today.

In those early days, companies that automated tasks such as accounting gained a competitive advantage. It wasn't long before it was possible to buy an accounting capability from a vendor who had packaged accounting software to meet the requirements of many different companies. When packaged applications were born, the time had come to stop reinventing the wheel. No longer did companies have to spend valuable resources creating the functionality they could now buy. Packaged software applications were also written for efficiency.

Although packaged applications made the automation of certain functions so much cheaper, they created problems of their own. Because they were designed to accommodate the broadest spectrum of users, they were inflexible. Trying to be all things to all people means that you can make fewer and few assumptions about who's actually using your product, and the product itself becomes more and more rigid. Enhancements to such applications were made only if they suited *most* of the customers. Custom changes to such applications were either impossible to arrange or very expensive. In essence, companies had to sacrifice flexibility for frugality.

Even something as simple as adding a new printing device could require programmers to rewrite some parts of these applications. When new custom programs were written, programmers also needed to write specialized code to pass data to or get data from the packaged application. Customizing anything turned out to be expensive, time consuming, and hard to manage.

Where packaged applications were not available to meet a particular business need, most businesses built customized applications. Sometimes businesses even built applications in hope of a competitive advantage, but such new creations ended up being as inflexible as the old ones. As changes piled on top of changes, it became impossible to transform these applications quickly when the business changed. The obvious and most limiting problem was that applications didn't integrate with one another. They didn't share data easily and they couldn't use each other's functions — unless you wrote custom code to connect one application to another.

In the early 1990s, the computer industry tried to address the problem by creating software that went by the name of *Enterprise Application Integration* (EAI). EAI was touted as the "new" new thing that would simplify software development tremendously by removing the requirement for custom coding. EAI had standard connectors that could connect some components together. In effect, companies began packaging the ways that applications could be linked to each other. This packaged connectivity proved useful for connecting application packages to each other, but it offered less help with custom-built applications. When custom-built applications were still needed, EAI didn't remove the need for coding, but it did reduce it.

However, there was a common problem at the heart of the EAI approach. The standard EAI interfaces, whether provided in a packaged form or with the addition of some custom code, could be designed only to react to and solve the "current situation." These interfaces themselves were not flexible to change.

For EAI, the emergence of the Internet as a computing infrastructure was the straw that broke the camel's back. Suddenly, companies wanted and needed to be able to use their applications in unanticipated ways. For example, the Internet provided the possibility for companies to link their applications with those of their partners and customers. Applications with limited connectivity were exposed to the wide world of electronic business and e-commerce. The watch word of the day was *dynamic,* as

opposed to *static* — no longer could programs be written for specific circumstances that would remain constant. Programs needed to be able to adapt to an ever- changing environment.

In an increasingly dynamic world, it became critical to use computer assets outside of their original packaging. The need for much more flexibility within corporate boundaries and between companies forced a different architectural approach. A way had to be found to enable applications to communicate and connect with each other without worrying about the implementation details. EAI products were too limiting.

This is why SOA has become such a hot topic (and why we wrote this book). The enterprise service bus is the next evolutionary step in application integration. In fact most EAI products evolved into ESBs. The ESB plays a central role in transforming how software is created and deployed in business. In essence, when you break the traditional packaged application into business services, there has to be a way to ensure that the pieces can work together dynamically. The ESB is part of the solution.

What's inside the Bus

The ESB can be treated as a *black box* — you don't need to know how it works, just what it does. You take your business services and link them into the bus. The bus doesn't care what a business service does as long as the service has been configured correctly. (We introduce business services in Chapter 2 and provide lots of real-world examples of business services in Part V).The ESB has the intelligence to connect services in the right way.

What actually happens inside the black box ends up being rather sophisticated. In effect, the ESB carries out a range of infrastructure tasks that would otherwise have to be written into the application code. To help you understand the brains of the ESB, we break down a reasonably comprehensive ESB into its component parts. The services offered by the bus are

- ✔ **Messaging services:** Support a wide variety of types of messaging, provide intelligent content-based routing, and guarantee message delivery. They can also split and combine messages.

- ✔ **Management services:** Can monitor their own performance, helping to enforce service level agreements by recording and responding to message latency. They can implement message priorities and apply global business rules across all the applications or components they connect.

- ✔ **Interface services:** Can validate messages against their schema definitions (which they hold in their version of a registry).They support Web services standards and provide application adapters for some non–Web services types of interfaces.

- ✔ **Mediation services:** Transform messages between the formats used by the sending and receiving applications.

- ✔ **Metadata services:** Related to mediation, these services can also transform data from one format to another by using metadata definitions held in their own version of a registry.

- ✔ **Security services:** Encrypt messages where needed and include a standardized security model to authorize, authenticate, and audit all ESB activity.

All the constituent parts of a typical ESB are shown in Figure 9-2, which illustrates how an ESB can link together two separate programs.

Keep in mind that not all ESBs are the same. In our illustration, we show an ESB with all its possible internal components.

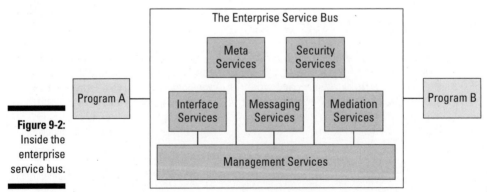

Figure 9-2:
Inside the enterprise service bus.

An ESB can actually take over many of the functions carried out by other SOA components. The *unique* services an ESB provides within a SOA are the *messaging services* and the *management services*. The other services it offers — the interface services or security services, for example — are also available from other SOA components.

Now, if you're wondering why an ESB bothers to offer services that seem to duplicate stuff available from other SOA components, the answer is simple. An ESB needs to be "full-featured" because it may not be part of a SOA at all and therefore cannot rely on the standard services offered by SOA components. ESBs are designed to connect programs to each other and manage the interfaces as automatically as possible, whether the ESB stands alone or is part of a SOA. If it just so happens that your ESB is part of a SOA, then its primary role is to manage messaging. The other services it offers could go unused.

ESB Components: Of Messages and Management, Security and Things

Because the most important services the ESB provides are messaging and management, we discuss them first.

Messaging services

The ESB is a messaging expert, so much so that it can manage whatever type of messaging you can throw at it. Now, if that doesn't sound particularly impressive to you, you're probably blissfully ignorant of the fact that there are quite a few different types of messaging out there. In order to fill you in on what's available, here's a handy list describing them one by one in a simple "Dick, Jane, and ESB" way — bearing in mind, of course, that Dick and Jane in this case are software components rather than people:

✔ **Point-to-point messaging:** This is the simplest messaging there is. Here's an example: Dick sends Jane a text message through the ESB to her cellphone, saying, "See you tonight when I get home." The message doesn't need a response. All the ESB needs to do is ensure that the message arrives.

✔ **Point-to-point request/response:** Here, Dick sends a text message to Jane via the ESB, asking her out to the cinema. Jane sends a message back through the ESB, saying "yes." This is a different situation because the ESB knows that Dick is hanging around waiting for a response. In fact, this is just like a transaction. The communication isn't complete until a response has been received. Of course, it can turn into a long conversation if they have to decide which movie to see, but the interaction is the same. The messaging activity isn't over until the conversation ends.

✔ **Broadcast message:** Here, Dick sends a text message to all his buddies at the office, saying, "I'm going home now, see you tomorrow." This is the same as a simple message, but more people are set to receive it, so the ESB has to do more work to manage it.

✔ **Broadcast request/response:** Imagine, sadly, that Jane simply does not want to go out tonight. So Dick sends a text message to a list with the cell phone numbers of every female he knows and asks each whether she wants to go out. This transaction will not be over until every one of the recipients responds — and if more than one says yes, Dick's going to have a situation on his hands. However, that's not the ESB's problem.

✔ **Publish subscribe:** Realizing the problems he may create if he just sends his cinema query out as a broadcast request, Dick instead decides to post a message on a board, saying, "I'm thinking of going to the cinema tonight; if you're interested in coming with me, let me know." The message board is only available to the eyes of those people who work in the office where it is located. They are the "subscribers" who are likely to look at the message board. This communication method is called *publish subscribe* because one person publishes a message in an agreed place and others regularly go there to check out what messages are posted there.

✔ **Store and forward:** Because Jane was very busy and didn't want to be interrupted, she turns her cell phone off. At 5 p.m., she turns it back on to discover that four text messages and two voice mails are waiting for her. The ESB that manages the messages to and from Jane's phone recognized that she was not available to receive messages and stored them up for her, forwarding them when she turned her cell phone back on.

And that's it. The messaging options listed above are the only kinds of message operations known to an ESB. Of course, you can make them more complicated by combining them with each other or adding complicated rules to the handling of a message and so on. In fact, if you've read a lot of other books about computer communications, you've probably run across a great deal of terminology devoted to just such complications — talk of synchronous versus asynchronous communications, for example, or discussions of whether messages travel by packet switching or circuit switching in packets via TCP/IP. We've tried to skip that stuff here because you really don't need to know or care about these details of messaging to understand SOA.

What you need to know about the ESB is that it's a versatile software component that manages all the complexities of low-level communications between components for you and can deal with any kind of message.

One final detail about messaging: It's important to understand that a good deal of what a computer does involves transactions — taking orders, making payments, updating customer details, and so on. Fundamentally, a transaction is a business event. When such transactions start, they must either complete or not happen at all; they mustn't "happen part way."

And how could a transaction "happen part way," you ask?

Well, as a simple example, in a typical transaction, a payment needs to be recorded and the customer account it affects needs to be updated. If the payment is recorded and then suddenly the software that has to update the customer account fails, the data is out of whack. The transaction only "happened part way" — that is, the transaction completed part of its task but not the whole job, making the reconciliation of the transaction impossible.

Making sure that this "happened part way" scenario never happens makes the messaging involved in a transaction quite complicated. And it is all made even more complicated by the fact that transactions need to execute quickly. For that reason, specialist "transaction engines," such as CICS from IBM and Tuxedo from BEA, are built specifically to manage very large volumes of transactions quickly and efficiently. Such transaction engines are sometimes referred to as middleware, too.

Keep in mind that an ESB is not itself a transaction engine, but it may connect an application to a transaction engine.

Management services

The various components in the enterprise service bus need to work together like a well-oiled machine. Remember the buses we talked about at the beginning of this chapter? Imagine if there were no bus driver. Needless to say, there would be problems with navigation, keeping order, and the like. Within the ESB, there needs to be a set of services that makes sure that all the necessary tasks are performed within the bus, whatever the level of traffic.

As with any traffic situation, things can and do go wrong. For example, one service might interfere with another, a transaction might stop without any visible reason, or smooth performance might suddenly become uneven. If something disruptive happens, services need to correct themselves and then start working again.

The management service that the ESB provides involves, first and foremost, managing itself — and in doing so it provides a highly reliable service for all the messages that it handles. An ESB is capable of balancing its workload across the resources available to it, and it is capable of recovering from the failure of some of the resources it uses. From a computing perspective, it looks after its own performance.

The management services that the ESB provides can be compared to the management services that the SOA supervisor provides. The principle is the same, but the SOA supervisor has the responsibility of managing more than just the messaging between components. It manages the end-to-end process, including every component involved. (We have much more information on the SOA supervisor in Chapter 10.) By comparison, the ESB manages only messages.

Interface services

When you move beyond self-management and message management, everything else that an ESB can do concerns making it possible for one program to talk to another. When one program talks to another, it most likely passes on some information and then gives a command. It is possible that no information is required — a command like "stop" would be one situation — but more likely than not, the system is going to want some informational tidbit such as the following:

```
Get me a credit rating: name = "John Doe" SS#
        ="672-38-8123"
Get me a credit rating:name = "John Doe"
    Social Security # =
```

This example makes the whole process look simple, but things can get pretty complicated pretty fast. (Check out our discussion of XML in Chapter 6 if you need further convincing.) The point here is that programs need rules on how to talk to each other, and before XML came around, many different methods were used for such conversations. An ESB definitely provides the means of connecting Web services to each other by using SOAP and WSDL, but it may also support other ways of connecting programs. For example, it might support the CORBA interface (*Common Object Request Broker Architecture,* a standard that relates to object-oriented programming) or the JMS interface (*Java Messaging Service,* a standard that relates to the Java programming environment). The number of different interfaces that an ESB provides is very important because the more different interfaces it provides, the greater the number of applications it can link together without requiring much coding.

In practical terms, the interface services are a set of adapters that allow different programs to connect to the ESB. In terms of SOA, the interface services are adapters. However, ESB adapters only invoke the specific capabilities that the ESB has to enable the passing of messages. SOA adapters can be more complicated and involve activities that are beyond the scope of the ESB adapter, such as the management of security credentials.

Handwritten left margin:
Corba

pros:
functionality
portability
(across
language
and platform)
good for
large
organizations
because good
w/ legacy
systems.

cons

IDL
must
be
learned

REMEMBER

does not
support
transfer
of
objects,
& speed

Handwritten right margin:
XML
pro:
quality,
low cost,
hi speed

con
complexity
cost of
set up.

Mediation services

You can think of a computing environment as being made up of computer hardware, the operating software, and the local management software. Computing environments vary widely, and connecting one to another is no simple matter. An ESB is equipped to mediate between such different environments — between an IBM mainframe and a Windows server, for example. These two environments are distinctly different in almost every way, but if the ESB is to do its job, it must be able to connect a program running in one environment to a program running on the other. This is a matter of translating between low-level protocols, and an ESB ought to be able to do this for nearly all kinds of computers, operating systems, and transport protocols.

The ESB also needs to be able to mediate the content of the message. If one program defines, for example, a date as being dd/mm/yy, and the one it is connecting to defines a date as mm/dd/yy, when a date is passed from one to the other, the format needs to be changed "in flight." The ESB mediation services do this.

If you're wondering which SOA component the mediation services correspond most closely with, it's the service broker. The SOA service broker enables two programs to connect directly to each other. It also does other things that ESB mediation services do not do. For example, it can search through registries looking for a service that a program needs.

Metadata services

Metadata is information about data structure and meaning. For example, if you hold data on customers, you also need to hold information about how you define a customer within your organization. You might be surprised at how many different ways your own organization defines a customer. Typically, you'll have a different way for each different application that involves customers. But if two programs are going to be able to talk to each other, they have to use a common definition for "customer" and "date" and whatever data they have in common.

The whole situation gets more complicated if you imagine your programs talking to programs from one of your suppliers. The only way to deal with this is to hold a record of customer definitions for every different definition that exists — which is precisely what metadata services do. In fact, the information they hold is quite similar to the information held in a SOA registry.

ESBs vary in how they handle metadata. Some ESBs hold an internal registry of all the programs that they can link together, and some use an external metadata service, such as that provided by a SOA registry. Some mix both approaches, holding a light-weight registry but depending also on an external registry.

Security services

Security is a big issue for computing in general. Therefore, you shouldn't be too surprised that an ESB concerns itself with security. You may not have a pressing need for security when you connect two programs that are both within your organization, but as soon as you connect to anything outside your organization (like your partners' programs, for example), security becomes a serious issue.

The ESBs that offer security services don't directly provide security themselves. They simply provide a framework for security software to plug into and capabilities to help the ESB navigate its way through a network without getting blocked by firewalls or any other kind of security mechanism. As far as ESB security is concerned, you need to think in terms of

- ✔ **Authentication:** Is this user (or message) genuine?
- ✔ **Authorization:** Has the necessary authorization been given to make this connection?
- ✔ **Privacy:** Is the ESB protecting information from being seen or copied by unauthorized users?
- ✔ **Integrity:** Is the data genuine?
- ✔ **Auditing:** Who did what to whom and when?

Although we have spoken of security services separately from mediation services, security services can be regarded as a special kind of mediation service.

In a SOA, the service broker has the responsibility of implementing security.

Running the Enterprise Service Bus

So far in this chapter, we've shown you what an ESB is and — at an admittedly high level of abstraction — how it works. As you can see, it is an important nerve center for SOA. In this section, we provide some further context for thinking about the ESB.

No ESB is an island

Large companies can benefit from a collection of ESBs rather than just one. These ESBs are linked to each other as a federation — a collection of ESBs that seek to provide an enterprise-wide service. (For more about federations, see Chapter 5.) You can think of the collection of ESBs as individual states united as one country. Each state has its own set of rules and policies. The collection of states is brought together with some unifying laws and policies so that they can work together when necessary.

When a company is getting started with an ESB, it might start with a single ESB designed to accomplish one task. Later, the company might add other ESBs as the SOA environment grows. Each ESB has its own set of rules and policies, but they are brought together under SOA governance — an enterprise-wide set of rules and policies that apply to all departments. (For more on governance, see Chapter 11.) In some companies, there may be only one ESB because the SOA focus is more limited. In general, the ESB is designed to connect things together and talk to other data, applications, and infrastructure between internal systems, partners, suppliers, and customers. Whew.

The ESB keeps things loose

In essence, the ESB is the container that enables the loose linking of software components and services. (When we use *loose* here, we mean that the ESB provides a layer that allows components to call and use each other's service in a simple way.) The ESB allows for the reuse of existing assets by enabling connections between them that were previously difficult to make. The loose coupling gives the ESB its flexibility, allowing the ESB to support an unlimited number of user interfaces ranging from a cell phone to an RFID device to a complex mainframe system. In addition, the ESB can support the most advanced and modular set of software components and services, as well as older legacy applications, and enables them to work together as peers in a large networked environment.

Breaching the perimeter

IT security on mainframe computers was based on a "moat and drawbridge" approach: Guard the perimeter to keep the bad guys out. This worked wonderfully well for decades. By contrast, PC security was based on a "no locks on any doors" approach. The thinking was that PCs were difficult enough to use without complicating them with security. This didn't work very well for very long. So as the PC grew up, it gradually added more security. It added perimeter security — that is, protection from everything outside the PC itself. Then the Internet came and exposed the weakness of the security for all to see.

The computer industry responded with firewalls and VPNs (virtual private networks) and intrusion detection systems and identity management systems. Ultimately the truth is that there really is no defensible perimeter. Now IT security is moving toward securing of individual components, including software components, data items, and whole files. In time, a security model for SOA will emerge that is based on the combination of identity management, data audit, and process authentication.

A bus is a bus

Most of us know the term *bus* as it is used in computer hardware — as a place where you can plug in different computer peripherals. Most modern desktop PCs have slots inside the case where you can plug in PCI bus cards. Older IBM-compatibles had ISA (Industry Standard Architecture) bus slots. Old-timers can probably remember terms like Unibus, Versabus, and Nubus, all of which described cards that could plug into computers.

A bus is a more general form of interface port. It is designed to accept a variety of devices. For example, older PCs had separate ports for a mouse and for a keyboard. That's pretty much all you could plug into them. Newer machines have Universal Serial Bus (USB) ports that can accept mice, keyboards, and any number of other peripherals including digital cameras,

video camcorders, disk drives and communications adapters. The use of buses was one of the factors that enabled the rapid growth of the computer industry because hardware designers *did not have to anticipate every possible peripheral that people might want to attach to their computers*. As long as the bus was well standardized, devices designed by different groups could be made to work well together.

The notion of a software bus is a newer concept. It is a software layer that allows different programs to talk to each other in a standardized way, even if they are on different computers, running on different operating systems, and written in different programming languages. We think the software bus will have an equally dramatic effect on the enterprise software industry.

The ESB delivers predictability

The ESB provides the software necessary to optimize the way information is distributed between different types of applications across multiple locations. It accomplishes this through a shared messaging layer that supports all critical types of messages within the enterprise. It provides the fundamental services to do this in a safe, predictable, and manageable way. In essence, it doesn't get upset if two services show up that seem to be mismatched. The bus is designed to figure out what is going on and to clear up the confusion — what this message is, to whom it should be sent, and under what circumstances. At the end of the day, the ESB also provides a common model for deploying, managing, and administering services.

Chapter 10

The SOA Supervisor

SOA is about end-to-end processing — all the time. Here's what goes on:

Someone (or possibly some software) requests a business service. The service broker goes into action, consulting the registry and then orchestrating the connection of all the necessary components of the service. It binds them all together, probably with the help of an enterprise service bus to manage all the messages and the service runs. Hurrah.

Now that this miracle of modern software architecture is up and running, though, what's keeping track of the whole set of computers and networking resources and software so that it continues to run without any problems?

Why, the SOA supervisor of course! (Not surprising, given the title of this chapter; were you expecting maybe a Ouija board?) It's a big role and, to be honest, the SOA supervisor can't do it on its own. It needs help from a whole set of infrastructure services to keep the situation under control. It needs help from "the plumbing."

The Plumbing

Throughout this book, we refer to the complex technical software that keeps a whole data center and network running as *the plumbing*. It's our view that you can find out a lot about service oriented architectures without having to know lots of technical details, so why not just think of it as a collection of pipes that run under the floorboards? It might be horrifically complicated, and you might need to employ a current-day Albert Einstein just to keep it running, but as long as you can pay his salary, it does stay running and everybody's happy.

But frankly, business leaders have never been particularly happy with the plumbing. Here's why:

Every now and then, the CIO delivers the bad news to the folks on the business side of things. "Business folks," he (or she) says, "you're going to need to spend millions of dollars more just to keep everything working the way that you want it working with acceptable levels of service." It isn't that the business folks don't believe him; they've been through the exercise in which they examine every item in the IT budget and get the CIO to tell them exactly what it's for. And it isn't that they don't end up doing more and more with IT every year. They may remember a time when they didn't even have e-mail and now an avalanche of it swamps them every morning; next quarter, they'll be implementing a new Voice-over IP system that's bound to save money on the phones.

The problem is that the company makes *widgets*. It manufactures widgets, it markets widgets, and it sells widgets. It's admittedly a big business, but the things that really matter to this business are its key business services: the widget manufacturing process, the sales process, the customer ordering process, the delivery process, and the after-care program. When a company invests millions of dollars in IT, it wants to know how it is improving these processes — and if, in fact, it is.

This has been a problem with IT since Pontius was a Pilate. You can spend millions of dollars on big servers or storage area networks (SANs) or high-speed networking or ERP systems or databases, but you can't easily tie the whole investment back to "the widget manufacturing process."

This genuine sore point became sore enough for many of the major IT vendors that they changed the nature of their technology products so that they focused on "aligning IT with the business." In fact, so many vendors did this that "aligning IT with the business" has become both an IT marketing mantra and an IT marketing cliché.

The truth is that IT was always aligned with the business, in the sense that technology was always purchased for sensible business reasons even when poor purchasing decisions were made. But the links between the business process and the technology were missing. The vendors of software management products (plumbing products) led the market in delivering the necessary change.

The change of direction did not happen because of a desire to accommodate service oriented architectures. In fact, it wasn't driven by SOA at all. It was driven by the need for service level management — the need to properly manage IT service levels in line with the business service they support. (We talk a lot about service levels in Chapter 4.) Nevertheless, this change of direction was very convenient for service oriented architecture, and, as this became clear to the IT industry, SOA and service level management started to play nicely with each other.

Layers upon layers upon layers

Figure 10-1 shows the three major layers of IT, which we like to think of as the IT layer cake. The plumbing layer is in the middle, and the first thing to note about it is that it is the least visible part of the cake.

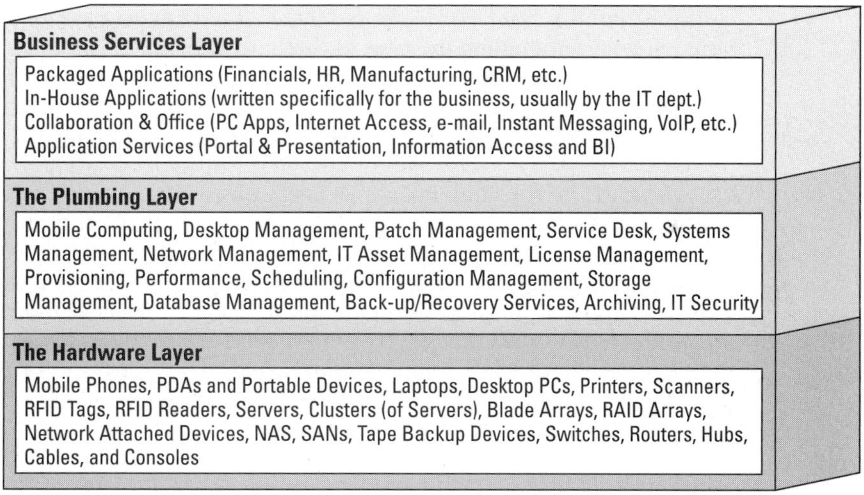

Business Services Layer

Packaged Applications (Financials, HR, Manufacturing, CRM, etc.)
In-House Applications (written specifically for the business, usually by the IT dept.)
Collaboration & Office (PC Apps, Internet Access, e-mail, Instant Messaging, VoIP, etc.)
Application Services (Portal & Presentation, Information Access and BI)

The Plumbing Layer

Mobile Computing, Desktop Management, Patch Management, Service Desk, Systems Management, Network Management, IT Asset Management, License Management, Provisioning, Performance, Scheduling, Configuration Management, Storage Management, Database Management, Back-up/Recovery Services, Archiving, IT Security

The Hardware Layer

Mobile Phones, PDAs and Portable Devices, Laptops, Desktop PCs, Printers, Scanners, RFID Tags, RFID Readers, Servers, Clusters (of Servers), Blade Arrays, RAID Arrays, Network Attached Devices, NAS, SANs, Tape Backup Devices, Switches, Routers, Hubs, Cables, and Consoles

Figure 10-1:
The IT
layer cake.

The bottom layer, the *hardware layer,* consists of things that you can see. You can touch them, turn them on and off with a switch, and kick them. The diagram provides a list of some of these things. None of these items are useful unless you can use them in conjunction with software.

The top layer, which we call the *business services layer,* consists of all the software that is directly useful to the business. This layer contains specific business applications or provides useful ad hoc services, such as presentation services (presenting an application's interface on different devices, such as PDAs and PCs, or through a portal) and inquiry services (services that allow you to search through [and find] information). This is the software that all the business users see, know, and sometimes love.

The middle layer, the plumbing layer, is what makes it possible for the top layer to run on the bottom layer.

We could give you a long list of every possible kind of product in this layer, with a description of what it does, and we would doubtless bore you to death in no time at all. So we don't do that. We just tell you what we think you need to know about the plumbing layer for SOA.

The plumbing service

The IT trend of "aligning IT with the business" is about service levels. You can easily link the costs of some of the plumbing layer activities to the applications that use them. For instance, the cost of activities like backing up and archiving files, including the cost of the hardware used, can be attributed to specific applications according to the actual usage of each service by each application. In fact, you can do this with a fair amount of the plumbing layer because what it does for an application is easy to understand.

But you can't tie the actual usage of *every* piece in the plumbing layer to specific applications.

You also need to understand the fact that attributing costs is not really about business applications anyway; it's about business services. To know how much the full IT costs are for a business service, you need to have an accurate map of all the applications that are used to deliver the service and all the hardware involved. Until the IT industry began to focus on service level management, such business process maps were rarely created.

The key point is that some business processes are a matter of life or death for the company, and some are not. Manufacturing processes, for example, usually fall into the "life or death" category, whereas HR systems rarely do.

Life or death availability

What do you think counts as "life or death" availability?

Some commentators think in terms of "five nines" as being the "life or death" level. Five nines means 99.999 percent, which translates to being out of action for no more than 5.25 minutes in a year. Others think in terms of "seven nines," 99.99999 percent availability, which means being out of action for no more than about 3 seconds in a year. The need for availability at such levels is rare, and that's a good thing because providing a "five nines" level of availability is very expensive, and providing "seven nines" is very, very, very expensive.

Providing such levels of availability can mean having devoted "hot standby" systems that are ready to run at any moment in the event of a failure somewhere and having software that will transparently fire up these systems and connect users to them when a failure occurs. It requires a lot of plumbing. It even requires a bank of diesel generators in the back of the building to guard against black-outs, brown-outs, and an outright collapse of the power grid.

But providing any level of availability for an application beyond about 98 percent requires making well-thought-out technology choices and organizing a little bit of plumbing. (As a rough guide, 98 percent is what you can get without trying — but that means an application is likely to be out of action for over 7 days in a year.)

Realistically, there will be a pecking order of importance among the various business processes of an organization, and the IT availability demands will be greater for the most important ones — within the range of 98 percent to 99.999 percent.

Response times and customer satisfaction

A long time ago, before the age of the PC, IBM researched the productivity impact of having fast computer-to-human response times. Officially, a *response time* is measured as the time between giving a command to the computer (by a mouse click or by pressing Enter) and the information appearing on your screen in response.

Any response time that is less than one tenth of a second may as well be instant because we humans cannot distinguish the difference. Anything that is "sub-second" is good for productivity, and anything worse than that has a negative impact.

But actually, it's a little more complicated than that because experience also depends on expectation. Nevertheless, most applications nowadays shoot for a one-second response time or better. Whether an application can deliver such a response time consistently depends on the plumbing.

The same pecking order that we mention in the previous section is likely to apply between the various business processes that an organization has. More investment of time and money will be made to deliver consistent response times for the mission-critical business processes.

Business service management

And so it came to pass that the vendors of plumbing products began to focus on delivering specific service levels to actual business processes. The much-hoped-for benefit was that organizations would be able to make their IT investments where they could make the most difference.

We have been at pains to point out that there is a great deal of plumbing underneath the floorboards of any IT network. From a service oriented architecture perspective, the aspects you need to be aware of concern

- **Monitoring service levels:** With SOA, service levels can and should be defined for all business services. There is no point in defining such service levels without monitoring them, so one service that the plumbing must provide is the monitoring of service levels.

- **Identifying faults and failures:** All faults and failures anywhere in the network, whether hardware or software related, have the potential to impact service levels for one or more business services. The plumbing products that provide this service are called *system management products*. They work by planting software "agents" on various computers to monitor local events, and these products also listen to and analyze network traffic in order to assemble a comprehensive picture of what is going on.

- **Fault management:** Depending on the actual circumstances, one of two different courses of action is taken if either a fault is detected or service monitoring information indicates that service levels are likely to be violated. Either the circumstances are reported to someone within the IT department — basically because the plumbing can't deal with the situation all on its own — or the plumbing figures out what to do and does it. In the real world, far too much is still reliant on human intervention, but the movement toward self-healing, automated remediation is well underway.

- **Automatic provisioning/remedial action:** Some plumbing products can respond automatically to some situations. You can find provisioning software that can automatically make extra computer resources available to an application (and hence a business service). Such software manages a pool of servers, deploying them when needed and removing them from service when they are no longer required. Cluster management software can share an application across a cluster of servers and automatically compensate if one of them bites the dust. It can also balance application workloads across multiple servers.

- **Performance modeling and optimization:** Some plumbing products can gather information on the way application workloads are changing and model different ways of using the network's resources to meet demands — both for specific applications and taking all applications into account. Such a capability is important for planning future capacity needs of an organization. It's also important when failures occur, and you may have to run a degraded service for a while. Such products can guide you as to which service levels to let slip.

✔ **Management reporting:** Consolidation and reporting products can gather relevant information about the performance of all business services so that senior management can know the status of the IT service.

The SOA Supervisor

If you've read the entire chapter up to now, we're pretty confident that you've read everything you need to know about plumbing to be able to make sense of the SOA supervisor, so we'll just go ahead and put the icing on this particular cake. In a service oriented architecture, the SOA supervisor is, in fact, the chief plumber. It *orchestrates* the plumbing.

We can't overemphasize how important this role is. Back in Chapter 2, we define a service oriented architecture as

> A software architecture for building applications that implement business processes or services by using a set of loosely coupled black-box components orchestrated to deliver a well-defined level of service.

The truth is that loose coupling is not as effective for delivering good service levels as tight coupling. The price paid in decreased effectiveness is worth paying, but it is still a price that has to be paid. That's why the SOA supervisor is important. It focuses on making sure that service levels are acceptable.

The SOA supervisor also has a great future. Right now, most businesses that are experimenting with SOA are implementing SOA in a limited way. They are not doing wall-to-wall SOA — and we don't recommend that they do. But as their ambitions expand, the job of the SOA supervisor expands because more applications are included, and the SOA supervisor simply has to keep more balls in the air.

Soon, some businesses will connect directly to other businesses through SOAs; it will be SOA to SOA. And at that point, the SOA supervisor is likely to take on legal obligations — because the service levels that it is charged with guaranteeing will be covered by legal contracts.

SOA supervising: The inside view

Take a look at how the SOA supervisor operates.

It is important to understand that what we describe here is the goal toward which IT vendors are moving SOA. In other words, it is an ideal that has yet to be fully achieved. But we'll go ahead and describe it anyway.

The first thing to say is that the SOA supervisor is active as long as any service within the SOA environment is operating. For all practical purposes, that means 24/7 with no holidays.

Our story begins with the service broker sending a message to the SOA supervisor saying that the service broker has in fact threaded together and started up yet another business process. We show the business process the broker is talking about, all happily threaded together, at the bottom of Figure 10-2.

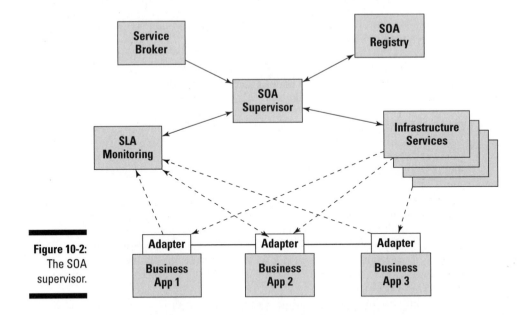

Figure 10-2:
The SOA
supervisor.

The SOA supervisor immediately consults the SOA registry to get the details of the full business process so that it can set up monitoring software to monitor all the necessary components. It delegates the job of doing the monitoring to a utility that we have labeled SLA Monitoring, where the "SLA" stands for Service Level Agreement. This component now activates agents that are local to the various application components shown at the bottom of the diagram. We represent the reporting of the performance of these components by the dotted lines.

The SLA Monitoring utility sends regular performance bulletins to the SOA supervisor, which passes them on so that they can be reported in real time to a console, which is probably manned by a bored operator. If everything is hunky-dory, and the service level agreements are being obeyed, that is all that happens.

However, should the SLA Monitoring utility provide information that indicates that some business process is running into problems and may be about to go belly-up, the SOA supervisor calls in the cavalry in the form of various infrastructure services that we describe earlier (for example, fault management and automatic provisioning). These services do what they can to save the day. This may involve a little load balancing or a little provisioning.

If a problem arises that needs some kind of human action, the potentially bored operator will probably be woken up by a nasty attention-grabbing noise and will be given detailed information about what the situation is and, possibly, where the problem lies.

Getting real

We don't want to mislead you into believing that the technology is more advanced than it actually is. We have described the role of the SOA supervisor as supervising the service level agreements (SLAs) and orchestrating an automatic response if any SLA violation looks likely to occur. Here's the reality in most enterprises today:

- ✔ Most enterprises don't have formally defined or well-defined SLAs.
- ✔ Most enterprises don't have a fully functional suite of infrastructure software.
- ✔ Most enterprises don't have maps of all their business processes and how they work.
- ✔ Most enterprises don't have a full inventory of all the computer equipment and software that they have deployed.

The truth is that most enterprises have quite a lot to do before they will be able to implement the kind of SOA supervision that we're describing here. It may seem like that puts a wrinkle in the works as regards SOA, but actually it doesn't. The truth is that, in most enterprises, the business applications are running reliably.

As organizations begin to adopt SOA, they will do it gradually. They will slowly move toward the kind of environment that we are discussing here. Right now, applications run reliably because organizations buy a lot more computer hardware than they actually need for the workloads that they run. And to be honest, in many companies, the loyal folk in the IT trenches are putting in long hours, living with beepers, and having sporadic nervous breakdowns to keep everything copacetic. The performance of applications is not meticulously managed in the way that a SOA supervisor manages a business service.

It is also the case that no IT vendors can claim to have a complete SOA solution right now, and this is particularly the case as regards managing the plumbing so that it is both effective and efficient. There are sophisticated SOA registries and brokers and sophisticated enterprise service buses, and there are also some sophisticated SOA supervisors that do provide an SLA monitoring service. But right now, a comprehensive set of well-integrated infrastructure services and monitoring services that link to a SOA supervisor and cater to every kind of computer platform is not yet available anywhere. But it will be, in time.

Part III
SOA Sustenance

In this part . . .

There's more to SOA than architecture. SOA governance, security, and development, for example, are all critical to the SOA new world order. In this part, we focus on these (and other) elements necessary to SOA life.

Chapter 11

SOA Governance

*W*hile a lot of organizations are starting to understand that service oriented architectures have the potential to transform the value of their IT assets, the ability to make SOA work comes down to governance. What do we mean by this? Well, in a broad sense, *governance* is just like it sounds — putting a consistent process in place to make sure there are checks and balances that ensure that the expected results happen. In the case of SOA, we're talking about keeping checks and balances between business and IT, between the business and government regulations, and between service and performance. Governance applies to human processes as well as software processes, and the consequences of failure are high.

The overarching principle behind governance is trust. All parties involved (the line of business managers, IT managers, software developers, business partners, and suppliers) must be able to trust that each party will execute its function to make the whole organization work according to established laws. Without governance, your SOA implementation will be a wild, untamed frontier. That isn't a very comforting thought, is it?

What Is Governance?

There are many ways to define *governance.* Governance comprises the organizing principles and rules that determine how an organization should behave. It is also interesting to note that *governance* derives from the Latin word for "steering." The idea of a process that focuses on steering is appropriate for our discussion of IT and SOA governance. SOA is dynamic, changing constantly. Therefore, you never really get to the end of the road. You simply keep steering your company in the right direction. All the policies and procedures — as well as the tools and programs that enforce policies and procedures — form governance.

Governance gives organizations — whether they are countries, towns, or corporations — a structure to make sure the rules of conduct between constituents are followed for the good of everyone. Country, city, and state laws and regulations keep civilization moving in the right direction. Without a set of laws, countries would slide into chaos. Needless to say, governance is a necessary fact of life.

To understand SOA governance, think about the general notion of how a government works. In essence, governments operate on a variety of levels. Local governments, for example, handle issues that concern the town or city, whereas national governments deal with matters of concern to the nation as a whole. In concrete terms, this means that policies related to how often garbage is collected are handled at the local city or town level, while policies related to national defense are handled at the country level.

Likewise, within a corporation, some governance issues are handled at the departmental level, while other issues require the attention of the corporate management team. Governance defines who is responsible for what and who is allowed to take action to fix whatever needs fixing. Governance also sets down what policies people are responsible for and puts in place means by which one can determine whether the responsible person or group has, in fact, acted responsibly and done the right thing.

We didn't write this book to discuss your local, state, or federal government, so we're going to focus on governance within companies. Working under the assumption that a good question or two (or three or four) is as good a way as any to wriggle one's way into a topic, here are a few questions (and example answers) to ponder when trying to imagine how SOA governance issues affect your organization:

> ✔ **What are the core values that define your business?** *"Our company is devoted to transforming the way critical medicines are made available without refrigeration to developing countries."*

> ✔ **How does your business deal with its customers?** *"Our goal is to make each customer a reference. We aim to solve a customer issue within 24 hours of notification."*

> ✔ **How does your business deal with partners?** *"Partners are a critical part of our company's strategy. We treat partners as an extension of our own brand. We do not compete with our partners."*

✔ **How does the company ensure that it treats shareholders fairly?** *"Our objective is to make shareholders successful by empowering every employee to help keep the stock price as high as possible."*

✔ **How do you structure your company so that the business principles and rules put in place by management are followed?** *"Management will articulate to every individual in the company what our company's principles and rules are. There will be ongoing meetings and interactions to make sure these principles and rules are well understood by everyone."*

Clearly, every company has a philosophy for conducting business and a set of rules for how employees within that organization are supposed to act within that philosophical structure. Therefore, the idea of corporate governance is a complicated combination of rules and regulations. In recent years, governments across the globe have passed laws to make sure corporations comply with binding legal notions of correct corporate conduct.

Governing IT

This whole governance business is all good in theory, but how do you put these ideas into practice? Can you say "IT"? There isn't a company in the industrialized world that doesn't use software as part of the process of automating aspects of how it deals with customers, partners, and suppliers. Efficient companies have gone to great lengths to automate as many routine (and some not-so-routine) processes as possible. Therefore, corporate governance is tied directly to IT governance.

IT governance is the way people make decisions and tie business practices to IT systems. IT governance includes the techniques and policies used to measure and control the way IT departments make decisions about their systems and the way those decisions are implemented and controlled. But IT is not monolithic. Like its counterparts in government, some IT systems are centralized and controlled directly by the IT department, while other systems are designed and controlled by individual business units. Still other systems are designed and controlled by business partners. One of the big issues businesses face is the need to have consistency across the company in terms of the business principles and rules that are implemented. This is a very difficult task if each department works in isolation.

The SOA wrinkle in IT governance

When organizations begin to move away from easily governed fiefdoms of separate software toward creating reusable business services that will be used by various constituents across an entire organization (and potentially beyond), it has a big impact on IT and corporate governance. Some rules and regulations apply in all circumstances, others don't.

Before you even start implementing SOA, you really need a SOA governance strategy. For example, say that you create a business service that calculates the commission structure for one product line. Just for fun, call this business service the *Sales Commission Calculation Service*. Your company now mandates that any time someone calculates a sales commission, he or she must use the *Sales Commission Calculation Service*. Within that business service are the business policies regarding commission rules, and it includes the process of paying big bucks that will have a major impact on the bottom line. It also must include any local, regional, national, or international regulations for appropriate business action (tax liabilities that are dependent on location, for example). As you can see from our little example, what is required here is more than a simple piece of code — it is the codification of business policy. The nature of IT governance changes as we move from coding to building services.

With SOA, organizations begin to change IT's focus from creating a single codified application to developing a set of business services that are loosely linked together. Therefore, *governance* takes on a whole different meaning. In essence, organizations must tie the integrity of those business services to corporate governance. As organizations create these services, they cannot be managed in isolation. For example, you can now combine the *Sales Commission Calculation* business service with a service that calculates the bonus for a salesperson based on seniority and performance level. In so doing, you suddenly find yourself in the brave new world of SOA governance.

Understanding SOA Governance

The previous sections in this chapter illustrate that SOA governance has a clear impact on overall IT governance. From an implementation perspective, SOA governance is a combination of policy, process, and metadata (data that defines the source of the component, the owner of the component, and who can change it). In many situations, an organization stores its definitions of rules within a registry so that everyone knows where to locate this important information. A SOA repository is a place where the organization stores information about what is inside each service. While the registry and repository are two separate SOA components, they are used in conjunction with each other.

Organizations that are experimenting might not put a lot of investment into their registry and repository. However, as companies begin to move from a pilot stage of SOA into real implementations across many different business units, the registry and repository become important factors in both scalability and control of the environment.

At this stage, organizations need to look at both SOA governance and IT governance. SOA governance is about looking at a holistic view of the processes and rules for creating a business-services-driven approach to business. SOA governance is as much about organizational issues and how people work together to achieve business goals as it is about any technology.

In contrast, IT governance is about the details of building business services, ensuring that the rules and processes are implemented correctly, ensuring that each service meets technical standards, as well as ensuring that the right interfaces have been implemented in the right way. It looks at the tools and processes at every stage from the creation of business services through their use and transformations over time. IT is building services to be reused in many different situations. Therefore, the SOA technical environment must be dynamic; there will be constant change. New business services that codify the way the business operates will be created, and new rules will be applied. These reusable business services are linked together to create brand-new applications called *composite applications*. These services and rules will have to be tested and designed according to processes within the company. The environment must be designed to easily deal with changes, such as new business services, new security requirements, new partner-generated services, and new innovative processes.

Moving to the reuse of business services is the heart of SOA. Therefore, it's important to think about the business implications of managing those services. If you use a service once and it's incorrect (for example, the calculation of a commission is written as 7% rather than 5%), the company could lose some money, but someone probably will catch the mistake (hopefully sooner rather than later). Now, if 20 different departments use that same service, that 2% mistake compounds quickly. The loss will have a major impact on the bottom line. Now, add another ten business services to the commission business service and link them together. The consequences of a mistake are even greater. If the company is public and tells the market to expect a profit and the company loses money instead because of a bad business service, well, the consequences aren't pretty or nice.

To avoid this type of business disaster, SOA governance has to be a part of overall corporate decision-making process. You must have a method in place to define and verify each business service. You must have a process for both business and technical professionals at the corporate, departmental, and IT level to be involved. You must also have a process in place to measure how effective each service is in delivering value to the business. Later in this chapter, we give you some help in how to set about putting SOA governance in place. Just hold tight.

SOA, What's Different?

In the past, business units and IT took very different views of what governance was all about. Business unit management looked at its customer requirements, its business practices, and its strategies and then established policies and guidelines for its staff to follow. Likewise, the IT department created policies and guidelines for everything from programming techniques to security requirements. While both organizations may have been working on the same issues, they acted as though they were autonomous organizations. And then there was a whole different layer of governance at the corporate level, hovering above the individual business units and IT. With SOA, such parallel universes are no longer an option — policies and business practices that impact the entire company need to be decided at the same level.

In a traditional scenario, the business unit certifies a new business policy, getting the necessary sign-offs from upper management. It then approaches the IT department and asks that a certain application be developed or an existing application be changed to implement that new policy. At this point, the IT department takes over and applies its own processes to writing the necessary code. Often, that application is designed in isolation from other applications. In addition, the IT department is responsible for its own development, testing, and certification of the code. The IT department turns to the business organization for "acceptance testing." Often, this type of testing involves a group of users sitting at a system and trying the application. When business management signs off on the finished product, the contractual obligation of the IT department has ended.

With SOA, life gets a little more complicated. By moving away from isolated, self-contained applications and data, SOA makes it possible to reuse existing IT assets. So, a truly effective SOA governance must be put in place so that organizations have real control over these business services. You must let everyone involved know the status of those services, within both the IT department and the business units.

As a SOA implementation begins to mature, hundreds of business services will be reused across many different departments. Because so many organizations will depend on the validity and quality of a service, a process has to be put in place to keep track of changes to services. For example, there might be a business service that calculates a 30-year mortgage. Suddenly, the governance committee has decided that the technique for calculating the 30-year mortgage must be changed. If there are only a few reusable business services, someone can possibly pick up the phone and call the departments that need to know about the change. (Not necessarily the wisest way to go, but still feasible.) However, if there are hundreds of business services, picking up the phone is a really bad idea. An organization needs a repeatable, documented process for keeping track of changes and informing all interested parties.

Remember that SOA requires a high level of trust. Each service needs to be so well constructed that anyone who needs to use that service can be confident that it will deliver the expected results. To reach this level of trust, there are a series of SOA governance steps you will need to put in place:

✔ **Establish a business services policy board made up of representatives of corporate, departmental, and IT management.** This board will certify that a service is the correct business practice and that it has been implemented in software correctly. For example, it will answer questions like these:

  • Is this the right way to process an order based on corporate practices?

  • Is this the way to calculate sales commissions?

  • Is this the way to calculate taxes on different products in different regions of the world?

  • Does the resulting code match the business practice?

✔ **Establish a programming standards board within the IT organization.** Many developers within IT organizations like to focus their attention on technique and cool new languages. Although mastering new skills and techniques is important, the IT department needs to focus on the use of SOA standards and the techniques for creating reusable business services. You need a peer review process so that IT serves the business in the most effective and predictable way.

✔ **Establish IT SOA governance best practices.** This is a combination of best practices and reality testing. For example, who is allowed to change a service? Who needs to be alerted if a service is changed? If a service is changed, does it have an impact on another service? How do you name a service so that its function is well understood by the business? Who decides which piece of code should become the standard service? How does the organization check the service for quality and performance? What is the process if something goes wrong? Who gets notified and how do problems get fixed? Without these checks and balances, SOA will not work.

✔ **Monitor the life cycle of services.** Because business services cut across technology, people, and processes, they require strong coordination between business and IT. Both business and IT must constantly monitor these services and their architecture to make sure that corporate governance standards are met.

The folks in IT are going to have their own (quite specific) set of obligations that they need to meet under SOA — obligations we summarize for you in this handy list:

- ✔ **Ensure the proper design of a service.** By *proper,* we mean insisting on a modular design process, consistent naming conventions, and standard usage of Web services interfaces.

- ✔ **Identify key implementation issues.** What do we mean by *key* here? First and foremost, IT needs to be vigilant when it comes to documenting how services are dependent on each other. IT also needs to create a reliable process so that an approved service is sure to be registered. It needs to create a consistent process for verifying the quality and integrity of a service, and it needs to come up with a consistent process for putting a service into operation. Finally, IT needs to implement a security strategy for ensuring that only the appropriate people and applications actually end up accessing services.

- ✔ **Monitor SOA services from a business perspective.** This is where all that talk about turning over a new leaf and working as *partners* gets tested. IT needs to create a consistent contract between itself and the business, and it has to establish an agreed-upon way to measure how successful the SOA implementation has been. In other words, IT needs to effectively track and report on results in a fashion that is comprehensible to the business side of things. And, after things are running (relatively) smoothly, IT needs to create a joint business/IT task force to implement a process for service improvement. (No more resting on one's laurels.)

- ✔ **Correlate your SOA strategy with regulatory requirements.** Regulations are as certain as death and taxes, so IT had better take on the responsibility of educating others on the way regulations are implemented in software. IT also needs to create a management process to monitor how software helps the company meet regulations. Finally, IT needs to put in place a well-documented process for ensuring that the right steps are followed throughout the lifetime of the software services.

It's very easy to get caught up in the technical details of implementing a SOA plan. SOA governance brings the focus back to the importance of the partnership between business and technology. Remember, the focus and objective of SOA governance is to identify the services that the business needs to conduct predictable and accurate business processes. When these are identified, it is the joint responsibility of the business and the IT organizations to meet the implementation goals. Therefore, you must have a centralized committee that focuses on the way the SOA life cycle works for the business. This committee needs to establish strategies for how IT policies are designed. It determines how SOA components are managed and maintained and how to achieve quality of service. This is the foundation for the governance strategy.

When organizations move to SOA, they are creating a dynamic and heterogeneous world across many different constituents. Without SOA governance, SOA will not be trusted as a business computing model. Without SOA governance, SOA actually introduces risk to the business.

Therefore, if you intend to create a SOA strategy, begin with your SOA governance strategy. The first task force you set up should be around governance. This will be time and money well spent. With successful SOA governance, you will create quality, trustworthy services that will make the company more efficient and effective. It will also ensure that you meet corporate- and government-mandated standards.

Chapter 12

SOA Security

*I*n the Dark Ages in Europe, when you wanted to be secure, you built a castle with thick walls and surrounded it with a moat. (Can you tell Robin wrote this chapter? He's the Brit.) Also, you needed a sensible number of soldiers to man the battlements. If you had a whole city that needed defending, such as London or Paris or Constantinople, you built walls 'round the whole city. If the city was attacked, all able-bodied men manned the walls, firing arrows and pouring boiling oil on the attackers. In those days, security was all about the perimeter . . . until cannons were invented, that is.

In the Dark Ages of computing — a time when only mainframes existed — the tactics were very similar. You built electronic walls and moats to defend the mainframe. You defended them with passwords and permissions rather than arrows and boiling oil, but it was a perimeter defense just the same. Even when networking began to make an impact, the same digital defenses were used. The whole networks — including the PCs — were like lots of little castles all connected together, all protected by local passwords and permissions. But then the Internet made its appearance and things changed utterly . . .

With the Internet, security problems exploded. Attackers were suddenly armed with a whole set of electronic weapons and tricks like password crackers, Trojan horses, viruses, and worms. But more important, they could attack anonymously from anywhere in the world at any time.

Right now, security in the computer industry consists of trying to build thicker walls and deeper moats. Firewalls, Virtual Private Networks (VPNs),

Intrusion Detection Systems (IDSes), and much else besides continue to guard the perimeter.

But the IT industry already knows that this approach to IT security is ultimately doomed. At some point, it will be necessary to protect on an individual basis all the programs we run and all information we store. The perimeter will not hold.

Who's That User?

We start to answer the above question by explaining the simple diagram you see in Figure 12-1.

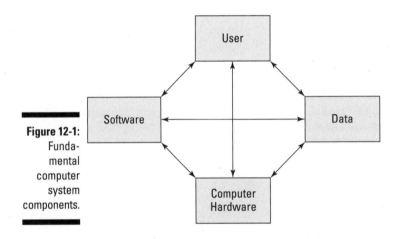

Figure 12-1:
Funda-
mental
computer
system
components.

Figure 12-1 shows the four fundamental components of any computer system. Admit it. It's a lot less complicated than a lot of people would like you to think. Yes, the truth is that there are only four components in a computer system, and one of them is entirely human: the user of the system. The other three components are software, data, and the computer hardware that runs the software and stores the data. See, it's all very simple.

So, from a security perspective, the fundamental question to ask before you allow any software to start up is this: Who is requesting this?

We discuss more security questions in a minute, but frankly, this is the most important one. The software that allows you to be reasonably certain that users are who they claim to be is called *authentication software*. When a user logs into a system, that user gives a name and goes through an authentication process. Authentication, like coffee, can either be weak or strong.

Weak authentication

Weak authentication is authentication by password and/or related procedures, such as asking a specific question that only a particular user is likely to know the answer to. This is regarded as weak because it isn't too difficult for a determined, clever person to get around such barriers. The clever individual needs only ferret out the information. Such authentication may be weak, but most authentication is of this kind and is viewed as good enough for most purposes.

Strong authentication

Strong authentication is based on having something that is unique. This can be a computer-readable card that is issued to you personally. If you lose the card or if it gets stolen, you simply report it. If you don't have the card, you can't get access. That type of strong authentication used to be the most common kind, but biometric readers are gradually replacing it. As it happens, you have many things that are unique to you, including your face, palm print, voice, fingerprint, and so on. These also count as strong authentication. Strong authentication is, as the words may suggest, very difficult to break.

So, if you authenticate someone when they log on to a computer, and you have software that automatically logs them out if the computer is inactive for a while, you can be pretty certain that when that particular "log in" requests something, you know who you are dealing with.

Can I Let You Do That?

If you already know who is making a request, all you then need to do is find out whether the user is allowed to do what she is requesting. Now, if our esteemed user has a perfect right to do what she has requested, you'd really rather not get in her way. She'll only get upset if you hold her up.

But finding out whether she has the right to do what she's requesting is not as simple as it may sound. In fact, it's so complicated that you need a whole system to manage it. Such a system is called an *identity management system*.

If you take another look at Figure 12-1, you see lines connecting the user to software, information (the data), and computer hardware. When users make a request, they are — implicitly, if not directly — asking to run some software and have access to some data and use some computer resources.

This could be a very simple situation — like running a word processor on the PC right in front of you to change a document you wrote yesterday. But it may not be. It may be a request to connect to several other computers and use software that straddles all those machines and that accesses a whole swath of information stored in several document management systems and databases.

Even if you can manage the complications in such a situation, there is also the possibility that, while a user is running such an application, he will try to do something that he doesn't have the authority to do. Consider the simple business rule that only a manager can approve an order with a value of more than $15,000. If a user who is not a manager tries to approve such an order, the order needs to be redirected to a manager for authorization rather than just being processed. This may not sound like much of a complication, and in fact it isn't, but it points to the fact that you need to know who the user is and what rights he has at all times, not just when he logs in.

The situation we just described is the situation you naturally encounter with a service oriented architecture. A user can be (and often is) running software that spans several computers that end up accessing a variety of data, and — to top it all off — the user may be subject to rules that govern what authority she has in specific situations.

So without further ado, we introduce you to identity management software, the software that determines what a user is allowed to do.

Identity management software

Identity management software does some very complicated things. It pulls off the trick of providing a single identity for a user that can be used throughout a computer network and that is enforced regardless of what the user tries to do. It also manages the rights and permissions that the user has so that the user is able to do only those things that he or she has been authorized to do.

The point is that it provides an identity service that can span a network — even multiple networks, if necessary. And that's very useful for SOA because a SOA really needs such a service. Identity management software wasn't designed with SOA in mind — it evolved quite separately. But, as luck would have it, it fits in very well with SOA.

So how, exactly, does identity management software fit into a SOA? First of all, consider the situation without SOA. Forget for a moment that the SOA registry, the service broker, and the tokens shown in Figure 12-2 are there. What you see is a user who logs in to a portal that connects to various business applications.

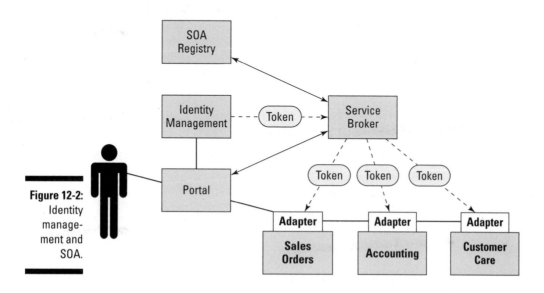

Figure 12-2: Identity management and SOA.

Think of a portal as a window that contains a menu of all the applications available throughout the whole network that the user is able to run. The idea here is that the user can home in on a particular application found on this menu, activate it, and then run with it.

The identity management software provides the portal with all the identity information it needs to connect the user to the application. This can be complicated because it can mean logging on to other computers and providing one or more passwords and doing it all securely. The identity management software knows what the user is entitled to run and knows what hurdles need to be jumped, so it can provide whatever validation is required at any point in order to get the user connected to the application.

Now consider the situation with SOA. You are no longer connected to an application but rather to a business service. Why are we making the distinction here? We make it because the situation can be a good deal more complex. Remember that, with SOA, you aren't necessarily dealing with applications anymore. You are dealing with components that have been connected together. Our user may or may not have a password for, say, the accounting application, but the user wants to use only a particular component of that application.

You may be thinking, "That's not too much of a problem; all you have to do is provide the user with a permission for that business service as a whole, and when everything is connected by the service broker, it should all work fine. You'll just connect it together in a way that gets around the need for a password so no component will ask for a password." If you thought that, think again.

Unfortunately, because accounting software is a financial application, it may be possible to do something quite irresponsible, costly, or illegal using just that component of the accounting application. If you don't provide the application with details of who the user is, you won't know "who did what" if anything bad happens. The user audit trail that the application had will have been disabled.

So, to avoid the possibility of such unpleasantness, you'd better provide user credentials to every component.

To understand how to do this, take another look at Figure 12-2. When the user requests a business service through the portal, the portal contacts the service broker, passing it a security token created by the identity management service. The security token contains credentials, including the identity of the user and the details of the access rights of the user. To add to that, the token is — and we're sure you'll approve of this — encrypted, so it can be read only by software you trust.

The service broker can deliver this token to every component the user accesses. When received, it can be decrypted by each component so that "who is doing what" is known.

Why this is a neat scheme

This is a neat scheme for a lot of reasons. For example, if you want to connect to the SOA systems of your business partners and suppliers, you have a ready-made scheme for exchanging credentials and granting permissions. If your business partners want you to provide information about who you are when you access their software, you will be able to do that. You just provide them with the means to process your credentials. And when they want to access your software, you either issue them security credentials or use their credentials directly. All you need for this two-way interplay to work is to agree to a common standard for credentials.

Think about the problems that can occur if you don't have this kind of authentication scheme. Consider a situation in which one of your business partners claims that one of your staff logged on to their system and caused some damage. You are convinced that you're innocent, but the evidence suggests that whoever did the dirty deed logged on from one of your computers.

The truth of the matter might be that some clever hacker spoofed your system, and it wasn't you at all. Alternatively, maybe it *was* one of your staff, but your security system simply cannot prove who it was, when it happened, or how it was done. Uh-oh, you're in trouble.

But if you had issued credentials in the way we describe, those clever security credentials would be able to prove irrefutably who did what and how. (It was Colonel Mustard with the laptop in the Board Room.)

Another reason it's a neat scheme has to do with the SOA registry. With a scheme like this, you can start making security policy and storing it in the SOA registry. The reason this is especially neat is a bit obscure, but worth finding out about, so bear with us for awhile.

All IT security since the dawn of IT security has been about applications. "You can use this and you can use that, but you can't use that over there." SOA moves IT and IT security into a different world, a world all about business processes. You don't really need to authorize staff to use an application, you need to authorize them for specific business processes. And you may need to authorize them only up to certain limits for specific business processes.

The point is that the authorization is not about an application or a component of an application. It's about a business process. You no longer store authorization rules in the application. You need to store them along with the business process metadata in, of course, the SOA registry.

If you're going to implement SOA, you're going to have to implement identity management. You may be able to start without it, but you won't get far. To put it simply, the time will quickly come when you have to know who the user of any process is. Without an identity management system that spans the whole network, you won't be able to know who your users are and what they're up to. And worse, it won't be safe to connect your systems with those of your business partners, suppliers, or customers. That's why identity management software is a foundation stone for SOA.

Authenticating Software and Data

People can make bad thing happen with computers, and software can make bad things happen with computers. Other than that, there's not a great deal you need to worry about. With identity management, you can take care of the people part; that is, you can ensure that you know the identity of everyone who's doing anything on your systems, and you can authenticate all your users, strongly or weakly according to taste. In short, you have the living/breathing types under control.

But what are you going to do about the software? Every time you read the news, it seems some computer somewhere is abused by vindictive hackers and digital thieves. Data is stolen, identities are stolen, and money is stolen. In one way or another, criminals are gaining access and running software that should be prevented from running. How do you stop it?

Right now, a lot of security is focused on building digital defenses around the perimeter, but this approach won't accommodate SOA in the long term. There is no way of getting around the fact that you are going to have to authenticate the software before you allow it to run. The remainder of this chapter spells out some ways of doing that.

Software fingerprints

One of the things that anti-virus software vendors do is have their programming teams come up with "signatures" of undesirable software (Trojans, worms, viruses, and other malware) so that the anti-virus software can recognize a virus when it comes across one. These signatures are software fingerprints, in the sense that they are unique to the virus. Every time a new virus emerges, a new fingerprint is created and distributed to the anti-virus software running on your PC.

All software can be fingerprinted by using a mathematical algorithm that reads the software and creates the fingerprint. If the software changes in any way — even if just the smallest possible part of it is changed — the fingerprint no longer matches.

Well, if you can use this technique to identify software that is bad, you can use it just as well to identify software that is good. The authentication of software identity can be carried out in a way similar to the authentication of user identity. You hold something that is unique to the software, and before you allow it to run, you carry out an authentication test to make sure nobody has tampered with the software since it was last used. This approach stops any illegitimate programs from running.

This is a security capability that can be used on all the software that a business runs, not just the software that's included within a SOA. The advantage of this kind of IT security product is that it isn't a perimeter security product. Many IT security mechanisms defend the perimeter only. Firewalls, VPNs, password login, security patching, and other mechanisms are really about keeping the castle walls intact. If anyone gets through them, they will probably be able to introduce their own software into the network and run it at leisure. Software fingerprinting makes such software invasions far more difficult.

Figure 12-3 illustrates how software authentication fits in with a SOA. Consider first that no business service will be put into operation without going through governance procedures. When a new version of a business service has been adequately tested and is ready, every software component of it is fingerprinted, and its unique fingerprint is updated. These fingerprints are stored in the signature file by the software authentication component.

When a request is made to the service broker to run a business service, the broker passes the address of each component of the service to the software authentication process, which then tests it and passes it (or rejects it). The service broker then executes each component as it is validated by the software authentication service, the components link together, and the service is available for use.

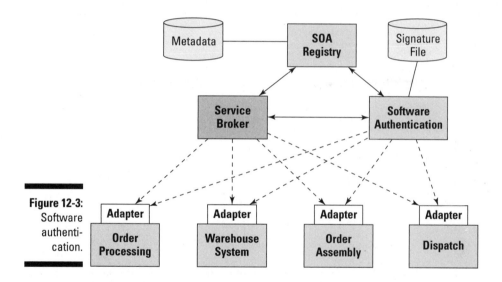

Figure 12-3: Software authentication.

Digital certificates

As long as your software suppliers guarantee the software they deliver to you directly, and you have effective governance procedures for the software your company builds, your primary security concern is with any software that you connect to (or any external software that you load directly into) your network in the normal course of events.

Quite a few computing mechanisms involve another organization passing you a software item that you then execute. It should be (and usually is) corporate policy never to accept any such executable item unless it comes from a trusted source. But how can you tell a trusted source from anything else when, as happens in many cases, software is just interacting with other software?

PKI

The PKI (Public Key Infrastructure) encryption scheme is used throughout the IT industry in a number of different security situations. With this kind of encryption, an individual gets two keys: a private key and a public key (which doesn't need to be kept secret). Anyone else can use the public key to send the individual secret messages that only he or she can decrypt, and it can also be used to verify digital signatures created by using the private key that can be attached to documents that can (but need not be) encrypted themselves.

Digital signatures are virtually impossible to forge. So if you receive some software along with a digital signature, you can know for sure who the source is and decide whether to trust that source. The PKI encryption scheme also provides a way to validate that data comes from a trusted source. All that is necessary is that the data includes a digital signature. And, of course, you can also use exactly the same mechanism if you want to pass software and data to your business partners and suppliers.

You use digital certificates. Digital certificates are security certificates that prove you are dealing with a trusted source and that any executables passed on by that source can be used automatically by your software. A digital certificate contains:

- A name (of a company or a person)
- A serial number
- The expiration date of the certificate
- A copy of the holder's public encryption key
- The digital signature of the issuing authority

The issuing authority, in the case of digital certificates, is an independent but trustworthy third party that checks credentials of companies and issues them with certificates to use. Certificates like this are kept in registries that are publicly available for software to access. The certificate is, in fact, a guarantee of authenticity from the issuing authority. It says that the named person or company really has this *public encryption key.* You know it is genuine because you use the public encryption key of the issuing authority to prove it to yourself.

Auditing and the Enterprise Service Bus

Security defenses for SOA consist primarily of authentication. If you know for sure who your users are, and you know for sure that the software you use, either internally or externally, is authentic, and you know that any external data you receive is authentic, you need only have one other concern — that your own staff isn't using your software in an entirely "legitimate" way, and so are able to defraud you. For example, if they have access rights to the payments system, they might simply start writing themselves checks. The software is legitimate and the user is legitimate, but the fraud still happens. However, such frauds leave traces. Your data should be able to tell you the truth, as long as you implement audit trails that can tell you who did what when. Audit trails are the surveillance cameras of computer systems.

Unfortunately, setting up audit trails is just about all that you can do to prevent internal attacks on a business. The reality is that you have to trust someone to carry out those business processes that require trust, such as procurement and making payments.

Naturally, you hope to be able to hire honest employees to do these jobs, but even if your staff selection isn't perfect, it's unlikely that you'll have any problems if you put a comprehensive audit trail in place and regularly monitor staff activity. In recent years, IT organizations have been implementing far more comprehensive audit trails than ever because of the Sarbanes-Oxley legislation and the penalties associated with the lack of compliance with respect to financial systems.

One problem with audit trails within a SOA is that the operation of the business service is split across multiple components. This may or may not be an issue, depending on the business service. However, if it is, the use of an enterprise service bus for all messaging will resolve the problem because the ESB can keep an audit trail of all the messages that are passed. (See Figure 12-4.) Additionally, if there is any concern about data privacy in passing data from one component to another — perhaps there might be some hidden listening software taking notes — most enterprise service buses will also be able to encrypt the data as it passes back and forth.

Beware of snake oil

We talk a lot about standards, and you're probably sick of hearing about them, but if there is one place where standards are absolutely crucial: security.

Security systems are notoriously difficult to get right. One minor design flaw can render an otherwise well-thought-out protocol easily penetrable. The history of cryptography is filled with stories of large organizations that thought they had a clever approach that turned out to be disastrously weak. From German and Japanese codes in World War II to broken copy protections on CDs and DVDs to flawed WEP encryption in wireless networks, the story keeps repeating itself. The only known method for ensuring that cryptographic systems are really secure is open and thorough review by large numbers of experts — a process that takes years.

Beware of companies offering proprietary encryption algorithms and protocols. There is no reason to risk your company on proprietary schemes. There are more than enough well-proven standards around for almost any application.

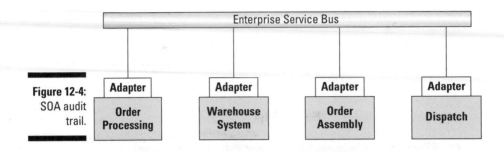

Figure 12-4:
SOA audit
trail.

The Big SOA Security Picture

In this chapter, we don't try to tell you everything there is to know about IT security. That would take volumes. Instead, we simply mention the security issues that SOA naturally raises. With SOA, you are likely to be linking together components that are spread across different computing environments. This stringing together of different components that were previously unconnected makes SOA business services more vulnerable to attack than other applications. Just spreading out software in this way creates a login nightmare.

In order to address this risk, three aspects of SOA business services need attention:

- ✔ Identity management
- ✔ Software and data authentication
- ✔ Audit trails

Software solutions are available in all these areas to address the security problem. Businesses that implement SOA need to implement solutions in these areas as early as possible.

Chapter 13

Where's the Data?

*I*f you've decided to dive into the world of service oriented architecture — thereby reaping the benefits of sharing critical business services across the organization — you need to consider how to maximize the trust and confidence you have in your company's data. You may decide to begin your SOA journey by eliminating some of the redundancies in businesses technology systems and software, but you can't stop there. The next step is to ensure that all the company's data is both *consistent* and *accurate*. This chapter shows you how to achieve both those goals.

When Good Data Goes Bad

Service oriented architecture represents a new way of thinking about everything in a company's IT structure, including how one thinks about data. It begins with the goal of achieving consistency between data sources. In order to achieve data consistency, you begin by separating your data from its tight dependency on the business applications that created it and update it.

Data is one of the organization's most precious assets, but these critical data stores are typically segregated by business function in *data silos*. Traditionally, business data has been managed in a way that tightly associates specific data definitions to specific business applications, such as finance, human resources, or operations. Take, for example, a sales force automation application that manages all your sales force data. This is likely to be a *silo* of data because the data structures will have been designed to satisfy the particular needs of the sales force automation application. Your customer relationship management system will probably sit over another silo of data — one that overlaps the sales force automation silo. Some organizations might have hundreds of such data silos scattered all over their enterprise. This may sound like an exaggeration, but it is not. If you have hundreds of applications, you likely have hundreds of data silos.

The problem is that an organization's data resources were not designed for global use by all applications. They were designed to suit one specific business application or, at best, several applications. The data was designed for a specific context. For example, the sales order processing system might record a person's name, address, date of birth and sex, but not their marital status, or what they do for a living. This is fine for taking orders and delivering goods, but not for the customer relationship management system, which needs much richer information about the customer.

When separate systems gather their own data, simple errors in entering data make it difficult, and sometimes impossible, to aggregate the data that has been collected about a customer (or any other entity). No matter how effectively data is gathered, corruption creeps in. The rate of error can sometimes be as high as 15 percent and it is never zero.

The siloed approach to working with data may provide great information to a particular business unit, but it creates some startling inconsistencies in data when viewed at an enterprise level. This happens because data is often defined to fit the precise view of a single business unit. So, one department thinks of the customer as the manager of a department that procured a service from the company. Another department defines a customer as the company itself. A third department defines a customer as the local office of that same company. How can you trust the information your business uses to make strategic decisions if poor-quality data keeps you from having a complete view of your customers or products? For example, you might underestimate the importance of one of your key customers if that customer makes purchases from several business subsidiaries, using slight variations of the company name and your system doesn't recognize them as a single purchaser.

Other inconsistencies in data are based on *semantic* differences. *Semantics* here refers to the rules that govern how one talks about data, just like the semantics of English govern how one conveys meaning when speaking English. A semantics of data is used to ensure that everyone in the business has a common understanding of the business information and rules — that everyone speaks the same "language," as it were. For example, one business unit might consider the word *customer* as referring to the local office of a particular company, whereas another unit might use *customer* to mean the entire corporate entity. These semantic differences in the use of basic business terms like *customer, partner, department,* and the like lead many organizations to devote significant resources to interpreting and reconciling differences in reports from various divisions or subsidiaries. (For a more technical take on data semantics, check out the "Data semantics" sidebar.)

Data semantics

Data semantics is the *meaning* of data. It's a meaning that goes deeper than definitions to include an understanding of the data in context with business products, people, or events. *Semantic interoperability* is an architectural quality that measures how people and technology understand data and how this level of understanding impacts the exchange of information. You have to understand data in context in order to make accurate and appropriate decisions.

Semantic interoperability means that both business managers (humans) and software applications (machines) can understand the subtler meaning in data. Humans and machines need to know something about how the data is defined or calculated and where it came from in order to determine whether this is the right data. Humans from different business entities need to agree on certain rules, definitions, and policies for critical data. However, there are times when a human may be able to make manual adjustments to account for slight nuances in meaning, but a machine cannot.

Much of the transfer of data in a service oriented architecture is done from machine to machine, without human intervention, so that you need the highest level of semantic accuracy or interoperability to really achieve trusted information. In the following example, the terms "balance" and "remainder" may mean the same thing, but the machine requires specific instructions to account for the semantic difference in the two terms:

✔ A billing application needs a customer balance. The application calls the data it needs *balance.*

✔ An accounting application supplies a customer balance. This application calls the data it supplies *remainder.*

✔ In order for the accounting application to automatically supply the billing application with the correct customer balance, an adjustment or mapping must be made between *balance* and *remainder.*

Reconciling inconsistent data can take a lot of time — and can result in missed business opportunities. In addition, imagine the confusion that often occurs when one organization buys or merges with another and tries to integrate the data. It's imperative to determine whether the soon-to-be-merged companies in fact share a certain subset of customers so that the customer can be appropriately served.

One of the main objectives of service oriented architecture is to make sense out of business chaos. This includes providing accurate information about the business — in the right form and at the right time — to everyone involved in the business. One critical step for making this happen is to ensure that each component of data can be used independently from its current implementation. With service oriented architecture, you need to begin to think of data as a reusable resource. We call this new concept *information as a service.*

Dastardly Data Silos

A database (or other data store) is called a *data silo* if it is tightly dependent on (and designed to manage data for) a specific application or a specific region or functional area of the company. The tight dependency between a siloed data store and the application makes it almost impossible to get a complete and consistent view of data across the enterprise.

Silos of data are a natural extension of how business applications have been designed for decades. For example, each department in a very large (fictitious) commercial bank (which we're calling Big Global Bank) has its own applications — such as the personal account system, the human resources system, and the mortgage origination system. Each of these applications uses and creates lots of data. Likewise, partners have their own sets of data about the products they sell and the customers they serve. In addition to all this data, Big Global Bank has recently acquired several other banks and must contend with overlapping sets of systems and related data, hampering business interaction and decision making. The mainframe systems that store the customer and product data from different departments and subsidiary banks cannot easily connect with each other or with externally located data stores belonging to Big Global Bank's business partners. This siloed approach to storing and managing data inhibits the flow of critical information at Big Global Bank.

Is it information, or is it data?

Often, the terms *data* and *information* are used interchangeably, and in general that's okay. However, people who spend a lot of time with data usually give these two terms slightly different meanings:

✔ *Data* generally refers to facts, like temperature and humidity.

✔ *Information*, on the other hand, is the collection of these facts in a specific context from which conclusions can be drawn.

So, if the temperature is high and the humidity is high little can be deduced, but if the temperature is high and the humidity is high in a given place for a given length of time, the conclusion could be that it will be uncomfortable for anyone in that place during that time. The facts — the actual temperature and humidity statistics — are the data. The conclusion that's drawn (uncomfortable weather) is the information.

Businesses use the term *data* to refer to words and numbers that represent what a business needs to know. For example, a data element like "Peter Jones" is an instance of a customer name, or "24601" is an instance of a style number. These pieces of data need to be placed in context, along with other pieces of data, in order to be used for analysis and decision making. Because companies use data to derive information to make decisions, and this data must be qualified and consistent, we think the term *information* sounds more appropriate. Hence, we use the phrase *information as a service* rather than *data as a service*.

Individual departments and bank subsidiaries have each defined data items for their own purposes — not taking into account the rest of the company's needs. So, when Global Bank needs to bring together data from one department with a dozen other departments in order to make new business decisions, they have problems. Definitions of everything from what a customer is to the names of products are different. The same customer may have different types of accounts, and Global Bank may not be able to associate all the accounts with this customer. Therefore, management simply cannot trust the data to be consistent and accurate when viewed at an enterprise level. When organizations like Global Bank discover this problem, they typically come up with ways to work around the problem on a case-by-case basis. Not only is this time consuming, but each situation also requires development teams to start from scratch — there is no reuse of expensive development efforts. They really need SOA.

Trust Me

Businesses like our fictitious Big Global Bank have become increasingly complex, resulting in many situations in which trust in data, and therefore trust among entities reliant on the data, has been compromised. Company mergers and acquisitions, electronic commerce, and economic globalization have all contributed to the increased level of complexity in organizational data. Government regulations like Sarbanes-Oxley and Basel II require organizations to make significant changes to the way data is managed to ensure accuracy, reliability, and auditability. But, in addition to responding to regulations, it makes good business sense for organizations to ensure the integrity and security of corporate data assets. A higher level of trust among companies, their partners, and their customers leads to more efficient business because transactions can be done more quickly and cost effectively.

In order to make data more reliable, consistent, and trusted, enterprises link data sources between departments or regions of their organization by using various data integration processes. Service oriented architecture is changing both the philosophy and the architectural framework for deploying the data integration software tools that manage the integration process. Some of the key processes required to bring the data together in a meaningful way include locating and accessing data from a data store (*data extraction*), changing the structure or format of the data so it can be used by the business application (*data transformation*), and sending the data to the business application (*data load*). Software programs that automate these processes are often grouped together as *Extract-Transform-Load* (ETL) tools.

Integrating data across business entities was previously done by creating a system of tight linkages or connections that were fixed in place and could not be easily changed. In many cases, they didn't (and still don't) provide for a two-way flow of information. Implementing a SOA approach enables the business to access, manipulate, and share data across the organization in a repeatable and consistent way. This approach provides the business with more useful information to help make sound business decisions. For example, the business knows more about John Parker Jones as a customer after the purchases of J. Jones, Mr. Jones, J.P. Jones, and John Parker Jones are aggregated. Service oriented architecture ensures that this aggregation can be done quickly and efficiently, and that the system is flexible enough to adapt to changes required by the addition of a new product line or subsidiary.

Service oriented architecture enables the business to put the priorities of the business first instead of holding the information hostage to the restrictions based on the structure of the IT system. The ETL and software tools for other data integration processes (data cleansing, profiling, data transformation, and auditing, for example) all work on different aspects of the data to ensure that the data will be deemed trustworthy. The following sections show how that's done.

Data profiling

Data profiling tools help you understand the content and structure of your data by first collecting the necessary information on the characteristics of the data in a database or other data store — a crucial first step when it comes to turning the data into a more trusted form. The tools then analyze the data to identify errors and inconsistencies so they can make the necessary adjustments and corrections. The tools check for acceptable values, patterns, and ranges and help identify overlapping data. The data profiling process, for example, checks to see if the data is expected to be alphabetical or numeric. The tools also check for dependencies or to see how these data relate to data from other databases.

Data quality

High-quality data is essential if a company is to make sound business decisions. The quality of data refers to characteristics about the data, such as consistency, accuracy, reliability, completeness, timeliness, reasonableness, and validity. Data-quality software makes sure that data elements are represented in the same way across different data stores or systems in order to increase the consistency of the data.

For example, one data store may use two lines for a customer's address, and another data store may use only one line. This difference in the way the data is represented can result in inaccurate information about customers, such as one customer being identified as two different customers. A corporation might use dozens of variations of the company name when they buy products. Data-quality software can be used to identify all the variations of the company name in your different data stores and ensure that you know everything that a particular customer purchases from your business. This process is called *providing a single view of customer or product.* Data-quality software matches up data across different systems and cleans up or removes redundant data. The data-quality process provides the business with information that is easier to use, interpret, and understand.

Data transformation

Data transformation is the process of changing the format of data so it can be used by different applications. This may mean a change from the format the data is stored in into the format needed by the application that will use the data. This process also includes *mapping* instructions so that applications are told how to get the data they need to process.

The process of data transformation is made far more complex by the staggering growth in the amount of unstructured data. A business application, such as a customer relationship management or sales management system, typically has specific requirements for how the data it needs should be stored. These data are likely to be *structured* in the organized rows and columns of a relational database. Data is *semi-structured* or *unstructured* if it doesn't follow these very rigid format requirements. (The information contained in an e-mail message is considered *unstructured*, for example.)

Some of a company's most important information is in unstructured and semi-structured forms, including things as ubiquitous as documents, e-mail messages, customer support interactions, transactions, and information coming from packaged applications like ERP and CRM. Many data transformation tools don't handle unstructured data very well, and if you need to incorporate the information into your integration strategy, a significant amount of manual coding may be involved.

Data governance and auditing

The primary role of establishing SOA data governance and auditing services is to enable and manage the enforcement of business and security policy as it is applied to data. The need for this technology is particularly urgent because of regulations like Sarbanes-Oxley. Data governance provides a level of accountability that is equally critical for business customers, suppliers, partners, auditors, shareholders, and regulatory agencies. This technology includes security services such as data encryption, digital certificate management, and authentication. It also includes processes for managing user privileges regarding data access control that determine who can see data as well as who can change the data.

As information becomes more loosely coupled (independent of any specific application), data auditing ensures that an organization can manage and adhere to requirements imposed by regulatory agencies and that access to data is kept confidential. It also helps the enterprise answer questions like these:

- Who has access to sensitive data?
- When was it accessed and by whom?
- How can I track data that may have been deleted?

Providing Information As a Service

When organizations begin to apply SOA principles to managing their data assets, they move from fixing problems on the fly to delivering information as a service. Information as a service is an architectural approach that loosens the tight connections between data and applications so that data can be controlled and shared across the enterprise. This approach allows businesses to reach a consistent view of enterprise-wide information that has previously been very hard to achieve.

By applying the principles of service oriented architecture, such as loose coupling of data to applications, businesses can increase the consistency and accuracy of their data. And they can do this in an efficient, cost-effective way without actually moving or redesigning the data stores that exist in their business today. In essence, you achieve the goal of getting at the data you need without performing major surgery. Although creating one massive centralized data store would help control data management and synchronize data definitions, it would be impossible to manage.

Data control

Control of data is a controversial issue in many companies. If you are responsible for a departmental budget or are responsible for meeting specific business objectives, you really don't want someone from another department manipulating your data. Businesses need to find the balance that lets managers retain enough control over the data that matters most to their department and also allows for a single, consistent view of customers or products at the enterprise level.

What the business needs is data that can be trusted and understood at all levels of the organization. The information as a service approach is designed to ensure that business services are able to use and deliver the data they need in a trusted, controlled, consistent, and flexible way across the enterprise regardless of the requirements specific to individual systems or applications.

As with so much of the SOA approach, the ability to provide information as a service is a work in progress. While no specific method will work for all enterprises, in order for information to be delivered as a service, the data must meet the following three requirements:

- ✔ **Consistent data definitions:** The meaning of data needs to be unambiguous so it can be interpreted and processed appropriately both by businesspeople and by machines.

- ✔ **Ensured quality of data:** Businesses should use whatever tools they need to ensure that data from many different sources can be trusted to be accurate and consistent no matter how the data ends up being used.

- ✔ **Data independence:** If the data is loosely coupled from its original sources, those data elements can be more easily brought together in different ways to meet many different business needs.

The following sections address each of these concerns in turn.

Consistent data and the metadata repository

To provide information as a service to everyone in the business — from sales to operations to finance and senior management — all the data the businesspeople need must be treated consistently across the enterprise. Consistent definitions and rules for data must be based on the way the business *as a whole* needs to understand sales, customers, products, and profit. If you have a right to view, change, and report on data, you should be able to get the quality data you need when you need it.

Information delivered as a service has been effectively certified by the enterprise as trusted data. This means you can trust that you and your counterparts across the enterprise are basing decisions on data that is secure, clean, and structured correctly. Everyone in the business is working with consistent rules about how the data is structured, accessed, and used. This common understanding of the data must extend across business units and regions to include information provided to partners and customers.

The definitions, mappings, and other characteristics used to describe how to find, access, and use the company's data are called *metadata*. Business services need to be able to access metadata in order to consume and deliver the data they need. Metadata is stored in the *metadata repository* — a container of consistent definitions of business data and rules for mapping data to their actual physical location in the system. This repository resides in a technical layer between the actual data stores and the business services.

The metadata repository is often referred to as a *metadata layer* because of its position in the information infrastructure. A more complete technical term for the metadata repository is a *metadata abstraction layer*. This is because it includes the rules, definitions, and mapping instructions about the data that are either replicated or separated from the data stores. The process of abstracting the data rules and definitions adds flexibility to the data infra-structure, which provides programmers with a way to loosen the tight con-nections between data stores and specific business applications.

The purpose of the metadata repository is to help you bring together all the components of your business in an orderly way without requiring you to replace your existing data stores. The abstraction of rules, definitions, and other instructions from the data stores provides your business with a way to achieve consistent data while still maintaining your extensive investments in data management assets. By abstracting data from the context in which it is held and used, you are better able to work with it in a variety of situations. The metadata repository ensures that the data is of the right structure and quality before it's consumed by a business service. The metadata repository also ensures that data from different sources can be linked together correctly. The semantics and rules that apply to all your company's data can be orga-nized, tracked, and managed through the metadata repository. For more on metadata repositories see Chapter 15.

Know Your Data

You should be as careful and curious about your business data as you are when meeting a new person at a party. The data definitions, data lineage, and other characteristics about the data in the metadata repository provide details about your data in the way that you might put together background details about a person you have just met. For example, last week, Elizabeth met Bob at a party. Initially, Elizabeth wasn't sure whether she wanted to spend the time to get to know Bob. She had no context in which to judge whether he was honest or thoughtful and would be a good person to get to know. Elizabeth began to collect data about Bob in a very simple way. She asked him a lot of questions. She found out his age, his hometown, where he lives now, and where he works. These are some of the descriptive characteristics about Bob.

She also found out that he went to college with one of her close friends, that he plays basketball with someone who works in her office, and that one of his co-workers is married to her cousin. This is the *lineage* — history about where Bob has been and some of the connections between Bob and other people. Now she knows enough to conclude that she would like to know Bob well, and she knows how to locate him to find out even more.

Think about data the same way. The metadata repository allows you to ask and get answers to the following types of questions:

- How is the data structured?
- What does the data look like?
- What rules apply to the data?
- How is the data used?
- How do you find the data?
- What does the data mean?
- Where does the data come from?
- Who has the rights to access or change the data?
- What is the context for the data?
- What impact will changing the data definitions create?

The answers to these questions provide context for data and enable applications to use data properly. The lineage or background history provided on the data answers the type of questions that Elizabeth wanted to know about Bob at the party. You need to know where the data has been and how it has been accessed, changed, and used to be able to achieve data consistency. (Safe dating, safe data.) A metadata repository helps you to understand the impact of changes to data. You need to be able to follow the history of changes to data and make the connections to the business services that use the data. This requires a link between the SOA registry and the metadata repository (detailed in Chapters 8 and 15).

Data services

Data services are all the technical processes that *qualify* the business data to ensure that it is trustworthy. These processes include the data integration technologies that we talk about earlier in this chapter (data profiling, data quality, data transformation, and data governance and auditing). Although businesses have successfully used software tools for data integration without applying SOA principles, using the data services approach gives you a more comprehensive — and more business-focused — view of your data. Data services bring all the modular data integration components together to deliver trusted information to the enterprise consistently and as needed. In the past, a data profiling tool or data-quality tool may have been applied to specific data stores on a case-by-case basis. The data services approach applies all these technical processes as required to the data requested by the businessperson. It is the automatic and integrated nature of this approach that ensures that all the data the business needs is accessible, accurate, consistent, timely, and complete.

The metadata repository is a critical part of the infrastructure that all data services need in order to work effectively. If sales, finance, and operations all need to get data about customer John Parker Jones for different business processes, the data services for the business ensure that everyone is working with consistent and accurate information. The data profiling and data-quality services, for example, look to the metadata repository to find and correct the different variations of the customer's name. The metadata repository provides data on the linkages between John Parker Jones and his various accounts. It also provides the security and access level so you can get this information only if you are entitled to do so. The metadata repository provides the data service with all the contextual information about the data to provide a complete picture of the customer.

Loose coupling

The third key requirement for delivering information as a service is to ensure that the data is available as a reusable resource. Loosening the dependencies between data and the applications where the data originated provides the infrastructure flexibility that supports reusability. Using a federated approach ensures that the data can stay in its original location. (More about federation in Chapter 5.) Federating data sources provides consistent rules and definitions so that data from various types of data stores can all work together. This means that the business can avoid changing the data and its location but can still combine data from a variety of sources depending on the requirements of a business application.

Service oriented architecture has the potential to allow businesses to grab the elusive brass ring of business achievement through flexibility and innovation. Achieving trust in data needs to be an integral part of any business's SOA. Even the most efficiently created, easy-to-use business services for payment, invoicing, or other business processes will not provide long-term value to your business if the data is misunderstood or of poor quality. Business services exist only to read, monitor, calculate, analyze, report, and otherwise manage the business data.

Implementing information as a service leads to increased business flexibility, business trust in data, and reduced costs. The integrity of the data is strengthened because when a business service receives or consumes data that is delivered as a service, the data has been effectively certified by the enterprise as trusted data. The ultimate goal of this approach is to provide a seamless way for the business user to access data that is both trusted *and* consistent with company rules and polices.

Chapter 14

SOA Software Development

A lot of this book focuses on how a SOA behaves when it's gainfully employed running business processes. Now, we're going to talk about building SOA services so that you can get all excited and get to work!

But don't get concerned. We aren't going to say much about programming languages, scripting languages, job control, compilers, linkers, interpreters, or code tracers. All that we need to say about such programmer tools is that in the world of SOA, they continue to exist. And the people who know and love them will continue to know and love them because they will continue to be needed for quite a while yet. The considerable skills of these talented souls are focused on all that fundamental code stuff buried deep within the enterprise system, and there's still going to be a lot of nitty, gritty, gnarly, intricate code to write for some time to come. But under SOA, all this kind of programming belongs under the heading of "plumbing" — that is, programming that business people and applications programmers can joyfully ignore. SOA sits atop the plumbing. Plumbing is not its job.

We characterize SOA as an architecture that separates the plumbing from business services, as indeed it is. But when you first adopt SOA, there is no single switch you can flip that magically separates these two aspects of software that in fact have coexisted for some time — coexisting to such an extent that they've become significantly intertwined. Lacking that simple switch, what ends up happening is that you begin to do things in a way that will eventually bring about this (much desired) separation. On a project basis, business management and IT must work together to determine where to start. When it comes to actually doing the work of creating reusable services, well, somebody has to get his hands dirty.

Often, the first thing that a business does in adopting SOA is to take some older applications and transform some of their business functions into Web services. In other words, they start to identify and transform specific components that they know can be gainfully reused. Which components should you choose? That's a great question.

So Many Components, So Little Time

If you try to turn everything into a reusable component, you will be, from our perspective, attempting to boil the ocean. We recommend against this. Starting a project to turn every interface option of every application into a service will create a great deal of unnecessary work. First, you need to understand all your applications in terms of how they relate to business processes. Replacing every interface takes a long time, and many of the interfaces that would be replaced might never be used.

don't reuse everything and replace every interface. Do only what you need by making a map of business process.

Instead, you need to model and record business processes on a step-by-step basis. For example, when the phone rings for customer support, the customer support person first does blah, blah, blah, and next does blah, blah, blah. She or he creates a ticket and the ticket is sent to tech support. When tech support gets the ticket they do blah, blah, blah. Every aspect of your business has some sort of process. Draw a literal map of the process and record what is supposed to happen at each step. Ultimately, you'll want to map every process, but you probably shouldn't wait until everything is mapped — unless you have a relatively small or uncomplicated business. Start with the biggest, most obvious processes or those you know need to be improved. SOA's a journey, remember, and you can begin with a single process, although you might be better starting with a few (not all).

In addition, you need to identify and map exactly which of your applications do what with respect to each business process. You can find software products that can help you do this. By doing this, you create a business process map of your applications. (Check out the sidebar, "Software component mapping and business process modeling," for more information.) If you're at a loss as to how to get started, we feel confident that any one of the vendors we talk about in Part V will gladly lend you a hand.

After you've built a business process map, you need to reduce the scope of action to the business functions that you identified within the specific applications you run. You might now be tempted to make all of these available as Web services so that you can reuse them as the need arises. But that's not such a good idea either. There's no point in making something reusable unless you are going to reuse it. So where do you start?

Software component mapping and business process modeling

We warn you, if you're unfamiliar with the jungle of software modeling products that has grown like a rain forest over several decades, you're going to be surprised by the many types and flavors of modeling products out there on the market. Some are little more than diagramming tools, some are for designing databases, some for designing programs, some are for modeling existing business processes and some are for building new ones. To make matters worse, some cover several such functions and some (usually referred to as *meta tools*) can actually be used to build modeling tools for modeling just about anything.

The mapping tools you choose to create a comprehensive map of software components will depend to a degree on the software tools used to build the in-house applications you already have. Your company could already have component maps created, for example, in UML (the *Unified Modeling Language*) using tools such as Rose (from IBM-Rational), AllFusion Component Modeler (from CA), Describe (from Embarcadero) and many, many more. There are over 100 such tools. If your company is already using tools of this kind, there's probably no reason to change.

Good question. To get to the beginning of an answer, keep in mind that you have to try to solve the problem from a high level. You have to think in terms of architecture. Remember that SOA is a *service oriented architecture.* At the beginning of the journey to SOA, none of the existing applications you run were created for this architecture. Ultimately, your goal is that all applications for which this architecture is suitable will be built appropriately.

However, for most applications, you have to continue (for a while at least) in the traditional way of doing things because you cannot simply convert everything all at once to run within a SOA, even if you desperately want to. It is inevitably a gradual process.

The adoption of SOA is not a process of tearing one building down to replace it with another. You cannot do that because the building you are trying to tear down is being used. Neither is it a process of creating a whole new building next to the one you are using. It is a process of renovating the building from within, starting in one place and then moving to another and then another, and doing this while the building is occupied.

And of course, this is no ordinary building. These are the computer systems of an organization to which we are forever adding extensions and new features and upgrading older parts.

In order to implement SOA, begin by choosing an appropriate IT project — one in which SOA can deliver some clear benefits but where the risk is relatively low.

New Shoes for the Cobbler's Children

From many perspectives, the way business applications are built under SOA does not differ much from the way that they are traditionally built. And, funnily enough (we thought you might enjoy that Briticism), the people that are building new business applications under SOA, at least right now, are people with experience building applications *not* under SOA.

So it shouldn't come as a great surprise that with SOA the software tools used to enable and assist development are not particularly different from the software tools that are currently in use. Indeed, as SOA is strongly based on reusing the applications that already exist, it doesn't make a lot of sense to abandon the software tools that built those applications. However, traditional software tools are becoming more sophisticated and more SOA-specific as well.

Figure 14-1 illustrates the situation with current software development. For SOA-specific projects, software development environments are still going to use a whole series of software development tools that are already being used in more traditional contexts, including modeling tools, programming tools, integrated development environments, app servers, databases, life-cycle tools, testing tools, and more. These are represented in Figure 14-1 by the Software Development box in the center of the diagram. Commercial IT uses such a variety of products that it is difficult to represent how a particular development will be organized, but you can be certain that there will be a collection of software tools for building, testing, and implementing applications.

With SOA, though, you can expect to see the following expanded capabilities added to existing tools or developed specifically for SOA:

- **Business process modeling:** Software tools that don't just design the application but also design the flow of work between people involved in the business process.

- **SOA application testing:** Software testing tools specifically designed for the complexity of testing composite applications.

- **SOA governance:** Software tools that ensure the coherent management of the application life cycle, implementing corporate policy and standards (that is, governance).

✔ **The SOA repository:** An information store that is the system of record for software development, holding all the source code, job control and much else besides for all applications.

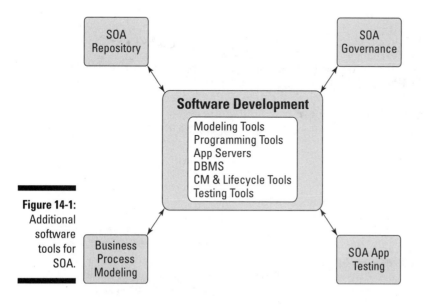

Figure 14-1: Additional software tools for SOA.

Software vendors improve their products regularly, and many vendors are currently enhancing their software development tools to embrace SOA functionality. The following sections show how these SOA tools fit into the new SOA software development life cycle.

The Software Development Life Cycle

The way organizations approach software development varies to some degree from organization to organization. In the early days of computing, most software was developed according to what is usually called the *waterfall model.* Under the waterfall model, software is developed linearly. After the decision is made to go ahead — which in the case of a large project may involve a feasibility study that defines the scope, cost, and expected benefits — the project proceeds through the following phases:

✔ **Requirements gathering:** Detailed discussions to determine the functionality requirements of the eventual users of the application.

✔ **Design:** The design of the application in terms of overall architecture, functional modules, data structures, and data flows.

✔ **Build:** Writing program code.

✔ **Testing:** Testing for functionality, performance, and robustness, including user testing.

✔ **Implementation:** The application goes into production and is available to users.

By the 1990s, a lot of people were dissatisfied with this process, primarily because the eventual users of an application never really had a chance to influence development between the requirements phase and the point at which they got their hands on the application during the testing phase. By then a great deal of time had passed and often problems spotted during this stage were caused by the fact that the requirements had not been well understood.

In reaction to the waterfall method, several different development life cycle models were introduced that tried to address this problem by involving the application users much earlier in the process. This approach was made possible by new software products that were designed specifically to build business functionality quickly so that a prototype could be built rapidly and changes to it could be made, in some cases, before the users' eyes. These new life cycle models went by the names of *RAD* (Rapid Application Development), *JAD* (Joint Application Development), and the *spiral model*. Although each of these was defined slightly differently, they all had the characteristic that the software development model involved what is known as *iterative prototyping*.

Iterative prototyping works like this:

1. After an initial design is created, a series of prototypes of the application are built in partnership with some of the eventual users of the application.

2. Prototyping then proceeds until eventually a version is arrived at that users are happy with. Procedures can be adopted to limit the number of prototypes, so that prototyping doesn't go on forever.

3. The application is then built based on what emerges as the final prototype.

4. Testing of the application proceeds as before until the application is ready to go into production.

In practice, if a project is well organized, three prototypes are usually enough to arrive at an application that satisfies users. Additionally, it's possible to abandon projects at a relatively early stage if it's discovered that the application will never work well enough for it to be worthwhile.

Figure 14-2 illustrates the differences between the waterfall model and the newer iterative model. Note that in the iterative model, application users are far more intimately involved in the building of the system, and they are thus able to intervene in a timely manner if the application under construction varies significantly from what was intended.

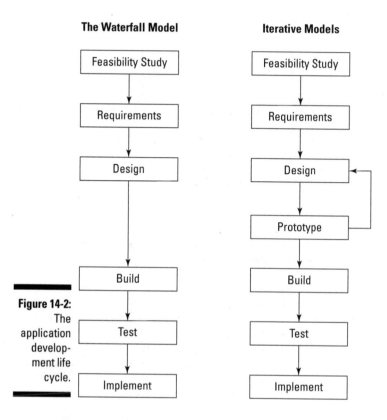

The Waterfall Model

- Feasibility Study
- Requirements
- Design
- Build
- Test
- Implement

Iterative Models

- Feasibility Study
- Requirements
- Design
- Prototype
- Build
- Test
- Implement

Figure 14-2: The application development life cycle.

Nevertheless, this iterative approach doesn't cure all ills. Its primary virtue is that you are combining people who know the business with people who know what technology is capable of. It does, however, have a weakness: With iterative development, what you are developing is an *application* or even a whole *system*. However, you are not designing and developing a *business process*. In practice, the iterative development process doesn't oblige either the business users or the software developers to design the whole business process. It only obliges them to develop an application that fits the current business process, or possibly a slightly improved business process. Getting software developers to think in terms of business processes can be tough, but there's a set of tools out there designed to do just that. They're called BPM tools (where BPM can stand for *business process management* or *business process modeling;* take your pick), and you can find out all about them in the next section.

BPM tools and software development

BPM tools focus on the design of the business process. (They aren't called business process modeling tools for nothing!) They model the business process both in terms of what various applications are expected to do and what the human participants in the business process are expected to do.

Before they were called BPM tools, software development tools that worked in this way were called *workflow tools* and were used primarily, but not exclusively, to model and build the activities and data flows in document management systems. Now, given the very strong trend toward BPM development, most such software tools have reclassified themselves as BPM tools, and their area of application is much broader.

One of the things that an organization may be tempted to do when it sets out on the road to SOA is to create maps of all its business processes. It may seem like a sensible thing to do because then you would have a map of the way that everything is done, from making a sale to emptying the trash. The danger in doing this is that by the time you have finished, some things — and maybe even many things — will probably have changed.

Nevertheless, it is a great idea to have a map of all the business processes within an organization. The best way to achieve this is the same as the best way to eat an elephant — bite by bite. When software development is done by using BPM within the context of adopting SOA, modeling the business process is a natural part of the activity. BPM development is naturally a kind of iterative application development, driven by a business analyst who has a good understanding of the business and who collaborates both with users and, if needed, with software developers.

In general, a BPM development life cycle, as illustrated in Figure 14-3, is similar to an iterative development life cycle (refer to Figure 14-2). It's important to note that it is a *business process* that is being built rather than just an application. After the initial feasibility work is done, the existing business process (or processes) is discovered and mapped — assuming that you are not building something completely new. At the same time, the requirements for the new business process are gathered. Iterative prototyping then proceeds, but it isn't just the application that is being prototyped; it's the working of the whole business process, including all manual activity.

When the final prototype is ready, the build and testing phases can proceed, and ultimately the new business process is implemented.

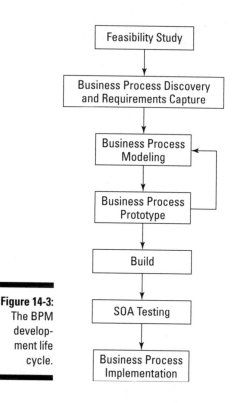

Figure 14-3:
The BPM
develop-
ment life
cycle.

Mapping the business process

After SOA is ingrained within an organization, the focus of software development activity becomes prototyping. However, at the outset, most organizations won't have maps of their business processes because there has never been sufficient motivation to create them. Part of the SOA journey involves creating such maps so that, eventually, the whole of the organization's activities can be easily understood at a detailed level.

For this reason, the discovery and mapping of business processes needs to be a part of all SOA development projects large and small.

BPM tools and other software development tools store their source code in repositories. Repositories are, simply put, a place to store things so you know where they are when you go to look for them. They help keep things organized and tidy and are a great help as soon as the number of people that need to know what's around is greater than one. In Chapter 15, we talk about the SOA repository, which is the place all good SOA components live. BPL tools have their own repositories, but as time goes by business process management and

SOA will become inextricably linked and which component accomplishes which function will inevitably shift. At this point in time, however, they're still separate.

In Figure 14-4, the BPM tool links together some components from existing applications, generating the linking code by referring to the interfaces published in the SOA registry. The BPM tool may also be used to build new business functions, in which case it publishes their interfaces in the SOA registry. It may also create instructions to direct a workflow engine. All the linking information, the source code, and the directives to the workflow engine are stored in the repository. Also stored in the repository is the business process map of the business process that has been created.

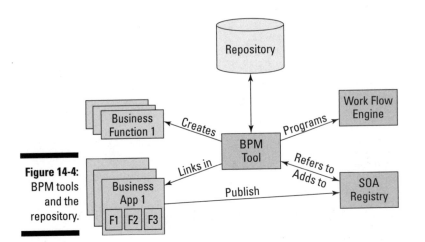

Figure 14-4:
BPM tools
and the
repository.

SOA and Software Testing

Software testing under SOA is easier than traditional software testing in some respects and more complicated in others. Because you ultimately end up with reusable components that have been thoroughly tested, your testing eventually gets easier. However, testing procedures need to change because of the potential complexity of composite applications and because SOA is a constantly changing environment, not the traditional stable environment for which most testing has been designed. There are issues that need to be thought through.

For example, if you transform components of existing applications into Web services, how do you test those Web services so that you know they are doing exactly what you expect them to do? Bear in mind that the original application was probably not written with the idea that it would be used as a collection of components. The program's code may be very complex and interwoven. Consider, say, something that's reasonably easy to understand, like managing a customer database. Suppose your order-processing application does this and you simply transform its customer update capability (add, amend, and delete customers) to become a Web service. You know the application, so you know that the program logic does what you want it to do (add, amend, and delete). But what else does it do? That can be a problem.

Unit testing of Web services

How do you find out if your handy customer update Web services component is destined to become a problem child? You could read the program code. It would be a good thing to do, to see if you can spot any logic that gets called that you may not want to get called when you do whatever it is you want the customer update to do — add, amend, or delete customers. But you need to do much more than read the program code if you really want to be rigorous. You have no choice but to test your customer update Web service in conjunction with the testing of the application it belong to — the order-processing application.

To do this testing, you could use an existing regression testing capability on the order-processing application (see our nifty sidebar, "Regression testing," if you're so inclined) while you test all the possible combinations of SOAP messages that the new customer update Web service accepts and responds to. (SOAP, in case you've forgotten, is the protocol that Web services use to send messages to each other.) When you have completed this test, all you have done is completed the unit testing of the Web service.

You need to do a test of this kind when you create any Web service for use, particularly if it derives from an old system. Indeed, procedures for doing so need to be laid down as part of IT governance.

So now consider the situation in which you are building a composite application by threading a collection of Web services together and adding some new logic of your own. Hopefully, every one of the Web services involved has been unit tested in the way we just described. The testing procedure should follow the usual cycle: create test plans, create a test bed, and test procedures (test design, specific test cases, specific scripts, test execution, reporting).

If you are not familiar with the software testing process, the description of the test cycle we just gave may have flown straight over your head. Actually it isn't too complicated. You need to understand that the testing of new software systems takes a long time, consumes a good deal of effort, and involves quite a few people. Roughly speaking, twice as much effort goes into testing a software system as goes into writing it.

Regression testing

If you're unfamiliar with the software testing process, you'll probably not know exactly what regression testing is. Lucky for you, then, that we've decided to let you in on the secret. The truth is that it is really difficult — some would say impossible — to test any program exhaustively, unless it is very simple. The reason for this is that in any reasonably sized program, there are actually thousands of possible paths for the logic to follow and it is a gargantuan task to test each one. It is also very difficult, if not impossible, to automate the testing of every possible path. This is why software bugs are so common. (We bet you've noticed one or two yourself.)

Nobody wants programs released into the world with errors in them. So software developers build test packs to test their programs in a kind of cumulative way. They build test scripts (which pretend to be users entering data) and test the program. When they find errors they may add more scripts. When they link multiple programs together, they add more. When they let end users try the programs, they capture the end-user activity and add even more. They test as much as they can before crossing their fingers and saying, "yes, it works," and putting the program into production.

They never throw the test packs away. Within a few weeks the users will be up in arms because they've found a whole nest of bugs, and developers will need to make changes and may need to make them in a hurry. So how do they test the changes they've made?

First they run the test pack that they gradually built up throughout the whole testing process just to make sure that the changes they've made haven't messed up something that previously worked. The process of doing this is called regression testing. Regression testing is testing what worked to see if it still works. If the regression testing causes no problem, they then test the changes they've made. They can then add the new tests they've made to the test pack so that in the future the regression test pack will also test for the bugs that were reported.

The reason for this is that you need to plan the testing activity and you need to build a complete testing environment that closely mirrors the actual environment where the program will ultimately be used. That environment is called the test bed. The various phases of testing need to be carried out until the system is proven to work reasonably well.

The fact that the Web services you are using have been unit tested should not make you overconfident of their behavior. Even if they didn't go wrong when tested individually, it's quite possible that they could go wrong when they're linked to other components. Your testing approach needs to allow you to break down the end-to-end transactions to detect the point at which failure occurs. This means being able to capture and analyze all the SOAP messages that are passed from one component to another.

From the point of view of testing activity, this is a more complex scenario than traditional application testing. Nevertheless, it can be automated. It is just that most current testing tools are not yet well suited for automating this kind of testing activity. Even when the tools are capable of doing this, developers may not have experience in this kind of testing.

Integration testing

The order of testing activities is no different with SOA. First, you do unit testing (testing of the individual components), and then you do integration testing (testing the components when they are integrated together). As with unit testing, there is an additional factor with integration testing. Remember how we told you that you need to do regression testing when you change a software component to prove that what worked before still works? Well, for the same reason, you have to do regression testing on the applications whose Web services you are using while you do the integration testing.

It is very likely that the integration testing will be easier than you may expect. After all, you've already rigorously tested all the interface messaging during unit testing. However, the need for regression testing makes integration testing a tad more complicated.

Stress testing and performance testing

The other two kinds of testing (stress/performance testing and acceptance testing) also need to have this extra element. You have to test that the original applications that provided components to the new application still perform adequately when the new application runs. You need to test everything that is linked together and test it so that it runs in the way that it will run in the "live" environment. The stress and performance testing tools that are used will be similar to those that have been used traditionally. However, you have the added complication that you will probably have to meet specific service levels, and so you will probably need to take detailed performance measurements.

The whole test bed

The testing process can get very complicated. In the pleasant but inefficient world of application silos, testing was relatively easy. The application wasn't sharing its resources with any other software and usually wasn't directly connected to other software either. That's why people in IT called them silo applications. They had their own hardware operating configuration, backup arrangements and everything. You tested the application by testing the silo.

You unit tested the components of the application, and then you integration tested the whole. Then if you had any qualms about the application's performance, you stress tested the whole thing and then gave it over to the users for acceptance testing. Creating the test bed was not a problem. You just imitated the silo run-time environment and built up a set of testing data, possibly borrowing some data from "live" systems.

The problem with SOA is that it's end to end. The silos have gone, and with them went the ability to easily set up a test bed. As you make your way down the SOA road, you need to have much more versatile test-bed-creation capabilities. Indeed you probably want testing tools that can create and dismantle virtual testing environments and draw data from live systems.

Virtual testing environments are the key to addressing most of these SOA testing issues. They provide testing tools that not only help to test the software you've written but can also use software to mock up large collections of server computers. These tools create an environment that models the real environment in which the application will eventually be deployed. After testing is complete, the virtual environment is switched off.

It may not come as a complete surprise to you to discover that if you are going to create such virtual testing environments, you are going to have to buy software to help. It's possible that you already have what you need. You could, for example, build virtual testing environments by using HP's Mercury testing tools or IBM Rational testing tools in conjunction with VMware, the popular virtualization technology. Additionally, a number of relatively new companies are selling testing tools of this type, including Akimbi, Surgient, and SQA Technologies.

Without such tools, it's going to be difficult to create an adequate test bed because you not only have to test the parts of the end-to-end application you have built, but you also need to test it while all the reused components are doing the other things that they normally do.

Stress testing and performance testing are made simpler with this virtualization capability. You probably want this kind of testing to be modeled around the complete set of end-to-end software that is involved, and this may span many different servers.

The reason the testing situation is manageable with most SOA implementations at the moment is that very few, if any, organizations are building complex end-to-end composite applications. Their projects tend to involve the integration of adjacent application silos or the adding of browser interfaces to core systems, plus a little bit of BPM here and there. When businesses get more ambitious, they'll discover just how complex SOA testing can get. Fortunately, many ambitious software vendors are grabbing on to this "market opportunity" with both fists and we expect to see SOA testing grow up right alongside SOA itself.

Chapter 15

The Repository and the Registry

In This Chapter

▶ Governance revisited

▶ Perpetually changing software

▶ Taking a little R 'n R

As the title of this chapter makes clear, the time has now come for us to discuss the SOA repository and the SOA registry — and their relationship to each other — in greater detail. You may remember that we had a lot to say about the registry in Chapter 8, and we mentioned then that it was close friends with the SOA repository. But before we can go down that path, we need to revisit our old friend governance. You may remember that we introduced the concept of governance back in Chapter 11, but now that we're introducing still more service oriented architecture components, it's time to expand a bit on that discussion.

Governance has become a big word in IT. It didn't use to be. In fact, if we sent you back in time ten years and told you to nose around a few major IT departments, you'd never hear the word "governance" mentioned. My, how times change.

If any IT hotshot from ten years ago were to ask you, in your time-traveling persona, what governance actually was (or will be), you could tell him or her that IT governance involves managing the relationships and processes that direct and control an organization's use of IT resources so that such resources can better meet the organization's goals.

In case you're wondering how governance differs from IT management — "Surely that's the same thing," we hear you say — we can only say that it really isn't the same thing, honest. We try to explain.

Over time, more and more business activities have gotten computerized so that nowadays almost everything that anyone does in an office anywhere seems to involve a computer. So many activities are computerized that the need to ensure most IT activities are carried out in a well-organized manner has become clearer and clearer. IT not only needs to be managed, it needs to be regulated according to a coherent set of policies. That's what IT governance is — the implementation and, if possible, automation of policies and best practices so that bad things don't happen to an organization's computers or applications or data.

In its never-ending struggle against the bad things that can happen to good computers, applications, and data (not to mention people), IT governance can involve a variety of activities, including

- ✔ Ensuring compliance of systems with Sarbanes-Oxley and other government regulations
- ✔ Adherence to IT standards
- ✔ Management of IT security
- ✔ Procurement of new technology

It's quite possible, and often wise, to formally declare corporate policy in these areas.

In the main, IT governance affects SOA in only an indirect way, but one area of governance impacts SOA directly — the governance of the implementation of new applications and capabilities. Here, the SOA registry and repository have critical roles to play, ensuring that services are kept findable, usable, and compliant with policy.

Ch-Ch-Ch-Changes

Nowadays, 80 percent or more of the typical corporate software development budget is focused on maintaining existing business applications, rather than building new stuff. If you decided way back when to build the applications in-house, you now need to have programmers on staff whose principal occupation is keeping those applications working. If instead you chose to go with wall-to-wall software packages — with little or no in-house software development — you now get to pay some software vendor to maintain the packages. Either way, most of the software budget goes toward tweaking what already exists.

Such a state of affairs has led to a situation where, if a software developer really wants to write new software capable of doing something truly original, his or her best course of action is to get a job writing computer games. Most contemporary software developers are actually maintainers of software.

Unfortunately, the word "maintenance" can be misleading and, in the case of business software, it truly is. Maintaining a building, for example, isn't usually onerous — you just fix the odd broken window, make sure the carpets are cleaned, replace light bulbs when they burn out, and so on. Some software maintenance is as simple as that, but most of it isn't.

Updates, updates, and more updates

A good deal of software maintenance involves making small changes to business applications so that they stay in line with business needs. The same is true with packaged business applications, except that the software developers aren't trying to meet one company's needs so much as they're trying to meet the common needs of all their customers. The difference is that the software developer is working for a software vendor rather than the ultimate user of the business software.

There are always changes to make. And that, in a nutshell, is the biggest complication in the whole universe of software. Software keeps changing — all of it, always.

And when we say all of it, we mean all of it. A typical mid-size organization runs thousands of different programs in its network. Aside from direct business applications, of which there are hundreds, you can also find system management applications, security applications, storage software, identity management software, network management software, database management software, office software, communications software, engineering software and more.

Not many of these applications are *static,* meaning they don't stay the same for any length of time. The ones your company builds itself keep changing because users keep asking for changes and errors keep occurring and getting fixed. Those applications that software vendors build keep changing because other customers (as well as your company) ask for changes and because the applications have bugs that need fixing. And all the other software that does all the complex management of all the applications and keeps the hardware functioning (we mean the plumbing of course) . . . well, it too keeps changing because it gets improved and because bugs get fixed.

Most software products come into a major new release every year or two, but in between times, every month or so, a vendor provides updates — *patches,* as they're called — to fix known problems. Think about it. Thousands of programs, most of them having changes issued every month and major changes issued every year or two. It wouldn't matter so much if they didn't all have to work together, but they do.

This is a problem.

Not so long ago, business applications were built to run on only a single computer. A good deal of the software running on that single computer would come from the actual computer vendor (IBM, Hewlett-Packard, Sun Microsystems, or whomever). The applications probably wouldn't share data with other applications and wouldn't try to connect to other applications. The software environment around each application was controlled and might change perhaps once a year. The software engineers really only had to worry about whether the applications worked or not. Change wasn't as frequent, and everything tended to work well together because it was all built for the same environment.

Those days are long gone. IT life isn't like that any more. Now, change of one sort or another happens quite frequently to virtually all the software across all the corporate network. This rate of change is accelerating and, to cap it all off, along comes Business Process Management, also known as BPM — not just software tools for business analysts but a tempting incentive for the business itself to embrace change as a way of life. BPM has the goal of changing business applications quickly — in days or weeks rather than months. How does an IT department cope?

The answer is, all too frequently, "Not very well." Sure, there are plenty of way-cool development environments and plenty of tools for the trade, but none of them was built with perpetual change in mind. And with SOA, the speed of change takes a quantum leap. Fortunately, SOA is ushering in new constructs that we trust will help development avoid ultimate futility.

The first thing in SOA's favor is that it separates the plumbing (the infrastructure management software) from the applications. This separation helps because it means changes to the software that manages the plumbing can be dealt with separately from changes to the software that performs the business functions that run on top of the plumbing. Operational staff and administrators rarely change plumbing software until they have to. The general rule is, "If it ain't broke, don't fix it."

When administrators have to upgrade operating systems, databases, transaction servers, and all the other software components of the plumbing layer, they usually choose to upgrade a large number of new versions at the same time so they can test the upgrades as a bundle before implementing them. Administrators also make such implementations gradually, server by server, whenever that's possible. And, as a matter of course, they make sure they have the ability to reverse the changes they've made if something goes wrong. Because software vendors can't test for every conceivable environment, things often do go wrong, and getting "current and working" in sophisticated environments is an ongoing challenge.

For a possible solution to this messy situation, take a look at Figure 15-1, which introduces the SOA repository into the mix. Here, SOA governance takes on the burden of managing the entire SOA software development life cycle. (We have lots to say about the software development life cycle in Chapter 14.) SOA governance's function is to automate, as far as possible, the management of the software development process so that the process doesn't spin out of control.

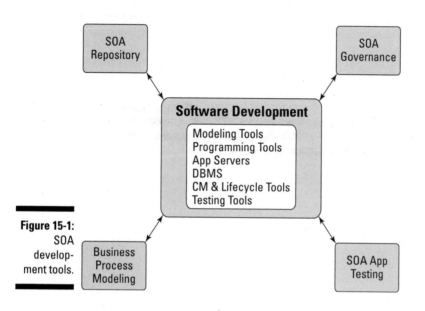

Figure 15-1:
SOA
develop-
ment tools.

SOA Repository

SOA Governance

Software Development

Modeling Tools
Programming Tools
App Servers
DBMS
CM & Lifecycle Tools
Testing Tools

Business Process Modeling

SOA App Testing

Meet the repository

In order to successfully carry out the (far from simple) task of managing the software development process, SOA governance relies on the SOA repository, which can best be thought of as "the system of record." It's indeed a repository, meaning a place where things are stored, and all the components used to build applications are stored there.

Repository and registry: Separated at birth?

You may very well be thinking, "But doesn't the registry do just what you describe the repository as doing?" The unequivocal answer is, "Yes and No." You can feel yourself in good company with a lot of software vendors who don't bother to make a clear distinction — in some cases, they even put the functionality of each into the same product and call it a registry/repository in order to avoid having to deal with the question at all.

To understand the difference between the repository and the registry, you need to understand the difference between "static" and "dynamic" and between "real time" and "not real time." Here we go.

Developers develop services. They put their nicely developed services into the repository for others to find and use. The repository keeps versions and history information, as well as other important information about each service. The repository itself is *static*, meaning it doesn't change from moment to moment. Yes, it changes when something new is added, but it's relatively stable. It is not changing in real time as the result of demands inside the SOA. It sits somewhat outside the SOA and supports the SOA. It is where services are introduced, but the repository isn't actively engaged in the dynamic operation of the SOA.

The registry relies on the repository in that it takes services from the repository. However, after the service is in the hands of the registry, the service is "in play," as it were. The location of the service may shift as required by the SOA, and the registry keeps track of where it is at all times. The registry is responding dynamically to the demands of the operational SOA. So although closely linked, the registry and repository actually serve different functions.

Dueling silos

In order to understand SOA governance and the roles of the repository and registry you need a basic conceptual grasp of the "siloed" nature of most software organizations before they embark on SOA. (We use "siloed" here as a shorthand way of saying that, in most companies, applications in one part of the organization don't talk to the applications in the other parts of the organization and they were never intended to do so.) A siloed world typically includes several different software development environments in use, all within one larger organization. Each software development environment has its own life-cycle procedures that depend, to some extent, on the platform (IBM Mainframe, UNIX, Windows, Linux, and so on) that it runs on. Packaged applications are managed in an entirely different way — that is, not as a software development environment, but as an administrative and management environment that must contend with new versions and patches to the applications delivered by the software vendors. Vendors don't usually deliver source code. They usually deliver just the new run-time version of the application.

In summary, the nature of software development and software maintenance is often extremely fragmented. You need multiple systems of record and multiple life-cycle procedures to automate the development-to-production process.

SOA provides a gradual movement toward integrating the silos. Just as SOA aims to integrate the application silos, it also aims to integrate the siloed nature of application development. The SOA repository is the primary mechanism that fixes the problem.

IT As Service Provider

The IT industry and IT departments have been gradually embracing the idea of acting in the role of "service provider" for quite a few years now. You're probably familiar with the concept of service providers if you get your Internet access provided by the likes of Comcast or Verizon — Internet service providers (ISPs), as they're called. You likely get a bill from your electricity service provider, a phone bill from your telecommunications service provider, and on and on. More and more, business people and end users view IT as a service that's provided. Indeed, most people want what IT delivers and want it reliably, and they aren't all that interested in how the service is delivered; all they're *really* concerned about is availability and the quality of service.

Managing complexity

One of the major motivations for viewing IT as a service is the complexity of IT operations. Twenty years ago, even large organizations had only a few PCs on desks, and most staff who had access to the few corporate computers used well-behaved but dumb terminals. Companies used far fewer applications and were thus able to keep their computing environments well under control.

Today's large organizations have thousands of servers, PCs, and PDAs (Blackberries, Treos, and the like). More devices come to market daily. Just about everything an organization does is tied to the computer network, or soon will be. The complexity of what needs to be managed has grown dramatically, and administrators have far less control. Beyond the manageability nightmare, the security vulnerabilities loom.

As a consequence of the complexity, the IT industry has evolved and adopted a set of standards for the governance of operational environments. These standards are collectively known by the acronym ITIL, which stands for the IT Infrastructure Library. The *IT Infrastructure Library* is a library of industry best-practice procedures that covers the whole operational (or plumbing) area of IT. The ITIL covers service support, service delivery, service management planning and implementation, ICT (Information and Communication Technology) infrastructure management, applications management, security management, and the alignment of IT with business. That's pretty much everything, for now. Most important, in this context, ITIL provides procedures for defining service level agreements (SLAs) and managing those SLAs — which is as good an introduction as any to the following section.

SOA and SLAs

A *service level agreement* is a technical definition of the availability and performance that an application is expected to provide to the user, as well as the performance bar that the operation side of IT commits to deliver.

In the majority of IT sites, service levels are only vaguely defined. This sad state of affairs is due to one simple fact: Traditionally, applications were implemented in isolated scenarios and they then continued on their (less than) merry way in isolation. If service levels were defined at all, they tended to be defined at the application level, within a particular context. For example, you may have had an agreement that the operational staff would provide 99.9-percent availability and that response times would average out at no worse than one second. You could meet such a service-level requirement by building a server configuration that was devoted to the service level application and could be counted on to deliver such performance.

This approach to guaranteeing a service level nearly always results in a significant overbuying of computer resources, and it simultaneously increases management costs. So it's no bad thing that such an approach is no longer possible with SOA.

SOA entails the reuse of software components as a matter of course. This makes it difficult to use a "one size fits all" approach to delivering service levels. For example, one context may require a very high level of availability and performance from a particular component. However, another context, using that same component doesn't need such high levels. This is an intricate problem and one that requires real sophistication to solve.

Consider, for example, the situation of making part of an order-processing application available to customers directly through the Web. When your own staff uses the application, it needs to be available only from 8 a.m. until 7 p.m. on weekdays. But when you make the application available over the Web, it needs to be available 24/7.

It may not be possible to run the application in that way. Perhaps the application was built so that it could back up its data only when it wasn't online. If that's the case, in order to use part of it as a component, the design needs to be changed. The point we're making here is that reuse needs to be carefully managed.

[handwritten margin note: Instead of buying more computer resources, reuse components by making service not one size fits all]

With SOA, you need to define service levels at the component level. And you may also need to define them *end to end*, meaning that you may need to define them for the particular contexts in which they are used. Setting and achieving service levels in detail is an inherent part of moving to SOA. Contending with service levels complicates the development process in some ways, but ultimately it pays off handsomely because, with this approach, you can accurately measure the performance and availability of business processes.

If you get to the point where you can express the operational aspects of a business process in terms of the service level delivered, you can make much more accurate decisions on how to run the computing side of the process. If, for example, a hosting company offers to run some of your software, you can simply compare costs on a like-for-like basis because the legal contract with the hosting company will be written entirely in terms of the service delivered.

Governance, the Repository, and the Registry

The repository is, as we note in the section, "Meet the repository," earlier in this chapter, the "system of record" — the SOA component that keeps track of all SOA services. Think of a typical application as consisting of an organized set of program logic that stores data in a database. If you think of software development as an application, the program logic is the governance part and the database or files is the repository.

The SOA repository contains (and provides access to) the source code of the applications that the company builds. The SOA repository also provides an audit trail of all the different versions of the application that have been created in the history of the application — a trail that leads from the application's creation right down to its current state.

Development repositories that attempt to hold and maintain a full record of all software development stages aren't new. Such products have been around for about ten years. Nevertheless, few IT sites, if any at all, have a fully deployed repository functioning as a coherent system of record that covers all the applications that the sites run.

Figure 15-2 illustrates the interaction of SOA governance tools with the SOA repository, as well as with the SOA registry. Software development proceeds according to the rules of governance, which manage the life cycle from design; through prototyping, building, and testing to implementation. And as new software is developed, using existing tools or new BPM tools, the repository stores all the business-process maps, designs, documentation, and program source code to create an accurate history of all software development.

At actual implementation, some of the information held in the repository is copied to the registry for operational use. Remember that the repository is the *static* — not changing in real time — system of record, containing the entire history and everything knowable about a particular service. The registry just needs the most current information about how the service works and any rules associated with it, including the interface descriptions. The specific service level agreements that have been agreed upon for an application are also stored in the registry for use in monitoring actual performance. Additionally, the registry holds the details of how the application is implemented in the operational environment.

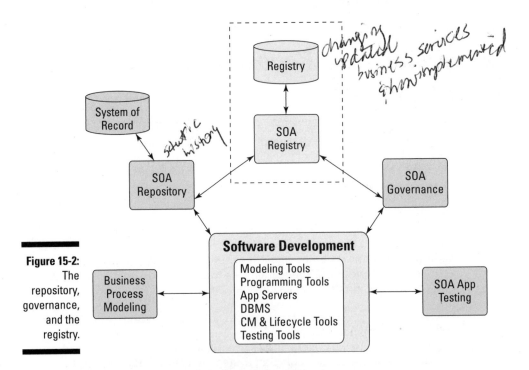

Figure 15-2:
The repository, governance, and the registry.

Packaged applications

You may be asking yourself how packaged applications fit into this picture — you know, those financial applications and human resource applications that your company bought from some big software vendor. If so, then full marks. (That's Brit for "Well Done," or "A+," or "Gee, you're smart!")

You don't have the source code for package applications and so won't be able to maintain a full system of record. However, if your application package suppliers provide you with full details of the component interfaces, you can store these details in the registry and may be able to reuse components of the application, as long as the software supplier is amenable.

It's important to understand that you'll find reusing components of packaged applications difficult, if not impossible, without the assistance of the application package supplier. The package not only has to be converted to conform with SOA, it has to conform as well with *your* implementation of SOA and *your* standards.

Suppliers maintain source code and apply their own governance procedures to their own software. If you want to bring that software within your SOA umbrella, it has to conform to your use of the registry and your approach to service levels. (This little example should make it clear why standards are so important; without standards, everything is a "custom job," and, if you've ever had to pay for custom curtains, you know what "custom jobs" will cost you.

Fortunately, it's in the business interests of packaged software suppliers to make their software easy to integrate. Ease of integration quickly becomes ease of adoption. Eventually, package vendors may be able to sell their software directly through registries on the Internet.

Reposing in the registry or registering in the repository

The potential for confusion between the repository and the registry is huge and likely to remain so because vendors of registries will doubtless add some of the functionality that a repository provides. Similarly, repositories will in time come with their own registries. The important point to understand is that the repository is the full system of record, and the registry is the real-time record of a SOA domain.

The SOA registry holds information about each business service that the business has approved for use and passed into production following IT governance rules. When the business service is implemented, a set of information is published to the SOA registry.

Exactly what's included in the registry can vary, but the following is a fairly comprehensive list of the kind of information that the registry may contain for each software component registered in it:

Most registries include:

✔ A description of the services the component offers.

✔ A full WSDL description of the interface or interfaces to the component. (For more on WSDL, see Chapter 6.)

✔ The location of the executable program/component.

✔ A specification of the service levels defined for the component.

✔ A definition of *usage rights* for the component — essentially a listing of who has what kinds of access to the component under what conditions.

✔ A definition of security rules that govern the use of the component.

The main functions of the registry are to publish and enable the discovery of services — either internally or externally — and to govern the real-time use of services. We explain each of these functions in a little more detail in the following sections.

The registry and internal publishing

Business analysts and application developers interact with the registry. They use the registry to discover, select, and connect software components together to form composite applications. The information that the registry contains helps the developer to understand what services (and what level of service) a specific software component can provide. The software tools that the developer uses, whether BPM tools or otherwise, use the technical interface information to formulate messages to interact with the software component.

The SOA registry provides a useful view into the organization's collection of sharable business services and software components. Now, you may be thinking that organizations have been sharing some applications across business units for years. This is true, but it has typically happened in an informal way, without control and oversight.

To take just one example, imagine that a software developer in the IT department for an insurance company knows that the property insurance group has a rate calculation application that other applications call upon regularly. The rate calculation tool is a service that applications have used so often that the developer keeps a set of documentation on how to locate this application and information on the rules associated with its use written in the margins of a printed copy. The developer also keeps additional history on who "owns" this business service and limitations on its use in an e-mail message. When the insurance company starts writing identity insurance, the developer easily locates this rate calculation and makes it available for reuse by the team preparing the IT applications for the new line of business. But what happens if the developer gets another job or the e-mail gets lost?

You also need to face up to the fact that different scenarios often ensue. Sometimes, business services are developed twice (or perhaps 20 or 30 times) because it wasn't possible to reuse an original service (because of evil dependencies) or because the developers that built the new application simply didn't know that another application somewhere else was doing exactly the same thing. A good example of this is the fact that very few large banks or insurance companies have a single customer database. Usually, they have at least three or four.

The registry provides an organization with visibility into what can be a very large number of business services. If used properly, the registry can help you use existing IT assets more efficiently. The framework that the SOA registry provides allows for continual growth, and you can publish hundreds or thousands of services in a registry.

The registry and real-time governance

A SOA registry has two types of users: software and people. On the software side, the SOA supervisor and the SOA broker interact with the registry in real time. (Chapter 8 is all about the registry and the service broker, by the way.) Technically, the registry is the central reference point within the SOA, and it defines the *domain* of the SOA, that is to say everything that the SOA includes. As such, the registry can also act as the central reference point for governance rules that need to be implemented when applications run.

The registry defines the rules for each component that's registered in it, including, as we mention earlier in this chapter, the service levels defined for a component, a definition of usage rights for the component, and a definition of security rules that govern the use of the component.

The SOA supervisor uses the registry's service level rules to report what's happening (or act on what's happening) whenever a trend indicates that service levels are likely to be violated. The SOA broker implements the rules relating to access rights when it initiates any new service or connects a new user. It may enforce such access rights via identity management software or other security software.

The registry and external publishing

Many of the IT vendors involved in SOA currently have the goal to publish registries to enable the use of software services by people or businesses outside the organization. Initially, such usage might only involve customers and business partners. Nevertheless, as soon as you allow any external user of any kind to connect directly to your software, you open up a set of potential liabilities, possibly for both sides.

Consider, for example, who should bear the cost if your software infects your customers' computers with a damaging virus or if connecting to your computer systems creates a security vulnerability for your customer that some evil hacker exploits. What if your software has an error embedded in it somewhere that somehow causes the customer financial loss? Some mutual contract can easily cover such legal issues, and for the time being, organizations will likely use such a contract to deal with these issues. The need to integrate software far more effectively — not only within an organization but also between organizations — is far too commercially attractive for such issues to prevent us from integrating.

When you open your registry for others to view and possibly use — allowing them to essentially integrate their systems directly with your software — you may be providing them with information that you want to remain confidential. Just consider the fact that if you had all your computer systems running under SOA, a detailed examination of the registry could provide a full picture of exactly how your company functions. Given that fact, you need to manage providing such access in a very secure way.

Now consider the ambitious goal of providing companies with the ability to link to your software dynamically. What would that mean? It would mean that one piece of software could read a registry entry, figure out exactly how to interact with another piece of software, and connect immediately. Currently, this is quite a distant goal, but pioneer software vendors will achieve it when they work out a way for the registry to store all the rules of connection (security, service levels, cost, and so on) in a way that software can evaluate and use.

SOA and Web services are heading toward this ultimate goal. SOA, as it's currently conceived, is actually capable of achieving that goal. All that currently prevents it is that the software components and the appropriate standards for them still need to be defined.

So imagine a simple business situation such as sending a package to a location across the world by using one of the global shipping services. Typically, the way it works today is that you check out the various options by using the Web (Fedex, UPS, DHL, and so on), comparing prices and arrival times. Right now, you have to go from site to site to do these comparisons because the Web page of each of the available services is slightly different, and in any event, how each Web site works can change at any time. But if these global shippers published their interfaces in a UDDI registry, the whole shipping process could be automated so that a user could automatically determine the best price and time.

This doesn't sound too radical until you consider the idea of new companies entering the shipping market and only needing to put an entry in a UDDI registry in order to compete for our business. The automated shipping process could simply look for new services every now and then.

Now consider applying this to everything a business sends, even if it's only sending an envelope across town. An automated system can consider every delivery service of any kind, according to the destinations they support. And, unlike its human counterpart, it will probably reliably make the best economic decisions.

Part IV

Getting Started with SOA

The 5th Wave   By Rich Tennant

"I assume everyone on your team is on board with the proposed changes to the system architecture."

In this part . . .

Starting a SOA journey can seem daunting. But, as the sages say, "A journey of a thousand miles begins with a single step." In this part, we help you take that first step by showing you some great places to start your SOA journey and some great ways to do it.

Chapter 16

Do You Need a SOA? A Self-Test

Given what you know of SOA by your innate perspicacity and by your diligent reading of our book, we think you're equipped to try to determine whether your organization is ready for SOA.

Readers of self-help books and lifestyle magazines are no doubt familiar with the kind of self-test that supposedly can tell you whether you're a really loving person, a person who's ready for change, or someone who needs to get a life. Well, in this chapter, we try to help you evaluate your organization's need for SOA. We ask you ten questions about your company. You score your answers by using the standard 1-to-10 scale — if your organization is at the high end of the spectrum for the question, you might be approaching 10; if the question doesn't resonate with you at all, you might be closer to a 1. When you tally up your score, each question gets a certain weighting because some factors are more important than others. At the end of the chapter, we help you weight and calculate your score.

Question 1: Is Your Business Ecosystem Broad and Complex?

"What's a business ecosystem?" you ask. Well, just as no species is an island in this collective enterprise we call Earth, no company can go it alone. Companies buy from suppliers and sell to customers. Beyond that, many companies have partnerships of different kinds — perhaps resellers who help sell the company's products, technology partnerships, and distribution partnerships. All these entities — suppliers, customers, and partners — create a business's ecosystem.

Even a small pet shop buys products and services from a variety of suppliers. It has to deal with payroll, employee management, and (potentially) partnerships with businesses that offer dog-walking services, veterinary services, and gourmet doggie dinners. The issue of complexity relates to scale. Again, if you're the owner of that pet shop, you may indeed have all the components that we just mentioned. But if you have only three partners, it may be just as easy for you to have a few small software packages that manage finances and your Web site. Setting up a small database to track your partners may be simple.

For the sake of our handy quiz, though, you might very well own a larger company. Instead of having a single pet store, you might have a large chain of pet stores across many different regions. Your corporation may own some of these stores, and other stores might be franchises. Your company might actually have a subsidiary that produces those gourmet dinners. Your company might have a major relationship with a vast number of suppliers of everything from birdseed to grooming supplies — so you have to worry about supply chain management. On top of that, new players come into the market all the time, so your company is likely to want to make acquisitions to remain competitive. Because your company is public, you also have to meet corporate governance regulations.

Now grade yourself. If you're more like the independent pet store, give yourself a lower score; if your company looks like a public company with a lot of acquisitions and partnerships, give yourself a score closer to 10. Somewhere in the middle? Give yourself a 5 or so . . .

Question 2: Is Your Industry Changing Quickly?

Not all industries are the same. Some industries change dramatically, and others are mature and stable. Why is this an important question to answer? Simply put, SOA requires an investment in time and effort — meaning it isn't something you should do lightly. If you don't need to change, stick with what you have.

For example, pretend you're in the construction industry, and your business is manufacturing cement. There are only a few large cement providers across the globe. The price for cement is relatively stable, and few new companies enter the market. Clearly, anyone erecting a monument or a building has to buy from one of these suppliers. Although you may certainly need software to help run your company, the need to change that software may be minimal because the industry is not changing dramatically.

On the other hand, if you're part of a media company, your industry is undergoing (and will continue to undergo) rapid changes. The Web has dramatically changed industry dynamics and has led to new products and services, new partnerships, and many mergers and acquisitions. To survive, media companies have to be able to turn on a dime.

So, if your company looks like the cement company, give yourself a lower score; if it looks more like a media company, go high.

Question 3: Do You Have Hidden Gems inside Your Software Applications?

You may not know the answer to this question — you may have to talk to folks in IT.

Many companies have built complex applications over the past 20 years. Some of this code involves, metaphorically speaking at least, the crown jewels of the company. It includes important, unique business practices that the companies cannot afford to lose. A simple example is Amazon.com's ability to implement a one-click purchase. Another example involves a real estate company's technique for calculating a 30-year mortgage based on a well-documented best practice in the industry. A pharmaceutical company may have created a software program that can quickly identify a molecule well suited for drug development. In many cases, these gems are tightly linked into one aging application that can't be changed very easily. If your company has a lot of intellectual property buried in these applications, it may be worthwhile to capture that code and make it live and breathe in the outside world.

So, if you think a lot of valuable gems are hidden in them thar hills, you should give yourself a high score. If your software holds relatively few valuable techniques or best practices, lower your score. Add a few points if your company understands the value of codifying rules or best practices as business services.

Question 4: Are Your Computer Systems Flexible?

This is actually a trick question. Most business systems have been designed to meet the needs of one particular business problem or one department. As company priorities have changed, developers have patched and repatched these systems — which means you end up with systems that don't easily adapt to changing business conditions. But some companies have done a better job than others in writing modular applications. The more modular your applications, the easier it will be for you to move to a service oriented architecture.

So, if your company had the foresight to create modular applications, give yourself a high mark. However, if you're like most companies, you'll have to settle for a low score.

Question 5: How Well Prepared Is Your Organization to Embrace Change?

Organizational readiness is every bit as important as the technology issues we discuss in the preceding sections. If each department wants to control its own technological destiny and is unwilling to create a company-wide plan for the movement to SOA, progress will be slow. If the IT organization is unable to communicate with business customers to create a mutually beneficial plan, you won't get very far. Technology gurus tend to be religious about their approach to technology and might not be willing to listen. Individual departments might be unwilling to share code, ideas, and processes with other departments.

So, be honest about the culture within your company. Are you set up to embrace change? Is there a mandate from the CIO and the CEO to invest in a new way of leveraging technology? Do various departments contain SOA evangelists who can serve as agents of change? Or are you stuck with the way you've always done things? If you're stuck, give yourself a low number; if you're on the path to culture change, pat yourself on the back and take a high number.

Question 6: How Dependable Are the Services Provided by IT?

You may have the best strategy on paper — you may even have started to modularize your software services — but you can still fail if the quality of service provided by the IT organization isn't up to par. For example, business needs a guarantee that the applications that they depend on are up and running at the level of performance that they expect and need. Poor quality of service will impact the ability of the IT organization to move to a service oriented architecture. Simply put, a poorly performing IT infrastructure will degrade business performance even more significantly if you move to SOA.

So, if you're a business executive, think about how often you're able to depend on the performance and quality of the software that you rely on. Do you frequently experience problems that get in the way of completing business tasks? Can you bank on IT to get the job done? If you answer "yes" to the first question and "hardly ever" to the second, give your organization a low score. If, on the other hand, you can depend on IT to deliver on their promises, give them your thanks and give your business a high score.

Question 7: Can Your Company's Technology Support Corporate Governance Standards?

Do your company's business practices meet mandated regulations, such as the Sarbanes-Oxley Act? Can you confirm that only people with the right authorization can change critical systems? Can you prove that regulated processes have been done in the appropriate way? Are the rules regulating your company's performance readily accessible to management? Public companies (and even private companies that interact with public companies) are being held accountable by government to prove that their business practices meet legal requirements. Companies are spending millions of dollars to reduce fraud and ensure accountability. Does your company understand the value of SOA in simplifying corporate governance?

We think there's a direct link between corporate governance and SOA. If your organization recognizes that SOA will help identify the critical business services related to governance in terms of processes and rules, you're in good shape to benefit from the move to SOA and likely have the type of enlightened management that immediately understands the value of the SOA journey. If you're enlightened, give your company high marks; otherwise, you know the drill by now.

Question 8: Do You Know Where Your Business Rules Are?

Business rules are everywhere in every company. Ironically, many companies don't realize that their legacy systems are chock-full of rules that dictate everything from the percentage commission a salesperson receives on the sale of a product to when a partner is eligible for a discount. Although this sounds straightforward, it isn't. Typically, rules are buried deep in existing applications. Rules might actually be written into the code of the application itself. Therefore, you can often have a hard time finding out if a new policy dreamed up by management actually gets implemented across the board in all software applications. For example, the vice-president of Sales might have changed the commission calculation two months ago, but the rule has been changed in only two of the five applications that include a commission calculation. In this scenario, you might ask, "So what commissions are we actually paying those salespeople?" If the response from IT is, "Heck if I know," you might have a problem.

If you have no control over where your business rules live within your vast array of applications, you have a problem and will have some work to do in order to move to SOA. If your organization has no handle on where the rules are buried, give yourself a low score. If you have an organized way to identify rules, even if you haven't yet changed the technology infrastructure, you're well on your (SOA) way — give yourself a higher score.

Question 9: Is Your Corporate Data Flexible, and Do You Trust Its Quality?

We've never heard of an organization that complains about too little data. Every application has data. Although most companies have no lack of data, they do lack the ability to move that data out of its home in isolated applications within departments. To move to SOA, you have to stop thinking about databases and data elements and start thinking about information services that you can use uniformly for many different purposes. But it doesn't stop there — those information services have to be accurate. Poor data quality is a killer! To move to SOA, you need superb data quality. There's no room for compromise in this area!

These are harsh words, but if your organization hasn't really started dealing with both information as a service and the importance of data quality, you're simply not ready for SOA. So, if this comes as news to you, give yourself a low grade. On the other hand, if this is old news and you're on the case, give yourself a high score.

Question 10: Can You Connect Your Software Assets to Entities outside the Organization?

SOA is all about being able to connect services to create everything from composite applications to flexible ways to link between customers, suppliers, and partners. The first step in preparing for SOA is to make sure that you're structuring your business and technical approach so that your partners and suppliers are planning the same way for the same outcome. Getting everyone on the same page requires joint sessions with suppliers and partners.

Think about what influence your management team has with its partners. Is your management aware of the need to have a flexible way to creatively plan for emerging opportunities and threats? If these ideas are new to your company and your partners, you may have a rough time planning a practical approach to SOA, so give your company a low score. On the other hand, if everyone understands the business goal, give yourself high marks.

What's Your Score?

Mark down and add up your points for each area to get your base score. Here comes the weighting — add to your base score the following points for each question:

- ✔ **Question 1:** If your answer was 3 or higher, add 5 points.
- ✔ **Question 2:** If your answer was 3 or higher, add 6 points.
- ✔ **Question 3:** If your answer was 3 or higher, add 5 points.
- ✔ **Question 4:** If your answer was 5 or higher, add 3 points.
- ✔ **Question 5:** If your answer was 5 or higher, add 10 points.
- ✔ **Question 6:** If your answer was 5 or higher, add 5 points.
- ✔ **Question 7:** If your answer was 5 or higher, add 10 points.
- ✔ **Question 8:** If your answer was 4 or higher, add 10 points.
- ✔ **Question 9:** If your answer was 5 or higher, add 15 points.
- ✔ **Question 10:** If your answer was 4 or higher, add 5 points.

If your score was under 34, you're just not ready for SOA yet. Go back and see where your scores were very low and start planning. On the other hand, if you score 11 or less, SOA might not be the right approach for you at all. You need to better understand your business drivers and needs before you invest in something that might not be right for you.

You will notice that there is a big range between 34 where you're not ready and 117 when you are in good shape to start. If you are somewhere in between, continue to work on the basics. This might mean getting some basic education on SOA or gaining a better understanding of where your business is headed.

If your score is between 117 and 150, you have some work to do, but you're at a good stage to start concrete planning for the movement to SOA. Look at where your scores are the lowest and start there.

If your score is between 151 and 174, you're in great shape. You've thought through the key issues and are on your way. If your score is this high, you're probably a ringer who's already pretty far along on your SOA journey. It's time to start sharing your expertise with your peers.

Chapter 17

Making Sure SOA Happens

*W*e're pretty sure that if you're reading this book, you're thinking deep thoughts about SOA. We think that's a good thing. You may also be trying to figure out how to get your organization from where it is now to where you want it to be, SOA-speaking. It's one thing to get everyone to agree that SOA's cool; it's another thing getting actual people to spend actual time and money to make things happen. So, don't be surprised if some of the people you need to convince ask what's in it for them. It's up to you to explain it to them. Well-paid corporate consultants call this convincing "getting buy-in." Political candidates look for "support." No matter what you call it, SOA isn't a one-person or even a one-department deal. SOA needs buy-in from constituents across your organization, and we feel it's critical to get buy-in from above — SOA must be driven from the top. SOA transforms business and IT culture, processes, language, and more. SOA means change, and change is rarely eagerly embraced. To make SOA happen, you need someone with authority insisting that SOA happen.

At the end of the day, the issues of leveraging great ideas and great technology are all about a) how you educate an organization and b) how you change the way people think. If organizations try to implement SOA the way they've always implemented new technologies, we think they'll fail. SOA is a different way to approach getting business value from technology. Making SOA happen requires business units and IT organizations to work in lock step, joined at the hip, side by side from here on out. It's indeed a new world order, and the sooner organizations can adapt, the sooner they can reap the benefits.

Don't get discouraged if this seems like a lot to undertake. The good news about SOA is that you can start small and build on your success. By demonstrating value with small projects that can lead into larger projects, you can show business and IT management that SOA is worth the investment. We find that success is contagious.

The Only Thing We Have to Fear is Fear Itself . . .

Thank you, FDR. One of the biggest hurdles to overcome in making SOA happen is fear.

Chaetophobia? Didaskaleinophobia? Ostraconophobia? No, not exactly. If you're afraid of hair, going to school, or shellfish, we can't help you. We think the fears that you'll encounter in your SOA mission are fear of change and fear of YASB — Yet Another Silver Bullet.

In the worlds of business and IT, many "this will solve everything" solutions have been bought with disastrous repercussions. The silver bullet is supposed to be the one thing guaranteed to kill a werewolf. The fact that people often see IT as needing a silver bullet ought to tell you something.

Technology vendors have been introducing silver bullets for as long as there have been technology vendors. These vendors always announce spanking new technologies with a lot of fanfare. The latest technologies promise to transform even the most mundane organization into a dynamo. These promises aren't all that different from the kinds of promises made by beer, cigarette, and cologne purveyors, but we don't want to throw the baby out with the bathwater or miss another opportunity for a cliché.

With technology, it's important to remember that technologies take time to mature. Though you may not have heard about SOA until recently, SOA's been around for quite a while, and the technologies that have lead to SOA have been in the making for a good long time. That's not to say that more and more SOA-specific technologies aren't emerging every day.

We liken SOA adoption to the early days of e-commerce. When companies first went to the Web to sell, all the sophisticated technologies that are commonplace today didn't exist. You had no shopping baskets or up-selling features, no fraud protection or alternative payment forms. Imagine if you had to be the person responsible for convincing folks that your company needed a Web presence. Those were tough battles — Web evangelists faced a lot of skeptics. Ironically, many of those skeptics were in IT. Companies tried things and made mistakes, and many gained by trying. E-commerce is here to stay and many early players garnered first-mover advantage that shook established competition to the bones. Do you remember life before Amazon.com? We do. Have your children ever seen a record store where they sold vinyl albums still in shrink-wrap? Ours haven't.

The Quality of Service Is Not Strained

To get buy-in, you have to sell. If you're the one selling SOA, focus on the benefits.

One of SOA's greatest benefits is the ability to improve quality of service. Does that sound a little too pat? Well, maybe an example would clear up what we actually mean when we say "quality of service."

Consider this example. Have you ever gone to a restaurant and everything seemed to work just right? You called ahead and asked for your favorite table. It was ready for you when you arrived. The host was polite and called you by name. The temperature in the room was just right — not overheated and stuffy, but not air-conditioned to frigidity, either. The waitress was friendly and brought you water, rolls, and a menu. Service was fast, but not too fast. Overall, it was a smooth, positive experience. If anyone asked you, you would declare that the "quality of service" was excellent.

This kind of smooth, satisfying, efficient operation is precisely what businesses can achieve by using a service oriented architecture. SOA adds predictability and regularity between business rules, policy, and software services. Therefore, one of the greatest selling points for SOA is that it can help management know what tasks a particular service is executing and what rules and policies are codified within these services. Being able to track this not only makes software within the company better but also makes corporate governance more predictable and less cumbersome.

If you're building services, you must design them to adhere to the following three requirements: They must be safe, they must be accurate, and they must be predictable. Safe means that the service itself is secure and doesn't introduce bugs and problems into the organization. Accuracy means that the service itself executes the function it's designed to execute. At the end of the day, accuracy is all about corporate governance. Organizations implementing SOA must be reassured that each business service is executing the right function in association with governmental regulations. Finally, each service must be predictable. If that service is designed to calculate a 30-year mortgage, it had better do exactly that each time it's used; likewise, a service intended to pay a claim needs to execute the same process across many different composite applications.

Failure to Comply?

Instituting and following a SOA approach will ultimately make an organization much healthier. When every aspect of IT is under SOA governance, regulatory compliance is a natural byproduct. So, if you know people in your organization who have been tasked with making sure that the company is adhering to guidelines for Sarbanes-Oxley, HIPAA, Basel II, GLB, Y2K, G8, P2P, XYZ, or any other regulatory or policy-based requirement, you may want to talk to them about SOA. After they understand what SOA can do for them, you're likely to have allies.

Educating Rita and Peter and Raul and Ginger

No sane person spends time or money on something they don't understand. One of the biggest mistakes that organizations make is to head straight to technical details. ("How 'bout those Web services interfaces!") In selling SOA, you need to explain the business benefits of the technology. Be prepared to answer questions such as

 ✔ **How will implementing SOA improve our ability to service our customers?**

 ✔ **How much will it cost? Will it pay for itself? How long will it take?**

Part of your education begins outside of your own company. It's important to find peers of your organization's managers in other organizations who have successfully taken the plunge. If a company that looks like yours has been able to begin their SOA journey, your management should take notice. One endorsement by a peer is worth at least ten well-crafted technology "Return on Investment" pitches.

Picky, Picky, Picky

After you have some buy-in (notice we aren't asking for unilateral, unanimous, unmitigated buy-in — just *some* buy-in), you want to pick a project that's relatively small in scope that can quickly prove the merits of SOA. Every organization has a lot of projects that would make great SOA candidates. Be careful to pick an important project that's doable in a relatively short time frame. We know of at least one company (that we aren't allowed to mention) that saved more than $40 million in just three months. Maybe you can't find something quite so dramatic, and you may need help figuring out what project will bring the quickest big yield. Our point is that you should pick your early SOA projects carefully. Early SOA success is critical to gaining more buy-in.

One of the most exciting benefits of SOA is that there isn't just one way to start. Depending on your business issue and the nature of your industry, you can achieve business benefit in a lot of ways. For example, are you in a company where a lot of knowledge is only in people's heads? Is there a danger that knowledge might walk out the door unexpectedly? Are some of the most knowledgeable people getting ready to retire? If you answer "yes" to questions like these, it may be important to start by working to extract the knowledge and processes that people carry around in their heads and make that information into business services with clearly defined interfaces.

On the other hand, you may have a situation where you have well-documented processes and rules — but they're scattered in different places in the company, and it's difficult for one of these services to access another. If that's the case, you may want to start your SOA-izing by implementing an enterprise service bus.

Other organizations may gain value from simply discovering exactly what assets they have in their IT systems. The point is to pick your starting point based on the issues that are most important to your company. (And remember that such starting points may not necessarily be the most sophisticated features of the organization and yet may still have significant business values.)

Revolutionizing IT

Traditionally, people who find themselves in an application development organization or an IT operations group are often viewed as ancillary to an organization. The organization uses IT staff as order takers. Business units approach IT when it needs an application designed and built. IT sends an analyst to meet with the business owner. Together, they create a specification for the application. Back in IT, developers happily start coding the application in the language or technique they love the best. At some point, the IT team will do a little testing on the code and then turn it over to the business unit for acceptance testing. In other words, the business unit is simply supposed to try out the application and give it their blessing. Sometimes, this process goes smoothly, and the application meets business objectives. However, in many situations, the vision of the business unit and the vision of the IT organization are like two countries with different cultures. Each group thinks they're doing the right things based on the dictates of their organization.

As SOA begins to become mainstream, IT will need to create a different set of jobs. For example, the application architect will be someone who's in charge of creating the environment where true composite applications can be designed. He or she will be the arbitrator deciding which business services should be codified and used throughout the organization. This is an important job because it requires an understanding of the value of the service, its reliability, and its ability to be generalized for many different uses.

A company needs individuals within the organization who both understand the business as well as how a SOA architecture is implemented. These people need to work hand in hand with developers who have the technical skills to create business services from existing software as well as those who can design new business services.

Organizations also need sophisticated SOA architects who understand infrastructure at a deep level. Software quality will become a much more visible task within a SOA environment. Too often, software quality doesn't get the respect it deserves. Under SOA, testing takes on even greater importance. Another likely new job will be focused on the manageability of the SOA environment. Because SOA is predicated on bringing services together in new applications, SOA will need professionals to look at the performance and management of these environments.

Foster Creativity with a Leash

After you start on the journey to SOA, things can start to get pretty exciting. Business people start to talk about the business services they want to create. Developers start learning more about cool languages, such as XML, and various Web service interfaces.

Because of the nature of technology, you may find that developers want to barrel forward and try all sorts of new products and techniques. Although it's wonderful to get everyone engaged, SOA needs to be managed carefully. For example, we talked to one organization where developers had gone wild and started creating 20,000 different business services. They started to code thousands of Web service interfaces — just in case someone needed them. Although this "more, more, more" approach seemed like a good idea at first, it soon led to a lot of pointed questions being asked, such as "What are we doing creating 20,000 business services?" and "Are these the right services?" and "Are they at the right business level?"

[handwritten margin note: don't creat too many services at once]

The truth of the matter is that the business services that the IT organization wants to create may not in fact be the *right* services. They may be too tiny and represent such a small business function that you can't easily find them and, more important, you can't easily reuse them. Therefore, in many ways, planning is more important than execution. Eager developers must understand that they can't work in isolation from the business units. SOA isn't about building systems the old-fashioned way, and it's easy to fall back into old habits. Resist temptation! Software developers need to work with business to determine exactly what business services need to be created and what those services should look like.

Another issue that can happen with enthusiastic employees is the desire to act heroically. A young development team might decide to break the rules and start coding on their own, creating a new set of facilities ahead of what anyone else has done in competing organizations. Indeed, this type of innovation can be very important in establishing market leadership. But, you need to remember a caveat — innovation and creativity always require a leash. *[handwritten: HA!]* Developers need to design non-mainstream innovation so that it can be changed when these capabilities become mainstream. Many innovative companies have shot themselves in the foot by building these innovative approaches directly into their systems without isolating these approaches from other components. Trying to get rid of old, hand-built technologies can cost you unless those technologies are written as business services or Web services without dependencies on other pieces of technology.

Banishing Blame

In traditional IT environments, business units typically make requests of the IT organization, and then sit back and wait for results. When results are late, unpredictable, or unsatisfying, business leaders let the IT organization know how badly the IT group has done in meeting business needs.

Under SOA, the role of the business changes dramatically. Successful companies create a business-led SOA team. With business services, business professionals more easily understand what it means to create business value from IT. SOA spawns a new culture that fosters collaboration between the business and IT organizations. In both organizations, new jobs focused on SOA will emerge.

For example, the role of the business analyst will change to absorb SOA and business services. Business architects that understand technology will have roles, and they'll begin to look at creating important business services as a revenue source for the organization.

Many organizations are looking at their business services and are seeing that their ability to offer software as a service is a surefire way to expand their business footprint. Likewise, these business services become the foundation for business partnerships. Therefore, new roles emerge within the business unit to work with partners, suppliers, and customers to make SOA the engine of growth.

Document and Market

SOA is a journey, not a sprint to a finish line. Therefore, you need to explain to potential SOA allies that each stage will provide results and business benefits over a number of years. To ensure that everyone is engaged, document the achievements of your initial efforts. Conduct reviews so that everyone sees the benefits. Tie those benefits into both cost savings and revenue enhancements.

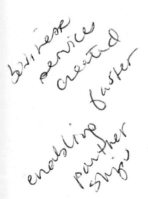

For example, by creating a business service, the company may be able to execute a new partnership in three weeks rather than three months. How much revenue will the company achieve because of this earlier start? How much happier is the partner with your ability to respond more quickly? Can you interview the new partner and get the skinny on their experiences in establishing partnerships, in general, as well as their (hopefully wonderful) experience partnering with your new, SOA-enabled company? In such an interview, be sure to be specific. Ask how that partner felt about the ability of the IT organization to respond quickly to their needs. Document both what has worked and how it worked — and don't forget to document what didn't work and why. This documentation is invaluable in the ultimate success of SOA in your organization. Having documentation of the benefits of the SOA approach will help you market your success throughout the organization and can be very helpful in getting the go-ahead for future projects.

Plan for Success

SOA's success depends on its widespread adoption throughout an organization. Although you definitely want to start with one smallish, manageable project, you still should come up with a larger road map that describes what you should tackle next. You want to be ready to leverage the success of your project to spread SOA, and you don't want to lose momentum by having to stop and think about what's next. Know, before you start your first project, exactly what your organization should be doing after you complete that project. Try to scope out enough of the future that — should you be the victim of overwhelming success — you're in a good position to take advantage of your success and move SOA forward.

You need to have a full plan — even if you're not ready to share it with anybody else just yet. Have a plan in place for the next project — perhaps in a different area of the business so you can achieve wider buy-in. Design a program to start introducing the company to the idea of creating a series of business services that everyone can start using. SOA can start from many different points and has no single one right direction. Choose a direction based on the business needs of your company, and keep moving forward!

Chapter 18

SOA Quick Start: Entry Points for Starting the SOA Journey

*I*f you've made your way through the self-assessment test back in Chapter 16 and are secure in the knowledge that you're a lovable person and that your organization is ready for SOA, it's time to plan your journey. We have two strong caveats about what you *shouldn't* do:

✔ **Don't try to boil the ocean.** Don't attempt to do everything at once.

✔ **If you are business management, don't turn SOA over to the IT organization and wash your hands of it. If you are IT management, partner with business management.** For SOA to be effective, it must be done from the top down. In other words, if you really want your SOA plan to succeed, business management and IT must work together.

So, how should you approach SOA? You need a SOA plan that combines a business perspective, a technology road map, and an organizational initiative. Instead of giving you a deep, philosophical discussion on these (and other) matters, however, we decided to give you some practical guidelines for getting started with SOA.

Map Your Organization's Business Structure

One of the biggest differences between planning for SOA and planning for any other technology initiative is that SOA planning forces you to think differently about your company, your industry, your ability to innovate, and the value of technology.

What does your company do, anyway? Are you in the retail business? If so, do you manufacture the products you sell, or do you sell products from a variety of manufacturers? Are you a financial services company? If so, do you put forth one type of offering or many? Do you have a strong set of partners that you collaborate with? Are you a distribution company? If so, what makes you different from other companies in your market? And what does it actually mean to be "different" in your market? Finally, how should an innovative company act tomorrow and in ten years?

Start your journey by stepping back and figuring out what your company is really about and how what you are translates into the core business services that define your business. Most businesses have key factors that have made them successful over time. SOA structure requires you to think from the perspective of reuse. In order to think from that perspective, you need to figure out a way you can structure the business as a set of services. Think about how to define your own business as a set of discrete services.

The good news is that you probably don't have to start from scratch. Many vendors have done a lot of work to create maps particular to specific kinds of companies, and those vendors are happy to help you get started. You probably don't want to try to tackle SOA without help.

Chances are, your SOA vendor can help you get started with a map for companies like yours. Compare one of these maps to your own company and then modify the particulars that make your company different from the model. *Voilà* — you now have a view of your company as a set of business services. This map helps you figure out where to start. When developing a map specific to your company, include the following steps:

- ✔ Discover and gather business requirements.
- ✔ Simulate and optimize the business process of your company.
- ✔ Determine what you need to measure in order to figure out how well your business is performing.

We know these steps sound simultaneously simplistic and grandiose. We apologize. It's the nature of the beast. SOA is chock-full of simple ideas that alter the world. These simple ideas represent a whole new way of doing IT-enabled business. They represent a new world order, and that new world order requires thinking in a new way for many organizations.

Pick Your Initial SOA Targets to Gain Experience and Demonstrate Success

If you try to move your entire company to SOA overnight, you'll likely end up living your own worst nightmare. Instead, start by reviewing the business services map to identify your first target. Select a specific area where you can leverage existing software assets, turn them into services, and create a plan that demonstrates the value of the flexibility you'll gain from SOA. You don't need to start with something huge. Remember, you're proving that SOA works in your organization and has real value.

For example, we know an insurance company that chose its Claims Processing department as its first SOA implementation. It turned the method of processing a claim into a business service called (ta-da!) Claims Processing. By making it easy to change provider information, the company was able to add new claims providers in a few weeks rather than the 24 months it took previously. This speed allowed the company to add new partners quickly and expand revenue. In addition, the company was able to offer this flexible and rapid Claims Processing service to other companies, providing a new source of revenue for the company.

We recommend that you pick a high-profile area where you can see results quickly. Demonstrating the benefits of SOA can make business change much less painful. You might have many good choices about where to start. One company might need to create a portal or a specialized Web site that brings key business services together to meet an immediate business objective. The portal view can help create an entirely different user experience within an organization. Another company may need to provide a single view of customer data so that various departments, subsidiaries, and business partners can find creative ways to grow revenue by focusing on customer opportunities to up-sell and cross-sell. Other companies may choose to focus on getting the necessary architectural components in place to support their movement to SOA. Still others may look at the manageability of various processes. Other companies may focus on the security aspects of SOA, while others will look at issues around governance.

Why you shouldn't wait

If you are a company CEO or high-level manager, you may be thinking this SOA stuff sounds complicated — and very new. Maybe I'd be better off waiting a few years until the vendors have all the angles figured out. Our advice: Don't wait. Because SOA is as much a philosophy of making technology work for your business as anything else, it is a fundamental shift in the way you work. You'll need time to find how to work across departments and turn your software assets into reusable components.

We could list hundreds of different options — all of them perfectly appropriate for a particular company or concern — but you, and you alone, know best what will have the greatest impact for your organization. Figure out what will get the biggest bang for your buck and go for it.

Prepare Your Organization for SOA

No matter where you start, all roads lead to the people. SOA is about how people across organizations work together to change the way they think about the intersection of business and technology. In this regard, the organizational issues are much more important than any single technology issue. Often, departments within organizations work in isolation, and corporate structures have been designed to emphasize departmental objectives rather than cross-departmental cooperation. For SOA to succeed, organizations need a new way to think about the value of technology, one driven by a corporate-wide effort to approach technology differently.

In order to kick-start such a new approach, we recommend establishing working groups that span departments. Separating work by different parts of the organization isn't going to fly. Information can't be owned by one department — it's a corporate asset; likewise with business services. Business services must be valuable across many different departments. We recommend that top management establish SOA as a corporate mandate and set up an organizational structure that encourages and fosters its development. Establishing recognition programs that reward cooperation between the IT and the business departments is a good starting point. If your company isn't at that stage, find high-profile departmental executives who can set an example. You'll need to approach different areas from different points of view.

IT developers need a different approach

Most IT developers are used to writing code that lives within its own enclosed world. When an organization begins the movement to SOA, developers need to start writing software based on the assumption that the software will be used in many different circumstances. Developers who come from the old school of doing things don't necessarily see this as an intuitive approach. Part of preparing the development organization is helping them understand how the business might use the components they'll be asked to build. Developers should be teamed with business professionals across the organization to help developers change to a more global perspective. It's also important to allow time for projects to ensure collaboration between a wide range of constituents across the organization.

Business managers need to look beyond their own departments

Business managers tend to worry about their own department's goals and objectives, and the metrics that they're judged on. SOA involves thinking creatively about business process and business measurements as they affect the enterprise as a whole. In order to appropriately identify key business processes, you need strong cooperation and collaboration between departments and divisions.

Business Partners Are Part of the SOA Success Story

In a highly competitive business world, no company is safe without partners. SOA can play an important part in making partnerships innovative. Any company that has a SOA strategy needs to implement their strategic plan in conjunction with their business partners. Partners may need to be educated on the value of the strategy and how it will help them take advantage of the combined strengths that partnerships can create. Some forward-thinking partners may have already started their SOA journey.

Don't Enter SOA Alone

SOA is a journey, not a one-time project that a single department implements to get a quick hit or quick success. It's a corporate-wide process to leverage technology in a way that reflects the business's key business processes, enabling business to change when needed without being constrained by technology. Therefore, don't approach SOA in isolation. Find yourself some help. Look for technology suppliers that have created successful SOA implementations for companies like yours. Admittedly, you probably won't be able to find a single vendor that can provide you with everything you need. Still, you should actively look for companies that can offer you an easy-to-implement package based on established standards that you can then add pieces to (or subtract pieces from) as your implementation matures.

Look for models of SOA success. What can you glean from companies that have already started on their SOA journeys? What would they do differently? What has worked well for them? How have they managed to get their people to work together toward a common goal?

Off to the Races

We hope we've given you enough to whet your appetite for SOA. We believe that a service oriented architecture will be critical for any business today that relies on technology to run the business. The world is changing rapidly, and SOA helps an organization keep pace. It's SOA that can help "future-proof" a company — making it ready and able to change when change inevitably comes.

In Part V of this book, we give you some examples of actual companies that have already put SOA into action. We hope you find them inspiring.

Part V
Real Life with SOA

The 5th Wave   By Rich Tennant

"They're pushing the company into a new, hip direction and asked if we would pimp the storage system."

In this part . . .

*T*he proof is in the pudding. It's time we put the pedal to the metal and gave you bunches of real-live SOA stories to help you envision your own SOA solution. This part contains the SOA strategies of eight top SOA vendors and gives real-life examples of actual SOA implementation.

Chapter 19

Big Blue SOA

Big Blue, in case you haven't heard, is the long-standing nickname for International Business Machines Corporation, typically referred to as IBM.

The company that would eventually become IBM was founded in 1888, which definitely makes it one of the more august figures on the IT landscape today. It has been a leader in the area of business technology since at least the 1920s. In fact, there probably isn't a single technology that IBM hasn't had its hands into over its long tenure in the industry. In its early days, IBM developed machines that actually automated calculations — their famous punch-card machines — which, at the time, was pretty revolutionary. In 1924, the company that grew through the merger of three small companies came into its own as IBM. Over the next decades, IBM was able to evolve into a force in mainframe computing. Over the decades, it added lines of smaller office computing systems and, in the 1980s, revolutionized computing for the masses with the development of one of the earliest commercially focused personal computers. Although IBM had long invested in software alongside its profitable hardware business, an emphasis on software and services began to take shape in the latter half of the 1990s and into the 2000s.

IBM and SOA

IBM's software strategy is particularly broad, with a focus on infrastructure software and services. Infrastructure software includes any software that helps ensure that software can be planned, developed, tested, managed, secured, and connected. In the early 2000s, IBM decided that it would focus on these infrastructure components and partner with companies that built industry-specific software packages, such as those dealing with customer relationship management, accounting, and supply-chain products. One major area of IBM, called IBM Software, creates products and partnerships within the area of enterprise software. Another major area, called IBM Global Services, provides business and technology consulting. Together, these two groups deliver IBM's SOA offerings.

SOA has become the defining strategy across IBM Software Group. IBM uses service oriented architecture to unify its enterprise software offerings and enable businesses and independent software vendors (ISVs) to solve business problems. IBM's product offerings involve every aspect of modeling, development, assembly of services, deployment, management, security, and governance of SOA environments.

IBM has decided to make service oriented architectures the linchpin of much of its software strategy for the future. SOA allows IBM's software offerings to integrate easily with the software currently deployed in clients' IT environments. IBM's Global Services organization has developed and codified best practices around helping customers more quickly implement a service oriented architecture — typically by using its own software and the software of an extensive network of business partners. IBM's partner program, which brings together independent software vendors, regional system integrators, and consultants, has a large SOA component.

It's hard to find an area of software that IBM doesn't focus on. It has a very broad technology platform that encompasses every aspect of SOA. We could write an entire book just on IBM's SOA capabilities. (Maybe next time.) Here's a list that gives a high-level view into the areas of SOA that IBM concentrates on:

- **SOA development services:** Such services include the ability to either create a new service from scratch or encapsulate existing code to create a business service. Within IBM's Rational division, the company sells application- and service-development technology based on the Eclipse framework (an industry-standard platform for applications development). Again, IBM's development-services technology is designed to help customers build business services either by encapsulating existing code to create a business service or by creating new services from scratch.

- **Infrastructure services:** Such services include infrastructure and platforms that support *loose coupling* — the "separating out" of tight linkages between components fundamental to service oriented architectures. The connective tissue includes software for messaging and brokering between services.

IBM has a large number of products in the middleware space branded as the WebSphere family of offerings. The enterprise service bus provides a mechanism for unifying many of IBM's connectivity capabilities. (Keep in mind that IBM's hardware products also form a foundation for enabling a SOA.)

✔ **IT service management:** Service management includes the ability to deploy, monitor, secure, control, and manage the highly distributed SOA environment. IBM's Tivoli division provides capabilities in this area.

✔ **Security management:** Without effective security, you may as well pack up your SOA hopes and dreams and toss them in the nearest waste bin. In security management, IBM's Tivoli division does double duty by providing capabilities for security and compliance of SOA environments across multiple application platforms and infrastructure. The security products from the Tivoli division focus on using both identity and security management to reduce costs and enable SOA applications to leverage "security as service." (Reducing costs is a good thing.)

✔ **Composite application creation:** IBM sees its ability to provide *composite applications* — where you use services as building blocks to create new applications — to a variety of customer environments as one of its true strengths. One of the most common ways to create composite applications is through portals and dashboards. IBM offers the WebSphere Portal Server and the IBM Workplace dashboard as key technologies that hold these composite applications together.

✔ **Information services:** IBM has a rich history of leadership in information management and integration technologies. IBM's information management solutions can publish information services that provide consistent, reusable information in a useful way to people, applications, and processes. In addition to its primary database platform, DB2, IBM offers many different products designed to manage a wide variety of information, including providing services for managing master data, providing information analysis and discovery, and managing unstructured content. IBM has also taken many of its information-integration products and unified them as a platform for delivering trusted information as a service. This platform is called the *Information Server.*

✔ **Governance of SOA environments:** With effective governance, you get a true accounting of best practices, methodologies, processes, tools, and technology. This accounting ensures that companies get the most business value from their SOA. IBM's SOA governance framework is designed to help companies establish effective governance by providing them with the methodology and tools needed to establish decision rights, define high-value business services, manage the life cycle of assets, and measure effectiveness.

✔ **Business process services:** This category contains technologies such as business modeling and business monitoring — technologies that align IT infrastructure to business processes. IBM's business modeling technologies help you deconstruct a business into discrete processes and functions so that you're better able to define the discrete business services in a SOA. IBM's business monitoring technology helps companies monitor business activities to ensure alignment to business objectives.

Seeing SOA

Figure 19-1 illustrates capabilities that you can use to implement a SOA environment. IBM enables customers to begin using their SOA approach from various entry points in this architectural framework.

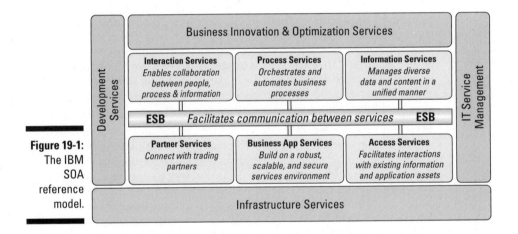

Figure 19-1: The IBM SOA reference model.

The unifying focus of the IBM SOA reference architecture is the enterprise service bus (ESB). The bus provides a mechanism to create links between the primary services that enable components to look and act as though they're part of the same environment. The ESB provides the ability to link interaction, process, information, partner, business-application, and access services. Each of these services is an integral part of the architecture, and each has a specific role:

✔ **Interaction services:** These collaboration services include portals, instant messaging capabilities, and different device interfaces, such as wireless devices and PCs. In addition, these services enable people in different locations or different areas of an organization to work together.

✔ **Process services:** These technologies enable you to orchestrate business processes so that you can link business services together in different ways. This linking or combining of business services creates composite applications — new applications built from (often previously created) software components that are used as building blocks to create new applications.

✔ **Information services:** These services enable organizations to use their highly distributed data as a *set* of services, resulting in more consistent data that can be reused in a lot of different situations.

✔ **Partner services:** The foundation for organizations that need to provide a mechanism to create online collaboration with trading partners.

✔ **Business application services:** Organizations use these services when they create their own Java-based applications.

✔ **Access services:** These services include the adapters and connectors to *legacy applications* — a company's pool of well-tested and well-used software applications that get the job done correctly, but are not easily changed.

✔ **Development services:** These services include the set of IBM Rational brand tools that model and design both the services and the code used within a SOA environment. Development services also include services associated with IBM's WebSphere brand of software products.

✔ **IT service management:** This broad set of capabilities scans security, federated identity management, and overall management of a SOA environment. IBM offers these services under the Tivoli brand.

✔ **Infrastructure services:** The set of services that enable a SOA environment to connect to legacy environments, including hardware and virtualization environments.

✔ **Business innovation and optimization services:** These services provide a high-level management view of the SOA environment. This business-focused view enables management to view key performance indicators, including a business management view of SOA services.

Now that you have heard about the software and services that IBM offers for SOA, it is time to see this in action. We focus on two organizations — one small utility called Delaware Electric and a much larger financial organization called the New York Stock Exchange. While these companies couldn't be more different, these cases demonstrate that there are lots of approaches to SOA, whether you are big or small.

SOA at Delaware Electric

Delaware Electric is an electric cooperative that serves 75,000 customers. Its entire staff of 140 employees includes an IT staff of only 4 people. Of the more than 900 electric cooperatives in the United States, Delaware Electric is one of the fastest growing — great news, of course, but its success hasn't always been easy . . .

Big Problem #1 occurred when the utility was deregulated. At that time, the government put a freeze on electric rates for five years, meaning that the cost of a kilowatt-hour was fixed — Delaware Electric couldn't raise the price. Now, electricity is a commodity like any other, and an electric cooperative's success depends upon delivering that commodity in a fashion that impresses its customers. Energy costs, on the other hand, are rising steadily, which means that Delaware Electric had to find ways to cut its own costs without compromising on service.

The onus of Delaware Electric's business predicament (and financial success) fell on everyone, including its Chief Financial Officer, Gary Cripps. Although responsible for Delaware Electric's small IT organization, Gary was first and foremost a businessman who viewed his primary responsibility as "keeping the lights on" — not only metaphorically, as in keeping Delaware Electric solvent, but literally for all 75,000 Delaware Electric customers.

Looking to IT to solve business problems

Looking for ways to optimize, economize, and deliver better service, Gary closely examined the various IT systems already in use at Delaware Electric. He found a lot of critical systems that didn't talk to each other. He looked around for some sort of packaged software that would solve the problems efficiently but found that none existed. "We simply couldn't find a software package that would handle the diversity of requirements that would provide integration for all of our business needs and would provide real-time services," is how he put it.

In addition, Gary wanted each department to be able to use the software that best fit that department's business goals — based on the best software available — and he understood that all these individual systems needed to be brought together if Delaware Electric was going to achieve the efficiencies required for a viable business.

With the help of IBM Global Services, Delaware Electric decided that SOA would help break down the barriers between various systems, allow them to leverage the critical assets they already had, and provide a framework for future requirements.

As Gary said, "The primary objective was to integrate our processes across the enterprise in order to become more member-centric."

That undertaking ended up being no small feat. Delaware Electric had many packaged applications that were critical to running the utility. Although each of these applications performed a valuable function, each was isolated from the next. Therefore, for example, they had no way to connect information about a service outage with information about which customers were impacted. They had an interactive voice response system, but it couldn't communicate with the system that tracked outages.

When applications can't talk to each other, people have to fill the gaps. Employees created manual processes to move between the various business functions separated by the individual applications. Faced with the necessity of cutting cost, these complex processes were a luxury Delaware Electric could no longer afford. Ironically, even if Delaware Electric had funds to add people to solve the gaps in business process, manual processes are inefficient and prone to error and would likely have had a negative impact on customer service.

Gary's team realized that they needed infrastructure software focused on integrating business processes across these isolated applications. Specifically, they wanted to integrate business processes within that part of the company responsible for everything that happens "in the field," that is, on customers' premises. For example, they wanted to be able to compare their customer information system — including the ability to load mapping data from a Geographic Information System (GIS) — with information coming from the State of Delaware. Delaware Electric needed to be able to compare this information in real time — especially when there were serious outages that could impact a huge number of consumers.

No need to go it alone

The management at Delaware Electric understood that they didn't have the expertise or the staff to undertake this plan. Instead, they worked with IBM Global Services to develop a strategic plan. Delaware Electric's management worked with three folks from IBM — one project manager and two developers. Working together, the team developed a customer-focused plan that identified key business processes. They then mapped the process plan to the various applications across the organization.

To manage power outages, they had to link the customer database and the field engineering database, and they needed a way to connect both of these applications with the company's interactive voice response system. All these systems had to be integrated with all the processes throughout the company. Delaware Electric's management understood that they could benefit greatly from changing the focus of their IT systems to support efficient customer service, but that meant shifting the focus away from the billing system that had been the primary focus.

The experts at IBM recommended using an IBM WebSphere enterprise service bus (ESB) as a way to link packaged applications to each other. In this first phase, Delaware Electric used Web service interfaces to hook its various packaged applications into the service bus. This phase required both the subject-matter experts within Delaware Electric and the IBM consultants working with the package software vendors to connect these applications into the service bus. As a result, Delaware Electric's PR department can say, "We can now provide more services to our customers."

The journey continues

At the time of this writing, Delaware Electric has completed Phase One of its journey. Its employees have integrated the outage management system with the geographic information system and the field management system. In the next phase, they will integrate the customer information systems into the WebSphere enterprise service bus. Within the next 18 months, they will install automated meter-reading equipment and connect that equipment into the enterprise service.

Reflecting on how Delaware Electric's SOA plan will benefit its customers, Gary says this:

> Imagine that you are an individual who is in the process of adding an addition to your home. You need the electric company to tell your contractor where the electric hookup is on your property and you need them to come out and work with the contractor to plan for the extension of power to the addition. With the new process and the enterprise service bus in place, you will be able to call Delaware Electric and have the clerk at the call center go into the application, look up your house, view where the hookup is, and tell you when the technician is scheduled to arrive. The call center clerk will not have to know how each of these systems works; he or she will simply be able to fluidly move from one function to another. The customer gets the information they need in a timely manner, and everyone is happy.

With the focus on customer service, the folks at Delaware Electric believe that SOA will help their customers minimize energy costs. With the new SOA environment, customers will be able to go to the Web and view their own energy consumption. They will be able to see when peak energy times occur and schedule major energy use (such as a printing production run) for a time when energy usage is low, thereby saving money. Gary continues:

> If a consumer has an electrical problem, I want my call center representative to be able to determine whether there is a problem with our system or a problem within the customer's home. If we have to dispatch a high-priced lineman only to discover that the problem is unrelated, everyone loses. On the other hand, if the call center representative can inform the customer that they should call their own electrician instead of waiting for hours to be told that "it's not my problem," the utility saves money by not sending out the expensive union employee, and the consumer has the right person fixing the right problem at the right time.

Now, that's progress!

Summing up

Delaware Electric's business problems were ripe for SOA — but it took an astute management to recognize the need and opportunity. The acute problem of needing to cut costs while at the same time delivering better service led them to take a close look at their entire company. Understanding that a great deal of their problems stemmed from the fact that the applications in the various parts of the company "couldn't talk to each other" — and that if they could, the whole company would benefit — was key to selecting SOA. In some ways, Delaware Electric was lucky — they recognized the value of innovation and knew they didn't have the resources to tackle it on their own. Buy-in from senior management is critical to SOA success.

NYSE SOA

Since that balmy day in May 1792 when 24 New York City stockbrokers and merchants signed an agreement to trade securities on a commission basis, the New York Stock Exchange (NYSE) has been trading business securities. The NYSE is physically located on Wall Street in New York City; however, the financial transactions facilitated by the traders on the floor of the NYSE bring together buyers and sellers of business securities from all over the world. In 2006, the New York Stock Exchange (NYSE) Group was formed when the New York Stock Exchange merged with Archipelago Holdings. The two securities exchanges operated by the NYSE Group are called the NYSE and the NYSE Arca.

Just as corporate governance has become a top priority for companies listed on the NYSE, these changes have impacted the way the NYSE does business itself. Meeting regulatory requirements and ensuring that member companies meet these requirements has always been a major responsibility of the NYSE. Recently, the Securities and Exchange Commission (SEC) approved the NYSE's new corporate governance standards for listed companies. In addition, the NYSE has reorganized their own approach to corporate governance, including changes such as the creation of a new, completely independent Board of Directors.

Business challenges at the NYSE

The recent creation of the NYSE Group, increased focus on regulatory requirements, and increased demand for tightened security of all IT systems has led to increased demand on the IT department for the NYSE. The organization has many software applications focused on supporting the demands for meeting regulatory requirements related to securities transactions. They also have many securities market data applications.

Traditionally, the development team assigned to the business division developed each application internally. The business analyst and software developer designed the application so that the final product would satisfy all the business objectives particular to that specific department. This process ensured that the applications satisfied the business objectives of the department, but many aspects of each application were redundant. (All these different applications required some similar steps so that there was a lot of redundancy built into the process.) The IT department wanted to use SOA to create reusable components out of many of these similar chunks of code and then be able to share those components and reuse them in various development projects.

Getting started with SOA

Firas Samman, Chief Information Officer of the NYSE, recalls that the impetus for getting started with SOA was driven more from the IT side than from the business side. His team got started with SOA to improve the way they developed software applications. The most important drivers for IT were to reduce costs and finish their development projects faster. The number one goal in developing the SOA platform was to eliminate the barriers to cost-effective and -efficient software development that had been created by the many distributed applications they had to deal with.

Samman wanted to find a way to help the development team communicate and share components across multiple applications. The initial focus wasn't on how their efforts at embracing a new technological direction would help them solve business problems. They simply recognized that they were effectively reinventing the same code each time they created new applications. (Many software applications with widely varied functions still need many of the same basic components, in other words.) The IT group at NYSE envisioned a development environment where software components would be shared and reused across multiple applications. So they decided to get started with SOA.

One of the first steps the NYSE took to begin their SOA journey was to create a special team responsible for SOA development. It was clear from the outset that the SOA implementation would be very different from a typical IT development project. In fact, it wasn't considered a project at all. The NYSE was clear that they were developing a SOA framework that would dramatically change the way software development would be handled. They were also clear that the SOA platform would consist of the IBM WebSphere Application Server (infrastructure for building, deploying, and running software applications) and IBM Lotus Domino with an LDAP server (a server running an Internet protocol — Lightweight Directory Access Protocol — that software applications use to look up information from a server) on the backend. The NYSE planned to leave legacy applications unchanged, while building all new applications as reusable services. Their decision here made it clear that they viewed the move to SOA as an evolutionary process.

The SOA IT team at NYSE began by developing services such as a directory service and a document service, because they represent common activities that many applications need. The directory service allowed different applications to share the use of information about NYSE employees. The creation of this service meant that information, such as how each employee should be contacted, was consistently provided to multiple software applications

All applications that need to retrieve documents and need to know where they're stored can use the document service. The NYSE IT team created a unified API (*application program interface* — a standard set of rules for the software to follow) so that any application could access any document that it needed in a consistent way. Now, the application doesn't care where the document is coming from, whether it be from relational databases, Domino files, DB2 databases, or other data repositories.

Documents are now effectively decoupled from the applications themselves. If enhancements are made to the documents or the applications, you can still access the documents in the same way. This decoupling makes the whole process more efficient.

Paying for services

Under the old way of developing software applications, each business unit was responsible for the cost of developing its own applications. Each application was tied into the needs of a specific business unit and was created specifically for that business unit. Maybe it was clear as to how much to charge each business unit, but everyone was paying more than they needed to because of all the overlapping code development and maintenance. The SOA way is more cost-effective for everyone. Now, the funds for software development come from the first application that requires the service. As more business services are developed, this base of existing services that can be shared across applications speeds up development and keeps costs under control.

Managing services

Samman's middleware services team is not the only team charged with building business services within a SOA framework. Project managers from various departments are encouraged to create software components as business services and contribute them to the SOA platform. All software architects get involved with business users during the requirements-and-design phase of building the service to ensure that the business service will work properly for the business, as a whole.

For example, a developer working on a regulatory application for market surveillance might meet with the business user to understand the level of action required, based on certain alerts that are set into the application. What level of detail or granularity is important to the business user? What does the business user need to know in order to do his or her job effectively? If the alerts programmed into the application are too detailed, the business user might overlook the truly critical alerts. After a business service is completed and properly documented, you can submit it to the SOA team, who can include it into a registry and make it available to others. All the management proper is done by the SOA services team.

With only 30 to 40 business services available at the NYSE, developers can still use somewhat of a manual process to search for services there. The

NYSE keeps an internal Web site with full descriptions and details about the services. Right now, developers are able to communicate from one team to another about the services, but in the future, they'll need a global registry to properly manage the use and accessibility of business services.

SOA helps developers

One of the major benefits to developers that has occurred since the move to SOA has been the extensive portal framework that brings together many disparate business functions in one place and supports collaboration.

So, what is a portal and how does it help SOA? A portal is a packaging framework of technologies that allow developers to quickly put connections to information stored in existing applications as well as pieces of applications together in a SOA container for users. The portal software is a fundamental way to create composite applications. A portal framework incorporates important services such as the ability to personalize access to information based on what job a person has (for example, an executive may be allowed to see more detailed information about customers than a data entry clerk can see).

To keep this example thing going, imagine that a team of developers from many different departments and divisions is involved in a software development project related to the relationship between the market trades that occur on the floor of the NYSE (people to people) and the electronic trading (machine to machine) — what the NYSE calls hybrid markets. The developers working on this project may not know each other or be in physical proximity, but they're able to work more effectively as a team by using the Hybrid Market portlet. The aggregation of information across the different departments occurs in this portlet and brings everyone up-to-date on the status of the project. The portal makes the design development process much more efficient for the developers. They're able to share and reuse code in this way, as well.

SOA helps the business

Business units at NYSE see the benefits of SOA in many areas, including the increased ease of collaboration resulting from SOA implementation. For example, regulatory examiners from the NYSE who need to check on how member firms are complying with regulations used to spend a lot of time using e-mail and the phone to get the information they needed to review the firm in question. Now, examiners no longer have to replicate a lot of this information on their laptop. They have a portal that they can access from the field that provides all relevant information. This change is very significant from a security point of view, as well. All the highly sensitive information stays on the backend system and it is not loaded onto the laptop, so even if an examiner's laptop is lost or stolen, very little will be compromised.

Business users tend to benefit from SOA in a more indirect way than do the developers. In fact, business users don't need to know or understand the technology, but the technology still has a positive impact on their productivity and efficiency. The NYSE intranet portal has over 30 different portal sites for various divisions and departments. The users are allowed to customize the pages on their portal. They may obtain an alert portlet or a document-management portlet and put it on their page. All these portlets have business services on the backend that provide the data and content for the portlets. Business users can create their own dashboards, depending on their needs.

NYSE summary

Samman says that there's more to come in NYSE's evolutionary process of SOA. The NYSE will expand the number of their services in ways that will make more applications available, benefiting member firms and partners. SOA has enhanced security for the NYSE, which is of critical importance as the NYSE expands their offerings to members and partners, or develops new business relationships with other trading centers. One of the key benefits of the SOA platform so far has been the improved communication with business users. Samman explains, "Slowly, the business user became aware of these services. Now they ask for access to the services. Communication is easier because we now share a common language."

Chapter 20

SOA According to Hewlett-Packard

*H*ewlett-Packard Corporation is one of the oldest computer companies going, having been founded in 1939 by two engineers, David Packard and Bill Hewlett. The company's first product was an electronic instrument used to test sound equipment. HP remained focused on the test and measurement equipment market for a decade and eventually expanded its focus into medical devices. At the end of the 1950s, the company entered the emerging electronic printer market and then segued into the computer field proper in 1966, selling its first computer to the Woods Hole Oceanographic Institute.

Many new computer products followed in the 1970s. By the 1980s, HP had become a major participant in the computer industry, with a product line that included desktop machines, portable computers, minicomputers, and inkjet and laser printers. HP grew significantly larger in 2002, when the company completed its merger with Compaq Computer Corporation.

HP's overall strategy has been rolled out under the rubric of Adaptive Enterprise, meaning that, with the right technologies, an enterprise can adapt to whatever business conditions demand. HP focuses on helping the IT organization align technology to emerging business needs. It finds that a service oriented architecture fits very well into its overall technology and business strategy.

HP's software business has evolved greatly over the past ten years. While HP has long considered software products to be a major part of its product line, its software strategy really began to take shape over the course of the last five years. As part of this new focus, HP has concentrated its software offerings around its suite of management products called OpenView.

HP OpenView is a family of solutions aimed at managing enterprise computing environments. HP offers products to manage computer networks, complex computing systems, and the applications that run on these systems. HP's definition of *management* extends to the management of processes, applications, middleware, the Internet, storage, and security.

HP doesn't sell its own middleware products or packaged applications. Therefore, it focuses on bringing together the pieces from myriad software vendors so that they can be effectively managed. By necessity, it partners with many complementary software companies.

What Does HP Offer for SOA?

HP approaches service oriented architecture in two significant ways:

- HP offers help in managing a SOA environment across a variety of middleware options, packaged applications, and data.
- HP provides consulting services to help companies implement a SOA infrastructure.

HP software is designed to manage all aspects of SOA. The company has developed SOA frameworks within its consulting organization focused on four target industries — network and service providers, financial services industries, manufacturing and distribution industries, and the public sector — and provides consulting services based on these frameworks to help companies with their SOA implementation. HP consulting works closely with platform partners such as Microsoft, BEA, JBoss, SAP, and Oracle. (You may notice that each of these vendors has a chapter of its own in this part of our book. Most organizations rely on multiple vendors to provide all they need.)

HP also works with smaller systems integrators, such as MW2, who bring together the middleware, registry, ESB, and development tools to provide a complete SOA solution to customers. In addition, HP offers the HP Nimius solution framework to provide the basis for an organization's e-business services implementation. HP has developed this framework for several industries, including electronic banking, insurance, mutual fund advisory services, and travel portal services.

The heart of HP's SOA management strategy is its OpenView SOA Manager. This technology provides an integrated way to synchronize and manage services and their IT resources. This software creates a way to enable customers to have a strategy in place to manage the business services created within the SOA model as part of their computing infrastructure components. This model enables customers to monitor, control, and manage business services and the relationships of those services to the underlying applications. By managing the relationships between all SOA components and the business services they support, HP helps businesses monitor and maintain SOA health. The goal of HP's OpenView SOA Manager is to mitigate risks in enterprise-wide SOAs by simplifying root cause — the process of determining the underlying reason for a problem — and business impact analysis — evaluating the relationship of business risk to business profitability.

HP OpenView's SOA Manager integrates with other OpenView products designed to manage a SOA environment. Here's a listing of the other products in the OpenView family and how they tie in with SOA:

- **OpenView Service Navigator** graphically models the relationships between business services and underlying IT infrastructure.

- **OpenView Select Access** provides role-based security and administration of business services, composite applications, IT services, and IT resources.

- **OpenView Business Process Insight** creates real-time models of key business processes, driven by data inputs from the OpenView SOA Manager.

- **OpenView Dashboard** provides views showing the performance health of the SOA environment tailored to the requirements of the business or technical user.

- **OpenView Decision Center** captures information about how well the overall infrastructure services are performing and determines the impact of changes to that infrastructure.

- **OpenView Asset Center** creates a list of every device and piece of software within a company's IT environment in order to keep track of all these assets.

- **OpenView Application Insight** brings together performance measurement for many SOA components into one view. The software monitors Web processes and transactions — online banking or online shopping or internal Web applications.

The SOA World à la HP

In order to help companies manage their SOA environments, HP has grouped the OpenView family of applications together in an integrated framework. Figure 20-1 illustrates how the IT business management, integration, automation, IT customer management, and service monitoring capabilities of OpenView products come together.

HP provides a SOA solution for customers in connection with several key partners, including BEA, Oracle, JBoss, and Microsoft. The HP OpenView products are designed with open standards so that customers can use them effectively with a wide range of SOA technologies.

Applications such as OpenView Executive Dashboard (included in the IT Business Management Applications group shown in Figure 20-1) are designed to provide the business with a high-level view into the overall SOA environment. Other products included under the IT business management category, such as OpenView Change and Configuration Management, represent infrastructure services that operate in the background to make sure that all applications within a SOA function together appropriately. These services manage the SOA so that an organization's applications that were not initially created to work together can be used and reused effectively.

Figure 20-1:
HP's
OpenView
for
managing
SOAs.

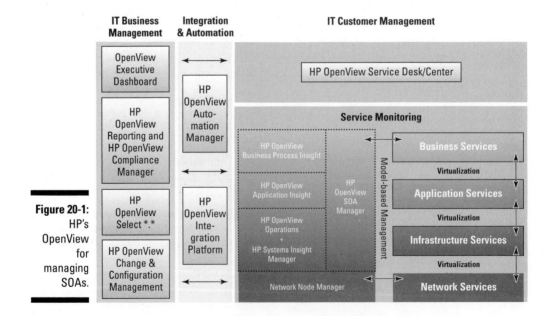

The next group in Figure 20-1 — the OpenView Integration Platform and OpenView Automation Manager applications — represent the integration and automation capabilities provided to manage SOAs. These technologies function as the glue that allows organizations to bring applications together consistently and efficiently. The OpenView Service Desk/Center functions as the nerve center for OpenView by providing the technology to track problems — as well as their resolutions — throughout a SOA. The OpenView SOA Manager is the central focus of the service monitoring capabilities, which also includes OpenView Business Process Insight, OpenView Application Insight, OpenView Operations and Systems Insight Manager, and the Network Node Manager.

Now that you've seen what HP has to offer, we'd like to show you how one Swiss insurance company put HP's SOA software into action to help it expand distribution channels in Europe.

Swiss SOA, Courtesy of HP

Helvetia Patria is a Swiss insurance company with over two million customers across Europe. The company has been in business since 1858. While it has grown and diversified over the years, a dramatic change in the company organization occurred in 1995 when a holding company was created to bring many insurance businesses together. The combined Helvetia Patria Group consists of multiple branches and subsidiaries located across six European countries. They sell a broad portfolio of personal and business insurance, including life, property and casualty, and reinsurance. In addition, the company operates different types of pension plans.

Helvetia Patria is focused on building on its strong brand identity in Switzerland and is intent on differentiating itself as an insurance provider with excellent quality and customer service. Helvetia Patria determined that expanding into new distribution channels across Europe would help them grow.

Business challenges

Didier Beck, CEO of ecenter solutions, a spinoff company of the Helvetia Patria Group, says the formation of the holding company in 1995 presented the company with many business challenges.

The individual business units are all based in different countries with different languages and cultures. (Switzerland alone has four official languages, so Helvetia Patria already had some experience with multilingualism.) Each business unit has its own products, technology systems, and marketing and sales departments. Helvetia Patria quickly realized that if it was going to capitalize on its established brand identity, all the new business units would need to become more integrated and market themselves in a consistent way. The business needed to be more flexible and responsive to changes in the industry if it was going to be able to bring on new partners that would help the company expand into new markets.

Technical challenges

Helvetia Patria faced several key technical challenges related to its business goals. The different business subsidiaries throughout Europe were connected by a technical communications backbone, but the administrative and financial systems were all disconnected.

IT determined that if the business wanted to add new distribution channels quickly and cost-effectively, the brokers, agents, and financial advisors needed to work with an integrated information system.

The current sales process was partly inefficient because agents based in different locations spent a lot of time manually integrating information between separate technology systems.

The business processes for channel distribution needed to be streamlined and optimized. The company had different software applications representing the different distribution channels — brokers, company-based agents, financial advisors, what have you. These systems were not consolidated, and the landscape was very complex. Helvetia Patria wanted to build more flexibility into the infrastructure so it could make rapid changes based on the needs of the business. In addition, it needed a way to provide some of its solutions to partners in order to expand the company's customer base and reach into new markets.

The move to SOA

Helvetia Patria created a new technology center called eBusiness Center with the mission of creating an integrated set of solutions that would streamline sales-oriented processes throughout the organization. It wanted Helvetia Patria employees, partners, and customers — located throughout six different countries across Europe — to all have access to consistent and reliable information about the business. The company worked with HP as its main technology partner. Together, they built a model of their insurance business.

HP built the SOA platform by using an industry-standard, open architecture. Together, they consolidated multiple applications and platforms, including Linux, IBM mainframes, and .NET.

The various insurance company subsidiaries were able to turn many of their existing and well-proven applications into reusable Web services. The programmers designed a new user interface and technical infrastructure. The IT team also added governance components and ensured that the technology accurately reflected the business processes. Some of the major product elements included HP Nimius software and BEA WebLogic Server.

SOA enabled Helvetia Patria to begin expanding its distribution channels in Europe. The company used a partner relationship with a bank that provided the bank's mortgage sales team with the ability to sell private building insurance along with mortgages. Helvetia Patria and its bank partner expected that, given the right tools and expertise, mortgage sales representatives would have a high success rate at selling building insurance to an established bank customer who was already completing arrangements for a mortgage on his building. Helvetia Patria used SOA and business services (including the aptly named Create a Proposal for Building Insurance service) to give the bank mortgage salesperson the tools needed to make the sale. A simplified version of the building insurance product was integrated into the mortgage product of the bank partner.

Helvetia Patria didn't want to force bank employees to go through an intensive training program on how to sell insurance. It wanted the product to be very easy to use. In fact, the Web services technology created a seamless transition between the applications so that a banker wouldn't even know that she had left her bank's application for a partner Web site. There are now 450 branches of the bank using the business service for creating a building insurance proposal.

According to Nick Stefania, Managing Director of ecenter solutions, SOA added flexibility to the process of trying out new business partner relationships and distribution channels. He said, "We found it difficult to know in advance if a strategic partnership would be successful. Now we have the flexibility to try out a partnership quickly, and then we have the option to deactivate the distribution channel if it doesn't go well." The business services created for the bank partnership are all reusable and can be easily applied to new channel relationships as they arise with little additional investment.

Didier Beck explained how the IT developers used legacy software code that Helvetia Patria's agents had used over the years to create proposals for business insurance. The developers took key pieces of this legacy code and encapsulated them so the resulting business service could be reused in different ways.

The IT team created business services for the most commonly followed business processes — the ones that were most likely to be shared and reused. Examples of some of these business services include:

- ✔ Create a Proposal for Building Insurance
- ✔ Collect Data to Calculate a Life Insurance Premium
- ✔ Compile Data for a Life Insurance Quote
- ✔ Calculate the Premium for a Life Insurance Product
- ✔ Print a Proposal for a Customer

The true beauty of the whole endeavor is the fact that many of these business services could be created by adapting legacy code to work within a SOA. IT started with the most common sales-oriented business processes that can be used across different products and across subsidiaries and created business services for them. They stripped the business process down to just the essential information needed for that service to function and then made sure to reuse that stripped-down version in as many other business services as possible. (Currently there are about 70 of these services percolating through Helvetia Patria. Talk about more bang for the buck!)

The move to SOA enabled Helvetia Patria to increase its business efficiency and create more consistent data on customers, their policies, and their claims. ecenter solutions built its solution in a flexible way to contain all the different life and non-life products offered by the many Helvetia Patria subsidiaries. The integration of these products helped to improve the consistency of the company's data.

In the past, each of the insurance products was designed and stored in completely separate sales applications. Now, there are common e-business applications for all lines of business. IT has created business services for life and non-life products that can be reused across the different lines of business. By putting components together in a flexible way, changes are much easier to manage. Now, when rate changes are made for a particular product, such as life insurance, the change can be made dynamically without changing the complete application.

Best practices

ecenter solutions has centralized much of the technical work required for Helvetia Patria to get its envisioned implementation up and running. ecenter solutions brought developers from the different subsidiaries together for six to nine months so they could be trained to work on the new SOA platform. Not only did many of the developers come from different cultural backgrounds and speak different languages, but they also had different approaches to developing applications as well. Bringing them together helped the team make sure that all were speaking the same *technical* language — the language of SOA. After the developers returned to their home bases, they were in a better position to focus on the development needs of their particular businesses.

One dimension that added a great deal of complexity to the Helvetia Patria implementation relates to security and data protection. The company needs to transfer sensitive data between different channels by using Internet technology while accounting for varied protection rights and rules. The company was able to put technology in place that would limit data visibility to those with a right to know. It had to account for situations where some information, such as a client financial portfolio, might be able to be viewed by one channel but should not be seen by another channel.

Next steps

ecenter solutions currently has approximately 70 business services and several hundred additional technology services to keep track of. The company currently uses a spreadsheet to keep track of the names and purposes of the services. This spreadsheet is also used to keep track of how often the business service is used and who uses it. This approach doesn't provide enough information or control over the services. During the next phase of Helvetia Patria's SOA implementation, the company will take steps to add more management capabilities.

Chapter 21

SOA According to BEA

*A*lot of smart software vendors are betting the farm on SOA. This chapter talks about one — BEA.

BEA Knows the Way to San Jose

BEA Systems, Inc., is a company headquartered in San Jose, California, that's focused on the enterprise infrastructure software market; that's to say software used by others to build business applications. BEA has made a major commitment to make SOA the foundation of its future product strategy.

The letters BEA are the first initials of the three individuals that founded the company back in 1995: Bill Coleman, Ed Scott, and Alfred A. Chuang (their current chairman and chief executive officer). The company is among the handful of software firms that generate over $1 billion in annual revenue, a milestone reached in 2004, and BEA claims some 15,000 customers worldwide.

BEA's original product lines were Tuxedo, a distributed transaction processing software suite, and WebLogic, an application suite based on the Java Enterprise Edition platform. Tuxedo was originally developed by AT&T, and its name stood for "Transactions for UNIX, Extended for Distributed Operations." BEA purchased rights to the product shortly after the company was founded and has continued its development since then. BEA acquired WebLogic in 1998. Since that time, BEA has enhanced the product so that it can be used as a Web services platform, supporting both Java and .NET.

Both Tuxedo and WebLogic have since been SOA-enabled, meaning that they now have services interfaces that allow them to become part of a SOA solution. BEA's future SOA strategy is based on AquaLogic, the umbrella name for BEA's suite of SOA applications and middleware, some of which BEA acquired and others they developed in-house. The company also adopts open source solutions when it considers them appropriate.

BEAginning SOA

The company recommends a sensible approach to SOA. As BEA sees it, execution is more important than theory. SOA isn't one big project; rather, companies pick a starting point and a two-to-three-year plan, and then they execute project by project. BEA has a neat slogan: "The power of *and* not *or.*" It's their way of saying SOA is an approach that you add to your existing IT solutions, rather than one that supplants those solutions. SOA migration is not a rip and replace proposition, but an evolution.

BEA analyzes SOA's potential in six dimensions:

- Cost and benefits
- Business strategy
- IT architecture
- Building blocks
- Projects and applications
- Organization and governance

BEA has found that organizational and governance issues — who's in charge and who pays — often determine the difference between success and failure in a company's first SOA endeavor. Getting senior IT management fully behind that first SOA project is vital. Otherwise, inter-group issues, such as deciding who pays for cross-business development, can hamper progress. Ensuring that everyone involved really understands the goals and priorities, and who's responsible for what, is ultimately a job for the boss.

BEA emphasizes the need to find aspects of IT systems that are *loosely coupled* — have minimal interactions with other systems so they can be made into services with minimal side effects — and represent business logic that you can "expose for reuse" by adding a services interface and making that interface available in the SOA service registry. Another BEA slogan is, "Reuse before extend before buy before build. Thou shalt steal and share."

As for costs and benefits, BEA recognizes that the first SOA projects will usually cost a little more than they would if done by using the conventional methods of a pre-SOA shop. There is a learning curve. Often, these additional costs are small enough that the project budget can absorb them. SOA adoption has clear benefits for IT, including reduced maintenance and shorter time to application deployment. Business benefits of the first few SOA projects can be harder to quantify. Early involvement of non-IT personnel with business responsibility is often crucial to success.

Blended development

BEA recognizes that open source is here to stay, and they developed an approach to incorporating supposedly free software into a business model it calls "blended development." BEA picks what it considers to be the best of breed in the open source world, projects such as Linux, Tomcat, Beehive, Spring, Kodo, and Struts, and uses them to add capabilities to its WebLogic suite. In some cases, BEA offers full support for the open source element it incorporates, even to the extent of fixing bugs in the open source code base.

The BEAig picture — SOA Reference Architecture

Figure 21-1 shows how BEA suggests its product families can be used to implement SOA. The bottom layer of the figure represents the different platforms — Solaris, Windows, Linux, and others — that may be providing the plumbing (hardware and operating system) for an organization's SOA implementation. BEA's WebLogic and Tuxedo products are shown at the application infrastructure layer. This includes the application server and enterprise service bus, both core elements in a SOA implementation.

A typical SOA implementation is bound to have third-party and custom applications built on various platforms. These may include packaged applications from software vendors like SAP and Oracle or custom applications from vendors such as BEA, Microsoft, or Oracle. The BEA's AquaLogic family of products is included in the service infrastructure layer. The major components of AquaLogic — including services for messaging, data, and security — are described below.

The top layer of Figure 21-1 represents the internal and external applications that need to connect across many applications within a SOA environment.

One benefit of SOA is that critical information on customers, products, partners, and employees can be shared and reused across many applications. BEA provides the interfaces that allow this information to be used as a service rather than tightly connecting each container of information to one specific application. This loosely coupled connection between services and applications holds true for internal services (supporting information provided within the organization) and external services (supporting information provided to or from outside of the company).

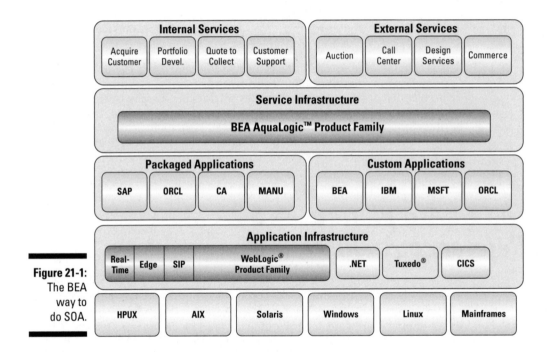

Figure 21-1:
The BEA
way to
do SOA.

You can find BEA's AquaLogic product family, their main product family to support SOA, at the heart of any discussion of BEA's SOA solutions. AquaLogic consists of the following (eight) major components:

> ✔ **Business service interaction:** AquaLogic Business Service Interaction (ALBSI) is BEA's business process management software suite. Fuego, Inc., a company in Argentina founded by Professor Emilio Lopez-Gabeirasan of Austral University, originally developed it. BEA acquired Fuego in early 2006 and maintains Fuego's development lab in Argentina.

AquaLogic Business Service Interaction supports six key business process management functions that allow you to

- Rapidly model any process, using a graphical interface or modeling language.

- Easily connect to back-end systems and applications that support the process.

- Create customized on-screen user work environments for easy navigation and task management.

- Manage enterprise process execution and exception management through a secure process engine.

- Monitor and measure real-time process performance through an integrated business reporting system.

- Optimize process performance through technology that isolates process problems and determines required changes.

✔ **Project Composer:** Project Composer is the newest member of the AquaLogic product family, but it wasn't yet released as of our getting this book to press. BEA views composition as providing a way for non-developers — mere mortals, in other words — to compose and assemble business applications by using existing services built by service-oriented developers. Details haven't been released, but we expect a visual programming interface that will let you select services from the SOA service registry and "connect the dots" to string them together into a business process.

✔ **Data services platform:** BEA AquaLogic Data Services Platform (ALDSP) creates and maintains data services within the SOA framework. (When talking about ALDSP, data services can mean anything from a conventional database with exposed services to sophisticated data transform tools.) ALDSP's tools deliver unified, real-time views of data from disparate sources across the enterprise. It automates the process of creating and maintaining data services with better performance, uniform management and control, better consistency, and easier reuse.

✔ **Messaging:** In a service oriented architecture, the enterprise service bus (ESB), in partnership with the SOA registry, is responsible for making sure that information gets where it needs to go.

In a BEA configuration, the AquaLogic Service Bus (ALSB) acts as the ESB. It includes operational service-management capabilities to speed services deployment and simplify SOA management in heterogeneous environments. BEA claims the ALSB enables rapid configuration of integration between services and the dynamic definition and management of routing relationships, transformations, and policies. It does this without requiring costly and complex development efforts, lowering the ongoing total cost of deploying and operating a SOA.

✓ **Registry:** BEA's AquaLogic Service Registry (ALSR) takes on the SOA registry role, which acts as a central location for managing the services life cycle. The ALSR makes a SOA more transparent by serving as the system of record, where services are published and discovered for reuse, either when composing new applications or in adapting current applications to changing market demands.

✓ **Repository:** In August 2006, BEA announced it had acquired repository vendor Flashline and plans to incorporate its products into BEA's SOA portfolio as AquaLogic Enterprise Repository.

✓ **Security services:** Security is a must-have for any serious deployment of SOA. AquaLogic Enterprise Security (ALES) allows security services to be shared and reused across the enterprise for better companywide IT security. ALES includes capabilities to more precisely control the protection of various application resources within a SOA environment.

✓ **User interaction:** BEA AquaLogic User Interaction (ALUI) is a portal middleware product that BEA acquired from Plumtree Software in 2005. It consists of a cross-platform framework and a set of tools that you can use to create a variety of interactive solutions, including portals, collaborative communities, and composite applications — all with search, publishing, and business process management features. It's designed to speed up the assembly of services into new applications, and it delivers these services to users through an intuitive interface.

Now that you get an idea of what BEA offers for SOA, let's take a look at a customer that successfully deployed BEA's SOA architecture to make their city hum.

SOA City

BEA's been hard at work putting SOA to work in a major metropolis. That metropolis prefers to remain nameless, so we'll hide some of the clues.

It takes a lot of people and a very complex technology infrastructure to provide services for the residents and businesses of any big city, but our mystery city turns out to be one of the largest financial centers in the U.S. while also having one of the largest U.S. city populations. So we're talking some major IT issues to resolve.

The IT organization for our mystery city's government wanted a better way to manage the many interconnected computer systems that they needed to run all the details of city life. Unfortunately, the complexity of the city's IT systems led to an office culture where people from business and people from IT didn't communicate well at all. To put it bluntly, the businesspeople didn't trust that IT could make their jobs any easier. However, the city's resourceful and innovative IT team used SOA and the BEA AquaLogic Service Bus (ALSB) to gain efficiency in (and reuse of) their computer systems, saving time and money for many city departments. Now, the business folks are impressed with the results they're getting, and there's a real buzz around the city departments about how everyone should "get on the bus."

The business problem

The CIO was concerned that IT developers didn't communicate effectively with the business users of the IT systems. We heard about a meeting where a developer and business analyst discussed the integration of a revenue department system with the ERP system. The developer and the business analyst each used a different language to explain the same business process.

The developer said, "I have nine database tables, and I need to create customers, and I need to balance them out." The business analyst responded with, "I just need to create an invoice." While the developer was thinking in terms of the actual APIs (Application Program Interfaces) that he uses to create software programs, the business analyst was thinking in terms of the overall business process. These differences in the words used to describe the same business process typically led to frustration and time delays in many IT projects. In addition to communication issues, the developer would often need to have repetitive discussions about key business processes — making a payment, for example — across many different departments.

The technical problem

Many of the time delays that gave the city's IT department a negative image among the business managers were related to the integrations required to connect all the city's information systems together. IT had recently completed installing several large enterprise software applications packages, including financial applications, Enterprise Resource Planning software (ERP) and customer relationship management (CRM) software.

However, IT also maintained separate IT systems for individual city departments. For each of the new enterprise-wide systems, it became necessary to create interfaces and integrations across as many as 25 to 40 different sub-systems. IT knew there was a more time-efficient way to manage the repetitive processes involved in the integrations.

Their first thought was to send all the integrations to a service bus, which would allow for reuse of integration processes across the enterprise so they wouldn't have to do the same manual steps over and over again. Next, they thought about one of their main goals in IT — how to communicate better with the business user — and that goal made them decide to take a look at SOA.

Getting started with SOA

The IT team hired consultants with experience in SOA to work alongside their development team and bring everyone up to speed on the new technology. They chose to create a Make a Payment business service as their first project because many departments used the same very structured payment process.

They chose BEA's AquaLogic Service Bus (ALSB) as the software platform for building business services because ALSB "allows you to orchestrate services, apply security, and apply rules at the business process level. There is really not a lot of development that needs to happen after those services are exposed, so a business-savvy analyst and a business process owner can orchestrate the services to build out a process." They also used BEA's WebLogic Integration, the AquaLogic Data Services Platform (ALDSP), the WebLogic Server, and the WebLogic Portal.

It's Alive!: Creating living, breathing business services

First on the city's checklist of things to do was to come up with a Create an Invoice business service. The IT developers and the business managers in the revenue department worked together to identify all the process steps required for this function. It was important that the business service would map closely to the actual payment process that the various city departments followed.

When all the mapping was done, the Create an Invoice business service ended up having nine Oracle Financial Application Program Interfaces (APIs) within it. Now, the business user doesn't need to know or care about the detailed APIs, and — after the business service is available for use — the technician doesn't need to worry about them, either. The developer works at the service-bus level and doesn't need to map all the way back to enterprise systems, such as the Oracle Financial engine.

The next service created was the crucial Make a Payment business service, which included 15 Oracle APIs. After these two services were completed, they could be used over and over in many different situations.

Now, when the developer and the business analyst meet to discuss an integration that involves making a payment, everyone speaks the same language. The business analyst describes the process of sending out a bill something like this, "I use the billing system to create a bill and send it to the customer." The developer responds with, "Okay, great. You need to create an invoice. I can use the Create an Invoice business service." Much easier!

When the business analyst says, "The next step in this process is for the customer to pay his bill," the developer has an appropriate response. She responds with, "I have a Make a Payment business service we can use." In the year and a half since the Make a Payment service was created, it's been used in approximately nine different applications, including purchasing a city residential parking sticker and making a quarterly tax payment online.

Life in the city departments after SOA

In the city these days, IT is better able to relate to users in a different, more business-focused way. IT used to say, "We need to collect data, we need to store it and build a database . . . " Now, they want to know why they need the database. When you understand the business process, you may take a different approach to software development — an approach that brings more value to the business.

This meant a certain amount of education on the part of the IT developers and the business analysts. The developers now stay away from the technical jargon and technical details about SOA in their conversations with business analysts. They talk more about the business drivers, business process, and the reusability of software. The business analysts figured out how to describe the workflow aspects of the business processes that they follow so the developers understood and had the appropriate level of detail.

Now, when business users talk to IT about a new project, according to the IT staff, the business analysts "almost have the application designed themselves." IT developers know the business services that are available, and they talk in terms of the business processes they need to follow. If IT needs to create a new business service, it often takes as little as 15 to 30 minutes.

Getting on the bus

The city is now at the point where everyone in the municipal departments wants to "get on the bus." SOA lets the business process owners actually own the process from a technical point of view, as well. For example, the parking ticket division only needs to know that the ticket has been paid, not how it was paid. The revenue department is concerned with how all payments are actually made throughout the system — if the ticket was paid online with a credit card or in person with cash. The business process owners in each department drive the business logic and set the security policies for the business services that apply to them. The policies are put in the service bus when the business service is created.

An administrative team oversees the infrastructure of the service bus and all that's in it. The security policies include different levels of agreement and control access rights to the business services. The business departments had to do a lot of thinking about security issues that they didn't deal with previously, leading to a better overall understanding about security needs.

Steps to success

The SOA journey has been very successful for the city's IT. Here are some of the reasons why:

- ✔ The CIO was very clear from the beginning about what he expected from the overall architecture and framework.

- ✔ The city brought in some outside hotshot developers with SOA experience.

- ✔ They created working partnerships between the in-house team and the consultants.

- ✔ The city made sure the in-house developers had plenty of opportunity to get involved and felt free to ask a lot of questions about the technology, business services, and the overall platform.

- ✔ The IT folks kept the whole program kind of quiet at first so that business users wouldn't pressure the team on delivery dates.

- ✔ All subsequent projects always fit the same road map.

- ✔ The city chose services they could handle without expending a great deal of effort. Don't start with the most complicated services because SOA proponents need to show success.

✔ They anticipated a learning curve and planned for it. Building the first service was an eight-week project that they could now do in two weeks.

✔ The city found that understanding the technology wasn't as challenging as rethinking the way IT communicated with business users.

✔ They took incremental steps, pushing the envelope a little more with each project.

✔ They were careful not to get too detailed in defining a business service.

✔ IT engaged in plenty of dialog with business users to get the process defined correctly.

✔ IT also found out that governance of the business services can be very complex, mainly due to the fact that the management of the business services is really a business function, not an IT function. The business process owner owns the business service. So, if another department wants to use the business service, they need to check with both IT and the business owner.

What's next?

Now that close to 200 business services are in use throughout the city system, some changes need to be made if the city wants to be in a position to effectively govern and manage the use of these services. IT needs to prepare for the future as the number of services may climb to as many as 25,000. Future plans include implementing a SOA registry and a metadata repository, and improving enterprise-wide data integrity.

Up till now, the developers have used a Web page to record the available business services and their descriptions. Given the increase in the number of available services, IT is beginning to use the BEA/Systinet Business Services Registry to catalog the services. (The BEA service bus does the actual services managing.) IT is also planning for software to manage the business services. The service bus gives some management capabilities, but not enough.

Over the next year and a half, IT plans to have all the metadata for all the systems in one location — a coordinated metadata repository. A metadata repository is built into the BEA framework.

Data integrity and accuracy is just beginning to get a lot of attention. IT recognizes that each division is very protective of its own data. No one in the divisions wants anyone messing around with their data. The city put a plan into place, so now that the business services are built and everyone is on the bus, IT can begin sending the departments reports showing the data-quality issues. IT built a centralized system that keeps the data federated, which means departments retain control of their data, but there's one system capable of tracking data-quality issues across all the data stores. The plan is to clean up the data with the approval and support of the departmental owners of the business data.

Summary

This city started from the point where business didn't trust IT, which put IT in the position of having to prove to business the value of what IT was trying to do. IT had to understand the business goals, in other words — and it was a far from painless process. People were skeptical. Now, they have reusable interfaces and great buy-in, and everyone wants to get on the bus. Now there is no longer a fear of integration.

Chapter 22

Progress with SOA

*I*n 1981, Joseph W. Alsop and several of his fellow MIT graduates founded Progress Software, a Massachusetts-based software company with over $400 million in 2005 revenue. The company initially focused on application and relational database development.

It turned out that one of Progress's first products included a language that made it easier for developers to create applications. This language, cleverly named Progress 4GL, was known as a *fourth generation* language, which meant that the computer commands were easier for programmers to understand than earlier, *third generation* languages such as COBOL. The company's early growth and success was predicated on its strategy of being in a better position to help software companies that wrote applications for specific industries.

Progress attracted a lot of software companies and software resellers as business partners as a result of this strategy. It found its niche partnering with companies that wrote software primarily for mid-size businesses. In the 1990s, as the client/server revolution unfolded, the company adapted its software environment to support this new technology approach. Therefore, the company was able to help its large base of partners adopt these more technically advanced technologies.

After Progress Software went public in the late 1980s, the company initiated an aggressive acquisition strategy to expand its portfolio of business application infrastructure software. It was able to transform itself dramatically through this process.

The company used its customer knowledge to purchase technologies that augmented its early messaging software. For example, Progress spent considerable energy focusing on how to access information that is based on XML.

The Progress story shows a company that played to its strengths and worked smart. As the company heads into the future, it should not come as any surprise that Progress strongly believes that working smart definitely means working with SOA. Read on to see what the Progress spin on SOA looks like.

A Progress-ive Approach to SOA

Products from the myriad of Progress Software's acquisitions have each been organized to support SOA around three market categories: application infrastructure, service infrastructure, and data infrastructure. For example, the Actional family of products and the Shadow RTE product (NEON), acquired from two separate acquisitions made in 2006, are included along with the Sonic product family in the service infrastructure family. The following list examines each category in greater detail:

- **Application infrastructure:** The OpenEdge division at Progress offers a platform for developing business applications. The platform includes integrated development tools, application servers, and application management tools, as well as an embedded database. OpenEdge supports SOA development and deployment technology.

- **Service infrastructure:** The service burden at Progress is borne by three groups of products:

  - *The Sonic product family* provides the Sonic enterprise service bus, along with an extensive set of products to help customers simplify application integration within a service oriented architecture. Sonic products include technologies for service orchestration, operational data management, and the integration of third-party relational data sources, packaged applications, and technologies.

  - *The Actional product family,* which finds the required services and controls actual business process flows, automatically adjusts to changes and visually traces the root causes of policy violations, wherever they occur. Actional was designed to recognize and monitor the activities of uncontrolled or rogue services to help customers eliminate the security and compliance risks associated with inappropriate use of business services.

- *The Progress Shadow RTE (real-time enterprise)* product family enables SOA-based integration with mainframes.

✔ **Data infrastructure:** The DataDirect Technologies division at Progress provides components to connect software to data. DataDirect relies on industry-standard interfaces to connect different types of systems, and all of its products support a SOA approach.

Progress places a great deal of emphasis on products that support the data infrastructure within a SOA environment, such as Progress DataXtend and Progress ObjectStore Data Services. One of the data-related products is DataDirect Xquery, which provides an advanced execution environment for Xquery. (Xquery is the XML-based query language that is emerging as a standard way to ask questions within a SOA environment.) This helps in the implementation of business services that work with and merge XML and data from relational databases.

Progress Proffers SOA

Since Progress first introduced the Sonic enterprise service bus in 2001, the company has pursued a strategy of offering a wider selection of SOA infrastructure products. Keep in mind that Progress was the first software company to offer an ESB, and it has used its first-to-market good fortune to good advantage. By 2006, Progress had over 300 large enterprise and government customers that had incorporated the Sonic ESB as the backbone of their SOA implementations, and Progress was acquiring 50–60 new accounts each quarter.

Progress hasn't wasted time by resting on its laurels; rather, it has worked hard to provide other SOA-focused products. The Sonic Workbench, for example, integrates several of the Sonic products together, including the Sonic ESB, the Sonic Orchestration Server, the Sonic XML Server, and the Sonic Database Service. Progress purchased Actional in 2006, based on the success of the Actional product's governing capabilities for Web services, and then proceeded to integrate the product into the Sonic family to provide a more complete SOA infrastructure solution for customers.

Progress has SOA-focused products in each of its product lines. All the products are designed to be used independently. However, much of the recent Progress acquisition activity has focused on building a more cohesive solution for customers so they will be more likely to use an integrated group of Progress products in their SOA implementations. Progress's goal is to provide a range of Web management services software for SOA environments, including service definition and deployment, process definition and staging, run-time visibility (the ability to manage components when they are assembled), and real-time optimization (ensuring that the services run efficiently).

In addition, several Progress products focus on helping developers find and correct errors in the development process for a SOA environment. One such product is the Stylus Studio Enterprise XML IDE, which is used to develop XML. This IDE tool — an *integrated development environment* tool to those of you who hate acronyms — helps customers find errors in various aspects of their SOA infrastructure. The Stylus Studio's Web services tools include a *call composer* (a tool that helps the developer test and use Web services interfaces), a Web services data mapping facility, a WSDL editor, and a UDDI registry browser.

The Sonic enterprise service bus is central to Progress's SOA reference architecture, as shown in Figure 22-1. The role of the Sonic ESB is to orchestrate the relationship and connection of business services to applications. Figure 22-1 shows how all the heterogeneous applications work together. The roles played by some of the other key products included in the Progress architecture are as follows:

✔ **Actional** for management and governance of Web services

✔ **Apama** to monitor and analyze event streams of data

✔ **Progress OpenEdge** business application platform for the development and deployment of Web services

✔ **NEON** products to create Web services for integration of IBM SystemZ mainframe applications

✔ **Progress EasyAsk** natural language search and query used to access business services

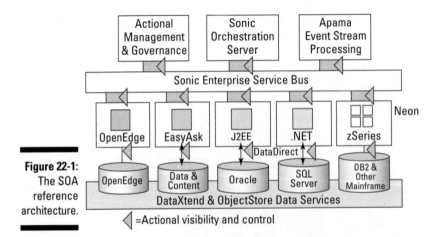

Figure 22-1:
The SOA reference architecture.

Accommodating SOA: Starwood Hotels

Perhaps you have stayed in one of Starwood's 860 hotels throughout the world. You may be more familiar with the brand names Sheraton, Westin, W, and Le Meridien. If so, you might have already taken the kids on a SOA vacation.

The business challenges

After Starwood's acquisition of Sheraton and Westin in the late nineties, and after successfully resolving various technology issues, Starwood established an aggressive program to improve guest service across all of its brands. The company wanted guests to associate the Starwood brands with very high standards of comfort and reliability. The Sheraton, for example, had maintained a consistent reputation for quality service outside of the United States, but the domestic brand image suffered from inconsistent service levels.

In order to develop consistency of service and improve the image across all brands, Starwood focused on improvements that would guarantee guest comfort, such as rapid resolution to problems, upgrading service, and introducing its SweetSleeper® bed. Admirable improvements to be sure, but Starwood also determined that centralizing customer data across the different properties would enable the organization to monitor guest preferences and provide a way to increase guest loyalty. In addition, as the Internet began to transform the way guests gathered information and booked hotel reservations, Starwood recognized the need to improve the functionality, usability, and scalability of the various Starwood hotel Web sites.

The technical challenges

Israel del Rio, Senior Vice President of Technology Solutions and Architecture for Starwood Hotels, set the following four main goals for Starwood's IT department in the effort to support the company's business goals of improving brand image, increasing customer satisfaction, and strengthening guest loyalty:

✔ Keep track of all customer preferences in a central database available to properties at all the brands.

✔ Manage pricing strategies consistently across all properties and brands.

✔ Provide room rate and room availability information to all channels — travel agent, Web site visitor, whatever — consistently and efficiently.

✔ Provide a way for each branded Web site to scale according to the expected increase in customer demand — more specifically, in response to different types of searches by guests over the Internet.

The creation of a new *centralized* data store for all the enterprise data was an important architectural aspect of the new plans. The decision was not an obvious one in the hotel industry, for in the past, Starwood properties and others in the industry operated on more of a stand-alone basis. The properties were often united under a specific brand like Sheraton, but operated independently. This meant data on everything from guest preferences to room availability to capital expenditure projects was highly distributed. Starwood wanted guests to trust that they were getting accurate information on hotel prices and availability and to associate the Starwood brands with superior quality and the expectation of comfort.

Gaining control over customer and hotel data at the enterprise level became the number-one priority. As potential guests began to flock to the Internet to aggressively shop hotel properties in search of the best deal in terms of price and guest services, Starwood knew it needed to be able to provide accurate information in real time in order to improve its competitive position.

IT management determined that creating a federated database system — one that relied on having separate data sources at each hotel — would be inefficient and too costly to implement given the wide range of data schemas and technologies already in use across the large number of Starwood branded hotels. The creation of a new enterprise-wide database would also be an extremely costly proposition, and Starwood decided it would use as much open source technology as possible to help control the expected costs for this project.

Starwood needed a reservation system that would effectively use the new data stores and scale to handle the various channels, including the growing online guest reservation systems. Starwood's legacy reservation system was based on mainframe technology developed in the late 1980s or early 1990s. While there is nothing wrong with mainframe technology, the legacy system was written mostly in hard-to-modify COBOL software and was not primed to easily support many of the emerging business demands.

Starwood needed a new approach to support new ways of doing business, such as the Internet, to improve customer relationships, and to ensure its brands' promises could be facilitated via technology. Starwood chose SOA as the road to refreshing its core technology but then went on to choose the Progress Actional family of products to help the company on this journey. Del Rio spoke of the benefits of the management aspects of Actional — using software tools to understand how the many components of a system fit together and the ability to monitor those components to ensure they work smoothly.

Starwood goes SOA

Starwood implemented its SOA in carefully crafted stages. The company decided to standardize with IBM WebSphere on Linux and initiate all new development outside the mainframe. The first stage involved moving their mainframe applications onto Linux — an open source solution — using a Java infrastructure. Starwood did not move all applications off of the mainframe at once, but used a gradual process. The first new applications were related to room rates and this required them to move basic room rate information and functionality off the mainframe. Two such new applications included the Guest Communication application and the Customer Response application.

Starwood used Progress Software's Actional product to provide agility or redirection of the business services. Starwood wanted to be able to redirect a service from one engine to another very rapidly and do load balancing. With Actional, they'd also be able to monitor the performance of the business services to ensure that all the components in the SOA are working together appropriately.

"Find a hotel property in Florida"

One example of a business service created by Starwood is the (ever-useful) Find a Hotel Property in Florida service. This business service incorporates business rules about pricing and availability that apply to choosing a room based on room type, length of stay, holiday seasons, and other factors. For example, the price per night for a three-night stay may be different than the price per night for a seven-night stay. A series of dates may be available for one room type, but not for another room type.

Starwood uses an object-oriented database to hold all the rate and availability calculations. There are millions of different rate and availability combinations that are actually precalculated for this business service and stored as cache. This pricing engine can be used in many different instances. The Find a Hotel Property in Florida business service can be used and repeated across the different brands. By putting a Web services interface (using SOAP) onto this code to make it into a business service, Starwood gained the flexibility to add new hotels quickly and cost-effectively.

The move to SOA enabled Starwood to scale its Web sites to increase the ease of use and accuracy of information to a skyrocketing number of guests researching and comparing hotel facilities and prices on the Internet.

A hotel guest planning a trip to Miami, Florida, might begin researching hotel availability on the Sheraton Web site. Another guest planning to visit Miami might use the Westin site. While the information and navigation on each of these sites looks and feels a little different based on brand variations, the rate and availability information is consistent. The guest can gather information on a property and book a room at any of the Starwood family of hotels in the Miami area by beginning at either Web site.

All the information is provided to a guest seamlessly. This means that a guest can start on Sheraton.com, see that there's a great deal on a Westin in Miami, and get more detailed information from the Westin.com site without being at all aware that he or she has moved to a different site. The search initiated by the guest finds the services needed to get the proper information to the guest. The Web services technology does the work in the background to make it easier for the guest to investigate as many options as possible in the search to find the right hotel at the right price. Starwood benefits because, with all these options, guests are more likely to stay on the hotel's Web site until they find what they want.

Del Rio attributes Starwood's ability to scale up to handle the increase in guest visits to its Web sites to SOA. "We are able to handle the large increases in guests coming to us from the Internet. Guests today are shopping around — comparing rates and the availability of offerings like spas or gyms. The rate of queries coming from the Internet has increased exponentially. Today, Starwood is handling approximately ten times as many shopping queries from the Internet than three years ago, and we are still using pretty much the same hardware."

Del Rio observed that, after Starwood's recent acquisition of Le Meridien, the IT folks were able to develop a new and more professional Le Meridien Web site in three months time because they were able to reuse many of the services and logic from the backend engine. If they had started to build such a site from scratch, it would have easily taken an entire year.

Discipline and SOA

Starwood Hotels has a generous spirit and is quite willing to share its SOA experience — as well as its practices — with you as you start your own SOA journey. The Starwood folks have these suggestions for you:

- **Start by locating as many tools as possible to help with your development efforts.** This is particularly important for information integration.

- **Begin testing early and test often.** There is a big gap right now in the availability of testing tools given all the complexities involved in a SOA implementation. Starwood has been learning on the job. Look for good testing tools.

✔ **Try not to create more business services than you really need.**
Sometimes developers create business services that are too narrowly defined in terms of the actual business process. Your services should be as broad as possible to get the job done. Some areas, such as reporting, don't need services.

✔ **Incorporate standards to help reduce complexity in your IT environment.**

Starwood has made good use of the monitoring and management tools provided by Progress's Actional product family. The software helped IT to locate problems in their SOA implementation and make corrections so the many components all work together. Del Rio recognized the contribution Progress Software's Actional product made to this development effort as follows: "The Actional software has been a godsend for us. The right management tools are so important, and this is an area where Actional has helped."

Chapter 23

The Oracle at SOA

*O*racle, founded in 1976, made its first big splash in 1979 when it introduced one of the earliest commercial relational database products. For the first decade of its existence, the company focused most of its energy on the database market, but in the next decade the company began branching out to focus on the development of applications, the Internet, middleware, packaged applications, and consulting. Part of this branching out meant being on the lookout for acquisitions that would expand its traditional market while, at the same time, open up new avenues for growth. Oracle proved to be pretty adept at the acquisitions game and has experienced considerable growth as a result.

Today, the company is focused on two primary technology areas: databases and packaged applications. Over the last few years, Oracle has managed to become a major player in the packaged applications market through its high-profile acquisitions, including enterprise resource management companies like PeopleSoft, Seibel, and JD Edwards. In addition, Oracle acquired other related packaged-software companies in areas such as retail management.

Oracle's vision for SOA included providing customers with a complete suite of SOA products. The company wanted customers to be able to get all the software they need for a SOA implementation in one place from one integrated group of software products without any missing pieces. This strategy would include acquisitions of companies with SOA products and internal software development.

One of Oracle's key acquisitions, from a SOA perspective, was its purchase of Collaxa, Inc., in 2003. Oracle built additional capabilities into the Collaxa BPEL (*Business Process Execution Language*) Server and integrated the software with other Oracle products to create the Oracle BPEL Process Manager. The Business Process Execution Language is a standards-based language written in XML, the foundational syntax for SOA. BPEL allows developers to define a business process so that different business services can be linked together or orchestrated to complete a business task. Using "process an order" as a sample business process, the steps needed to "process that order" are the business process. BPEL is the language used to provide the instructions for processing that order.

Oracle introduced the Oracle BPEL Process Manager in 2004 as a way to provide customers with a SOA and integration platform. Oracle wanted to provide a solution for both publishing and orchestrating business services. (*Publishing* a service means taking a part of an existing system and adding Web service interfaces so that they can be used as a business service. *Orchestrating* a service refers to the development and management of software that models the processes followed by the business.)

Oracle already had the Oracle Application Server (which supports a Java-based development platform) for enterprise grid computing (the ability to use a group of small computers as though they were a single large system) and SOA, but it needed a complementary product to provide the orchestrating and executing of Web services and business processes.

The BPEL Process Manager provides the complementary SOA integration platform as well as a framework for the deployment of Web services and the automation of business processes. It includes a BPEL modeler, a BPEL engine for executing business processes, a framework for developing Web services, and services for integration.

SOA Fusion

Oracle brought its Oracle Application Server and BPEL Process Manager together under the umbrella term *Oracle Fusion Middleware*. These products provide customers with an integrated way to publish and orchestrate business services. Then it threw other Java-based SOA software products into the mix, resulting in a full portfolio of products for developing applications and business services, integrating data and applications, and deploying applications and Web services.

Although Oracle Fusion Middleware definitely includes new code based on emerging SOA standards such as XML and BPEL, many of the technology components of Fusion are based on existing Oracle technology offerings. The Fusion Middleware family also includes a business-to-business server for Oracle customers to connect with their partners, portal software and other tools for business intelligence, collaboration, data management, identity management, and content management. And, just for the sake of completeness, it has some tools for managing and monitoring the health of business services and the SOA environment.

You have a lot of tools to keep track of, so it may help if we provide you with a handy list of the various and sundry Fusion features. Here is said list:

- ✔ **Fusion provides for an integrated service environment as a mechanism to develop services.** Application developers use this environment to actually create business services. It enables them to develop, compose, and orchestrate these services into a business process. Tools for doing so include JDeveloper — the Oracle application development framework — and TopLink, which is a data services framework for accessing both relational data and data in an XML format. Oracle JDeveloper (based on XML) is a development platform that allows developers to model, create, discover, assemble, orchestrate, test, deploy, and maintain composite applications based on services.

- ✔ **Fusion has at its core an enterprise service bus intended to integrate applications.** The Fusion enterprise service bus, like all ESBs, is used as a centralized mechanism for passing messages between components and for transforming messages from one format to another.

- ✔ **Fusion makes use of a service registry that can locate each service and manage the life cycle of the services.** The service registry, based on the UDDI mechanism, provides services that include handling SOA governance and managing life cycles. (UDDI is short for *U*niversal *D*escription, *D*iscovery and *I*ntegration and it's important for SOA because it stores the locations of services so they can be used in composite applications.)

- ✔ **Fusion works with a BPEL-based (standards-based) orchestration engine for tying services into business processes.** Orchestration services control workflow and manage business process. Oracle's Business Process Execution Language (BPEL) Process Manager enables business processes to be modeled, automated, and monitored. It can be used to develop new integration solutions as well as to interface with existing ones.

- ✔ **Fusion has a rules engine that enables customers to store business rules to be used in applications**. IT can use it to find, store, and automate business policies.

- ✔ **Fusion has a robust Web services management and security offering.** Management services are located on a dashboard from which you can monitor and manage security services (and the interactions between these services) in an SOA environment.

✔ **Fusion offers strong data management services.** Such services include support for the major data formats, including SQL, XML, and the XML-based query language called XQuery. Fusion's data management services let you distribute data and include a metadata repository within the Oracle database.

✔ **Fusion offers portal services.** For those of you out there who need a portal refresher, portal services provide a preintegrated environment to build *portals* — a software environment that brings together data and components of information from different applications so they can be displayed in a unified way — that can be customized for different end-user groups in the organization. The portals provide business intelligence and collaboration capabilities to business and IT management.

The Oracle SOA Reference Architecture

All the Oracle SOA components — Oracle Fusion Middleware — described above are illustrated in Figure 23-1. The Service Assembly Framework shown in the center includes the Oracle Application Server. This solution is used to develop, integrate, and deploy applications, portals, and business services and is designed for *grid* computing — the ability to present a series of smaller computers as though it were a larger system and SOA. Various component parts intended to enhance collaboration — software to facilitate and manage business process and rules — are integrated within the Service Assembly Framework. The Oracle Collaboration Suite includes a range of tools for bringing disparate groups of people together.

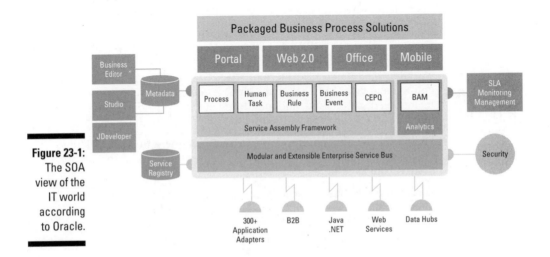

Figure 23-1:
The SOA view of the IT world according to Oracle.

The Oracle Business Intelligence Suite covers Analytics, shown adjacent to the Service Assembly Framework in Figure 21-1. This suite of products includes solutions for dashboard development, proactive intelligence and alerts, real-time predicative intelligence, and mobile analytics, all important for monitoring a SOA environment. The software is designed to operate with a company's existing data sources and systems and is designed to provide information to technical staff responsible for monitoring the environment based on service level agreements (SLA monitoring management). Metadata works in conjunction with the Service Assembly Framework ensuring that there are common definitions in use throughout the SOA environment. Business Editor, Studio, and Oracle JDeveloper represent the SOA tools available to developers.

The enterprise service bus (ESB) is an integral part of the SOA platform. It routes and distributes events between applications and connects existing IT systems with business partners. There are many adapters provided to connect services that may be outside of the SOA environment. In a SOA architecture, services are loosely coupled together in a flexible way. The ESB accesses definitions and other important data about the services from the registry to create this fluidity in the SOA environment. In addition, the ESB facilitates the accessibility of security services required to protect the SOA environment.

Data quality is at the core of SOA and of Oracle's SOA strategy. Oracle's Data Hub products are focused on managing data quality. The Oracle Customer Data Hub is used to centralize, update, and clean customer data. It can be used independently of other Oracle applications.

The Oracle SOA Architecture makes allowances for whatever method or technical environment the end user will be using to access applications. This flexibility is illustrated in Figure 21-1 in the layer showing Portal, Web 2.0, Office, and Mobile as the different types of end-user access. Oracle Portal is a framework for building, deploying, and managing enterprise portals as referenced in the top layer of the diagram, Oracle and its business partners are building industry-specific business process solutions that are based on Oracle's SOA platform.

In the next section, we take a look at how one company has used Oracle's SOA infrastructure to create a flexible platform to more easily change the business. Given the highly competitive nature of the telecommunications industry, SOA was the answer to Helio's needs.

Oracle SOA@work

Helio, a midlevel player in the mobile communications field, was created in 2005 as a $440 million joint venture between SK Telecom and EarthLink. (SK Telecom brought the full force of South Korean advanced wireless technology to the table — handsets with customized multimedia capabilities for communication, social networking, and gaming, for example. Earthlink brought its established business as a well-known Internet Service Provider (ISP) offering both wireless voice and data service. Helio provides devices (and related services) at the more technologically advanced end of the mobile communication field to young and youthful-thinking consumers.

Things hit the ground running in May, 2006, when Helio went live over its high-speed 3G network. The company expects to find a very large (and long pent-up) demand among the younger market for mobile communication technology that will take their wireless connection experiences to a new level.

The U.S mobile market has been slower than the broader global markets to make some of the latest technology readily available — a result, in part, of the lack of a standardized communication technology in the U.S. For example, the high-speed third generation (3G) network that was first introduced commercially in Korea by SK Telecom in 2002 was not brought to the U.S. until 2005.

The business problem

Helio is betting on the fact that exclusive, high-end mobile devices and exclusive services like MySpace Mobile and Helio OnTop will prove so compelling that young people will rush to take full advantage of the features in these new devices. As of July, 2006, MySpace had over 85 million users, all of whom constitute a potential target market for Helio's MySpace mobile offering. This exclusive arrangement provides users with a way to connect to their MySpace account from wherever they are. Helio OnTop, on the other hand, is a programmable, direct feed of channels including news, entertainment, and other information that shows up constantly on the user's device screen. Helio is totally focused on building a brand around mobile service that the young, hip, and connected consumer must have to be socially cool and in the forefront of all the latest technology.

Speed to market was the top priority for Helio. Because it is a business based on bringing the latest and greatest technology to a notoriously fickle market of young consumers, the company knew it needed to act very fast. As soon as the joint venture formed in 2005, Helio began to plan and build the business and IT infrastructure needed to support this new service. One of its top priorities was to build a scalable and reliable infrastructure that would support all business logistics. Early analysis led the company to believe that it would be much more efficient and cost-effective to outsource the logistics services for device distribution support to a third-party trading partner. Right from the beginning, Helio wanted to allocate the majority of its resources to the goal of becoming a great mobile services company. The company did not want a situation where the logistics of building the physical infrastructure interfered with its focus on adding value to the systems and services it provides.

The technical problem

Although Helio expected that outsourcing logistics would be of great benefit as it ramped up its business, this plan added an extra layer of complexity to the work of the technology development in the six-month period prior to the "go-live" date in May, 2006. The department knew it would be challenging to build the IT infrastructure and virtual logistics systems needed internally while creating the framework for integrating with the physical logistics of the third-party partner. In effect, this meant deploying an Enterprise Resource Planning (ERP) system and, at the same time, augmenting it with a highly integrated environment. Brandon Behrstock, Senior Director of Financial Systems, and his IT team at Helio began by evaluating their technology options. Because of the team's familiarity with Enterprise Applications Integration (EAI), a technology they considered a more conventional approach to integrating between multiple applications, this option was considered first. However, the team was concerned that the time spent on traditional EAI would result in a long, cumbersome process that would not allow them to meet their "go live" dates.

In addition, the financial services team at Helio felt that the formal development methodology associated with EAI would not allow the requirements to evolve as the technology system developed. Brandon explained that, although his team was concerned about meeting a very tight deadline, they were also pretty excited by the way this situation challenged them to think creatively and broadly about all the innovative technical choices available. They felt they had greater flexibility than in a more established organization where they would face many hurdles from legacy technology. They were working in a "green field" environment, without any entrenched technology, and so they were a little freer to find the right technology to meet their needs.

Getting started with SOA

The Helio team embarked on its SOA journey with very high expectations and with technology from Oracle. The team chose to implement Oracle Fusion Middleware 10g based on the following three factors:

✔ The technology comes encapsulated in its own preexisting orchestration and development environment that allowed them to develop and test business process flow.

✔ They could rapidly build a prototype to determine if the approach would work.

✔ The graphical development environment user interface appeared highly flexible and easy to understand, which would increase the speed of software development.

Mr. Behrstock said, "We found the development cycle using the Oracle Fusion Middleware to be very flexible, and knew that would be the only way we could make it through rapid deployment when we didn't yet know all our final core requirements. Because we were running so fast, there was no way we could go through all the step-by-step phases of a traditional requirements-design-build approach." Instead, Helio sped up the process by beginning to build some of the most common business services immediately and then followed a process in which the project could be conducted in small increments in order to collect all the requirements while development was already underway. Mr. Behrstock said, "Oracle's flexible environment allowed us to develop, test, and deploy a highly sophisticated platform in just four to five months. This saved us about 50 percent in time and money, and now we have an incredibly scalable and controllable environment that allows us to support our logistics and inventory in the channel. The environment even allowed for changes to the requirements later in the development cycle without causing the delays that these changes would incur in a traditional environment."

The Oracle SOA products they used included the Oracle ebusiness Suite and Oracle Fusion Middleware 10g, which includes the Oracle Application Service, the Oracle BPEL Process Manager, and Oracle Discover. The Oracle BPEL Process Manger provides the orchestration. These products put the power of business processes into the hands of the end users by means of various end-user reporting tools. Oracle Fusion allowed them to quickly build a flexible, declarative (that is, without having to program), extendable environment to manage of all their business processes without building any orchestration or error-handling systems. The graphical Process Manager proved invaluable in creating and correcting business processes without coding.

Helio found that the SOA approach of having the Web services and orchestration together gave it a good way to manage all its processes. The team liked the flexible nature of the approach because they found they could easily build a reusable business service in a declarative development environment, call the business service from any process, and monitor all the business processes in a graphical user interface. They could see results and control them very quickly. After they combined the business services with some of the user-oriented reporting tools in the product suite, IT felt that the SOA approach with the use of Web services interfaces combined with the creation of business services enabled them to put the power and control in the hands of the users who needed the information the most.

Getting started and up to speed on the new technology was very easy for Helio. The six-person ERP systems team was very experienced and had deep knowledge of much of the Oracle platform, but the developers were initially unfamiliar with Oracle BPEL Process Manager. After spending just two days in classes, those new to the environment were able to begin contributing and collaborating with experts right away. The development of business services for the entire logistics environment — a necessary first step in any SOA implementation — got underway immediately.

These business services included key business logistics processes like Procure to Pay and Order to Cash, enabling support of procurement, device shipment, and receipt of payments from resellers. One of the benefits of the Oracle Fusion software was the flexibility it gave to make changes as needed regarding the integration with the outsourced logistics provider. For example, some business services, such as Orders for the Sales of Devices to the Resale Channel, might initially be processed internally. If Helio's sales increased, however, the company might want to move the responsibility for this business process to an outsourced service or to new business partners.

Although each business process may start in one department, it can quickly cut across many departments; new systems may be added, others may be outsourced. All of this means that maintaining fluidity between internal and external processing is crucial if you want your company to grow quickly and efficiently. Helio recognized this and acted accordingly. Helio doesn't think its logistics provider has ever integrated with customers quite so quickly. The company was used to deploying smaller initiatives over time and usually to using more traditional ways of integrating applications such as using Enterprise Applications Integration (EAI) environments.

Monitoring the health of a SOA

Overall the monitoring capabilities of Oracle Fusion Middleware 10g have proved helpful to everyone in the business. Helio has used the health monitoring information for systems operations and other end-user reporting and notification capabilities for the business. Oracle Discoverer (a component of the Oracle Business Intelligence product) is used to provide reports for management to give rapid insight into how the business is doing. Helio has also provided multiple dashboards for different business management and technical end-user groups with a need to monitor the key aspects of the business from the supply chain to sales to technical maintenance and systems operations.

Mr. Behrstock was pleasantly surprised at the robust monitoring and troubleshooting capabilities of the Oracle suite. It provides his team with a powerful technical (yet graphical) interface for tracking every process in its flow. The red and yellow signals on the graphical interface are easy to read and very informative, making it easy to locate errors. There are also sensors and notification functionality provided as part of the BPEL process interfaces. Mr. Behrstock said, "We are able to find issues earlier and control processes better. We have full visibility into the data and processes, which allows us to monitor the business and see how we are performing."

Next steps

Implementing the new technology by using a SOA approach helped Helio get to where they wanted to be in time for launch. The team members also expect that the reusable business services and the technical infrastructure they have created will provide them with the flexibility to support future initiatives. One new initiative on the horizon is the opening of several retail stores. These stores would need on-demand access to customer and inventory information. Helio feels that with the power of the Oracle BPEL tool, it can reduce the complexities of additional integrations such as a point-of-sale system or integration to support new retail stores. Reducing the complexity means faster, more cost-effective results. Mr. Behrstock is confident that "with this tool we can integrate just about anything and bring it up quickly in a scalable and reliable fashion."

Chapter 24

Microsoft and SOA

● ●

In This Chapter

▶ Much ado about Microsoft

▶ MS SOA

▶ Meet Jack Henry

● ●

*W*e think you know pretty darn well who Microsoft is, but in case you don't know all the details, Bill Gates and Paul Allen founded Microsoft in 1975 in Albuquerque, New Mexico. The company's first product was a version of the popular computer language called BASIC for an early microcomputer called the Altair 8800. But the company really emerged out of the shadows in the 1980s when it was contracted by IBM to create a version of the DOS operating system for the original IBM Personal Computer.

Microsoft was able to use its market position to evolve its operating system franchise with the development of Microsoft Windows in 1983. It was a commercial success in 1990 with the release of Windows 3.0. Again, Microsoft used this successful launch to continue to add products to its portfolio. These products included Microsoft Word, Excel, PowerPoint, and Access, all of which were eventually packaged as Microsoft Office.

Over time, Microsoft moved from the desktop and office focus to a focus on the enterprise. Over the years, it added products such as the Microsoft SQL Server database and various middleware platform technologies such as Microsoft.Net and the Microsoft Live Communications Server, with a focus on enterprise computing. In addition, Microsoft offers its Microsoft Dynamics suite, a series of packaged software offerings dealing with supply chain management, customer relationship management, and financial management. These software solutions work with Microsoft Office products and use the capabilities of Microsoft technologies like Microsoft Servers and Microsoft.NET.

Microsoft identified the significance of service orientation and Web services, including the building of applications that rely on abstraction (See Chapter 13 for more on abstraction) and the passing of messages. Microsoft has expanded and developed its application platform to support these key goals and industry trends.

NET SOA Microsoft gives customers who enable a SOA the freedom to implement their technology platform in a variety of different ways. Microsoft's philosophy is to provide different components that customers can combine to meet their unique needs. The company takes a very individualized approach to customer SOA implementations, so it should come as no surprise that consulting services are a very important part of Microsoft's SOA strategy. Microsoft Consulting Services and Microsoft partners, like Geniant, are often involved with customer implementations. Microsoft sees one of the key customer challenges to be adding Web services interfaces to existing software components so, by adding process rules, they can be combined with other services.

Some of the Microsoft products that support SOA include:

- **Microsoft Windows Server**: An infrastructure platform for connecting applications, networks, and Web services.

- **Microsoft Dynamics**: Software used to automate financial, customer relationship, supply chain management, and other business processes.

- **Microsoft BizTalk Server**: Microsoft's business process management (BPM) server known as the BizTalk Server. It includes tools to design, develop, deploy, and manage a company's business processes. The BizTalk Server has an integration layer used to add Web service interfaces to a company's applications as services for their end users and trading partners. In addition, BizTalk Server includes the underlying infrastructure for exchanging messages between services or components and an engine that manages the communication between different services.

  To be more precise, the BizTalk Server, the Windows Communication Foundation (WCF), and other integration tools on the Windows platform handle the messaging technologies required for integrating services. The BizTalk Server functions as an integration and business process server. The Windows Communication Foundation is the framework for building Web services in a secure way. The two combine to provide messaging, message validation and transformation, business process orchestration and management, and business activity monitoring and rules management. Microsoft provides the integration technologies included in BizTalk Server as an alternative to an enterprise service bus (ESB).

✔ **Microsoft.NET**: A development framework for building new applications and Web services. The .NET framework (pronounced "dot net," by the way) is technology that cuts across vendor-platform boundaries. Microsoft and other major technology vendors (IBM, BEA, and TIBCO, to name a few) recognize how important this is to their customers. The vendors collaborated on extending messaging capabilities across multiple vendor technologies, and each one did individual research and development in this area as well.

Microsoft.NET incorporates standards such as XML that are used to connect systems, applications, and devices in a SOA environment. The .NET framework allows developers to create an environment comprised of different software languages that work together. Developers have a wide choice of programming languages, giving them more flexibility. This makes it easier and more cost-effective to build applications that integrate with legacy applications and the applications of customers and partners.

✔ **Microsoft SharePoint Services:** Windows SharePoint Services acts as the foundation for collaboration across client and server environments and is a component of the Windows Server. It is used to create Web sites for sharing and document collaboration and provides a platform for application development focused on well-established sharing and communication services like portals and Web-based conferencing. Microsoft has been developing additional applications by using the Window SharePoint Services platform as a base. For example, Microsoft now offers a collaborative portal application called the Microsoft Office SharePoint Server, which is based on Windows SharePoint Services.

✔ **Windows Workflow Foundations:** This is both a programming model and a programming engine with all the tools necessary for the development of both human and system workflow systems. Examples of these workflows include process flows based on business rules, workflows for systems management, and composite workflows within a SOA. The components include a .NET Framework and an in-process workflow engine.

✔ **Windows Communication Foundation:** Windows Communication Foundation is a set of .NET technologies focused on the communications infrastructure needed in a SOA environment. These messaging technologies (the stuff that lets the various components of a SOA talk to each other, for starters) simplify the development and running of systems. They include standards-based support for secure and reliable messaging under multiple environments. These work with Windows Vista™ as well as with Windows XP and Windows Server 2003.

✔ **SQL Server Database Services:** Microsoft SQL Server provides information as a service. As companies move to a SOA and they begin to turn their business processes into services, the traditional database must change or the business will lose many of the benefits of this new approach. It is not enough for the applications to communicate with each other; the business, their partners, and customers all need to communicate with the database *in the same way.* The data must be made available as a service to allow this communication. Microsoft's SQL Server includes a service broker that, along with the XML capabilities of the server, can be used to create database services. Business rules can be implemented by using Microsoft.NET.

Banking on SOA

Jack Henry & Associates (JHA) of Missouri provides technology systems to financial services firms. The company has been in business since 1976, when it started out by selling software to small community banks to help them with their core data processing and information management requirements. As ATM usage and then online banking grew in importance, JHA added lots of related applications to its core systems to include functions such as ATM management, electronic banking, and debit card and electronic check processing.

JHA provides services to help companies with the deployment of their hardware and software. In addition, many of their customers outsource a portion of their financial processing activities to JHA. JHA has approximately 7000 customers. About 34 percent of these customers are small banks and credit unions deploying the core systems and about 66percent are banks and other financial institutions deploying ancillary products. JHA's core banking software applications remain strong with its traditional customer base of small to mid-size U.S. banks and credit unions. However, much of the future growth is expected to come from the larger banks and other financial institutions that are interested in JHA's growing portfolio of complementary services and their outsourcing capabilities.

Over the course of the past few years, JHA has pursued an aggressive strategy of expanding its offerings for the electronic banking and Internet security needs of their core customers. It has done this both through internal software development and by acquiring some 14 companies over the course of 2005-2006. Its expanded portfolio of offerings (in combination with the company's move into SOA) has positioned it to provide services for an expanded market of larger banks both in the U.S. and internationally. It has also broadened offerings of software and outsourcing solutions to expand its industry focus to include insurance and healthcare. JHA is a public company with 2005 revenues of $535.9 million.

The business problem

JHA has five core banking software packages for banks and credit unions. The complementary applications have been added to the core banking products in a way that makes them tightly connected to the base application. This is a traditional approach to software development, and it worked well for a time, but JHA recognized several limitations to this approach.

First, a customer had to buy the core product in order to benefit from any of the ancillary solutions, and this fact limited JHA's market for these solutions to their traditional customer base of small community banks and credit unions.

JHA determined that many of the supplementary capabilities such as Internet banking, security, cash management and item processing, and electronic check processing could stand alone as strong offerings that would appeal to larger banks throughout the world. If JHA wanted to broaden its market reach to include larger financial institutions, it must decouple the supplementary applications from the core. (Many of these larger banks have extensive legacy systems and are not interested in switching to the core JH software products.)

The second major limitation of its traditional approach to software development was the time and expense of integrating new applications into the core products. JHA needed a way to reuse software code instead of repeating the same procedures over and over.

The SOA solution

After the company realized how important it was to decouple the tight linkages between its core products and the growing number of complementary products it offered, it considered the technical implications of actually carrying out this decoupling. The number-one priority for the company was finding a fast, efficient, and cost-effective way to integrate all the new technologies with its product suite so JHA could make them available to existing customers as soon as possible.

Although the emphasis was on what was best for its existing customer base, the solution JHA came up with also had to provide a better way to bring its products to a larger market. In order to achieve both of these goals, JHA had to consider many related technical challenges. Its top business and technical priorities moving forward were as follows:

✔ To share information across all the newly acquired companies

✔ To increase reuse of software code

✔ To speed development time

✔ To roll out new product releases more easily

✔ To create more robust interfaces and better backward compatibility

✔ To create an open standards approach for software to increase JHA's compatibility with as many partners and third-party vendors as possible

✔ To ease integration with business partners

The next sections spell out how JHA went about handling these priorities.

Expanding opportunities for growth with SOA

JHA originally looked at SOA as a way to integrate technologies quickly into its product suite and serve the needs of its existing customer base. It listened to customers and heard that they were constantly challenged by the demands of integrating products from various software vendors. Customers wanted to shift resources away from application integration to core business practices.

Debbie Wood, the General Manager of Marketing and Industry Research for Jack Henry & Associates, said "Around the same time that the company was looking at SOA for our own products and our own customers, we also made a strategic move within the company to start selling outside our own customer base. We found that we could go to non-core customers and sell non-core products, but that this strategy would also require a SOA solution."

JHA recognized that it had the potential to sell more of its products if it made them more open and more compatible with other third-party products, including those of their top competitors. This was a competitive differentiator that could open the door for future growth. This shift in thinking allowed the company to envision that if it could make its products more open — thus allowing them to connect more easily with a host of other vendor products its customers used — it would make those products more desirable.

SOA provided the pathway for JHA to move in its new strategic direction of openness, integration, and compatibility with other vendor solutions by implementing a SOA strategy. Because of the adoption of open interfaces, JHA was more easily able to develop and acquire new technologies to create better quality software for its small banking and credit union customers.

An aggressive acquisition strategy like JHA's is always expensive. It would have been a high-risk strategy for JHA if it had to restrict its market opportunity to the traditional customer base. The SOA approach is what made the JHA business strategy achievable and cost-effective. SOA helped JHA to act on a plan that allowed the company to bring the best technology to its existing customers and, at the same time, expand into new markets that would drive the company forward and allow it to compete in a larger marketplace. JHA decided that they wanted Microsoft technology on their side and found a Microsoft strategic implementation partner to get started on their SOA journey.

Working with Geniant and Microsoft technology

JHA contracted with Geniant, an IT consulting firm based in Texas. Geniant is a Microsoft Gold Partner with extensive expertise in SOA. In 2004-2005, Geniant assisted JHA with the development of a pilot project to construct the framework for its SOA implementation.

jXchange is the name chosen for the JHA platform. Two to three people from Geniant worked on the pilots and then collaborated with four people from the JHA IT staff over the two and a half year development period for this project. JHA decided to deploy the Microsoft.NET platform because it was in wide use and, after seeing the results of some pilot projects, the company determined the Microsoft solution would be a cost-effective approach.

JHA also knew that most of its core customers had some sort of Microsoft network deployed so that the technology would be familiar to its customer base as well. The products deployed for this initiative included the Microsoft.NET Framework, Microsoft Windows Server 2003 (as the operating system), SQL Server 2000 and Visual Studio.NET 2003. In addition, Microsoft Web Services Enhancements (WSE), a set of developer tools provided as an add-on to the .NET framework, was used to help speed up the development process.

The software developers for jXchange wrote the program in C#, using an XML messaging layer. They used UDDI — a SOA directory service — to help find and publish business services. The JHA team felt they were able to keep development time short while improving software quality with the .NET platform. JHA now has an integration development group that includes a staff of 18 IT architects and additional support staff. The work of the development group is centered on jExhange and some other integration duties.

Creating business services

JHA is in the process of putting XML-based interfaces on its software components for its various product lines. This has allowed JHA to create new product offerings by combining these components in different ways to meet changing business opportunities. Kevin Sligar, Integration Development Manager for Jack Henry & Associates, said, "This is a significant effort. We are currently well into the process of service-enabling our flagship product so it will be available for third-party usage. We are also working to service-enable our core credit union product. It already has a messaging layer, but it is not Web-services based so we will be working on that as well."

The company will convert all JHA products from proprietary technology into standards-based products so that it has a complete integration platform for third-party products. This eliminates the need for all sorts of customized interfaces between third-party vendors that JHA or their customers formerly had to create. The service-enabled products are now composed of flexible, reusable containers of code representing important business processes.

Examples of these codified business processes or business services include: Get Account Balance, Place a Stop Hold on an Account, Transfer Funds, and Make a Deposit. Both Internet banking solutions and telephone response solutions can use Place a Stop Hold on an Account. In the past, each of these two solutions would have used separate embedded code to place a stop hold on an account. Now each of these solutions can call the same business service, saving on software development time and maintenance.

The move to SOA required JHA's developers to think about software coding in a different way. The consulting and development support from Geniant personnel was very helpful because they had a lot of experience with SOA. JHA's developers were ready for this transition. They understood how some of the limitations of the traditional style of development prevented IT from keeping up with the goals of the business.

From day one on this project, IT was determined to increase code reuse, and the technical team recognized that creating interoperability between products — setting things up so that two different components could be easily linked together without complex programming — was the way of the future. Sligar said his group was looking to the future and notes that, ". . . to be service-enabled means our products will be able to enjoy a long life cycle."

Senior and executive management at JHA also connected with the SOA vision. Sligar said that senior management was behind the move to SOA and felt that ". . . to be open to our customers' needs and to fulfill those needs we needed to be able to service-enable our products." With business and IT supporting this initiative, it clearly became a top priority, even preempting other projects.

Some concern existed, however, that because it was creating products that could fit into virtually any standards-based technology environment, JHA was exposing the company to a greater degree of competition. However, its experience has been that the use of open standards and SOA has helped it close more deals more quickly. For example, in a competitive selling situation, the sales team for JHA's document imaging product find their jobs easier now that they are able to say the integration will be fast and easy because they have service-enabled the software.

Some of the most immediate benefits of the move to SOA are the shortened development times stemming from the increased reusability of software code. According to Sligar, "Software code reuse is one of the top benefits of SOA. We basically design and code the functionality one time to be used by many in a format that is common to all."

The company is beginning to see these benefits take hold. Sligar continued, "We can see golden apples at the end in that ease of use and ease of integration and maintenance are the goals we are shooting for and we can see that they are attainable." The company has attracted and retained customers that it would not have without a SOA strategy. Sligar advises other companies moving to SOA to understand that SOA does not happen overnight. After you jump in, you must be ready for the long haul, but the benefits will be worth the effort.

Chapter 25

SAP SOA

*I*n the real world of enterprise IT, you might find products from every major SOA vendor all within the same organization. We encourage you to embrace diversity. Understand the strengths of various offerings so that you can make informed decisions. That's what the big kids do.

You and Me and SAP

SOA's not just for Americans any more. German software leader SAP has joined the throng of software vendors plying SOA software. In fact, many of the largest companies throughout the world use one or more offerings from the SAP software product line to store and manage information from key functional areas, including operations, finances, sales, and human resources.

SAP (short for Systems, Applications, and Products in Data Processing) was originally founded in Germany in 1972 by five former IBM employees who visualized an opportunity to provide businesses with a packaged solution of financial business processes. The former IBMers decided on this business plan after observing the repetition and similarities that occurred in software programs created for their consulting clients. The adoption of the software that came out of their vision (Enterprise Resource Planning software, also known as ERP software) was fairly rapid among large enterprises, and SAP grew very quickly. In the 1980s, SAP expanded their software offerings to include the MySAP Business Suite of solutions for Customer Relationship Management (CRM), Supply Chain Management (SCM), and Supplier Relationship Management (SRM).

Today, with 33,000 customers worldwide, SAP thinks that many of their customers could gain additional efficiency and flexibility by implementing a service oriented architecture to overcome some of the inherent challenges of integrating information across diverse applications.

SAP developed the first versions of their ERP system at the end of the 1970s, and they designed it to run on mainframe computers. You can imagine that the ERP system has gone through a number of changes in the course of the three decades that have since flowed under the bridge. In the 1990s, the ERP system was based on a client/server approach including UNIX and Microsoft platforms. It evolved to embrace Internet technologies and can now offer, with the introduction of its NetWeaver software program, its own integration software for use across its various software modules.

Enterprise Service Oriented Architecture

SAP's most recent transformation involves the addition of a service oriented architecture strategy called Enterprise Service Oriented Architecture (Enterprise SOA) to its offerings. Enterprise SOA is a framework built on top of SAP's NetWeaver middleware and then combined with what SAP calls its "composite application environment." SAP customers can combine component parts to meet specific business objectives without having to start from scratch. Using this architectural approach, SAP itself is beginning to build new packaged functionality to meet new customer needs more quickly. They're accomplishing this goal by creating composite applications from SOA-based building blocks.

By putting themselves in SAP's hands, companies have been able to retire aging and ineffective homegrown applications and move to new packaged enterprise applications that SAP has designed around best practices. Companies that needed help in establishing consistent business practices found that using SAP's structured approach was a practical way to move forward.

SAP is continuing to transform their applications and middleware structure for SOA. Here's their plan:

- ✔ SAP will continue to transform its ERP platform into a set of modular business services.

- ✔ SAP has started to work with complementary software partners. These partners are expected to use SAP's NetWeaver platform in order to do business with SAP. Fast workers that they are, SAP already has several hundred partners.

✔ SAP is leveraging its knowledge of specific industries (such as automotive, life sciences, insurance, and so on) to add new, smaller packaged software offerings that can work well with its ERP system software.

SAP's ERP applications should become a lot more flexible in the coming years. The key to success, from the customer perspective, will be to insist that all these approaches focus on interoperability and ease of implementation.

Figure 25-1 gives you a bird's-eye view of the SAP reference architecture for Enterprise SOA. SAP's NetWeaver platform, smack-dab in the middle of the figure, provides the foundation for the architecture. Its main component is the Enterprise Services Repository, which SAP views as the central piece of this architecture and one of their key offerings.

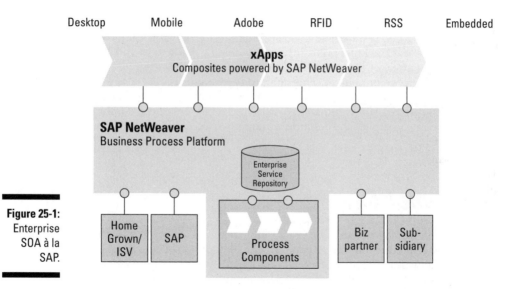

Figure 25-1: Enterprise SOA à la SAP.

This repository is the container for all the data needed to design a new business service, including data about the business process. Each service is created with an appropriate and accurate understanding of the rules of the business. The repository includes pointers to the location of existing business services and descriptions of how to create the linkages between different policies, metadata, and other business services.

The tier labeled xApps in Figure 25-1 refers to the packaged composite applications that SAP and their partners create and sell as software products for specific industries. You (and other applications) can access these composite applications in many different ways. The headings shown at the top of the figure (computer desktops, mobile devices, Adobe technology, RFID tags — radio frequency identification, RSS — really simple syndication used to deliver content, and embedded devices) represent the different user interfaces.

SAP provides adapters for connecting many types of applications into the SOA platform, including homegrown applications (applications developed by an organization's own developers), applications developed by independent software vendors (ISVs) and applications purchased by the organization, as well as applications developed by SAP, SAP's business partners, or an organization's subsidiary business(es). Applications written by SAP and their business partners are more tightly linked into NetWeaver and Enterprise Services Repository, as illustrated in Figure 25-1. The process components represent the business processes described by the application.

SAP customers can create their own new enterprise services — ones that meet the very specific needs of each of their organizations — but they can also use the Enterprise Services Repository to access and use an expanding inventory of enterprise services created and provided by the Enterprise Services Community. This community is made up of SAP customers who may create business services for their own organizations and then make those services available to share with other members of the community. These enterprise services include commonly used business processes, such as Create a New Order for a Customer or Hire an Employee.

Whirlpool Does SOA

You can find Whirlpool Corporation's appliances in homes throughout the world. The company's product line includes a full line of major laundry and kitchen appliances, such as washing machines, refrigerators, and dishwashers, as well as smaller appliances, such as mixers. The products are manufactured in close to 50 different locations worldwide, and those products are sold through distributors and retailers in over 170 countries under a total of nine different brand names. In addition, Whirlpool manufactures appliances for the Sears Holding Corporation, and those appliances are then sold under the Kenmore brand. With some $19 billion in annual revenue, that's a lot of appliances.

Because many consumers view appliances as commodities, the price competition in this industry can be fierce. With prices forced lower, Whirlpool's budget for innovation was necessarily tighter. Whirlpool controlled costs by driving increased operational efficiencies. Its growth strategy focused on building customer loyalty through product innovation.

Whirlpool IT ponders the problem

Esat Sezer, Whirlpool's Chief Information Officer, told us how the company embarked on a plan to implement SAP's Enterprise SOA to help achieve these corporate goals. He started off by noting that the IT organization at Whirlpool was very complex, based as it was on the challenges of keeping track of many different products and brands produced and distributed throughout the world. (To make things even more complex, Whirlpool acquired Maytag in 2006 for $2.6 billion, which added yet another level to the IT infrastructure.)

As Sezer saw it, the enterprise needed to integrate many different sources of information from different locations to monitor and optimize procurement, operations, and distribution on a global basis. The company knew they needed to improve access to information on customers across the different brands to help the company innovate based on a customer's needs and changing life-style. Whirlpool also knew that they needed more efficient access to operational information across the different manufacturing centers to successfully develop appliances that were different from their competitors' offerings.

Whirlpool IT management had a clear understanding of where they wanted the company to go, but they were left feeling stuck. IT developers had to spend so much time maintaining and working around the complexity of the IT infrastructure that they had little time to develop innovative solutions. Whirlpool was already successfully using SAP's ERP, SCM, and CRM solutions. The company looked to Enterprise SOA to help IT align their goals and priorities with the business priorities.

One example of how Whirlpool implemented SAP's Enterprise SOA is in the area of product information synchronization. Whenever Whirlpool introduces a new product, all the business partners they trade with need quick access to the new product information so they can update their own systems. The trading partners need to enter product description details for each new unit of inventory, including such information as unit price, color, dimensions, and promotional activities.

In the past, Whirlpool made sure that all the information got to the right places by using point-to-point file transfers, meaning product description data went from Whirlpool to each business partner. This file transfer process demands a lot of time from Whirlpool's IT staff. In addition, the IT department needed staff with experience in many different technologies, such as Electronic Data Interchange (EDI) and networking, in order to keep up with this process.

Whirlpool made a decision to outsource this capability to SAP. The company uses SAP R/3 — SAP's most popular version of its ERP system — to manage the master data. Now, the updated product data automatically goes into the Master Data Management (MDM) tool in SAP's NetWeaver. The MDM tool takes the data and moves it into the electronic exchange infrastructure managed by the Uniform Code Council (UCC). (The UCC is an association that provides and administers codes to help businesses keep track of products. The organization provides the UPC or bar codes that you find on the packaging of most products you buy in a store.) All of Whirlpool's trading partners subscribe to the UCC electronic exchange, which uses industry standards to transfer information on products between companies that supply and purchase those products.

The Whirlpool IT staff had been so caught up in the maintenance of the company's technology systems that there were too few resources available to achieve the kind of technical innovation that the business needed to achieve its growth goals. Now that SAP has brought Enterprise SOA to Whirlpool, IT has become more efficient and developers are able to focus on projects that make the company more competitive.

Making Whirlpool work better on the Web

Most consumers of Whirlpool appliances today begin their search for product information on the Web. Whirlpool is well aware of this fact and recognizes that the future growth of their company in many ways depends upon their ability to provide a high-quality online purchasing experience for consumers. Due to factors that will soon become clear (see the following paragraph), providing such a quality experience was very hard for Whirlpool to achieve — at least before Enterprise SOA came along.

In the past, each brand had their own consumer Web site, each developed with a different technology. Maintaining the various brand Web sites was very inefficient. In addition, there were "never enough artistic abilities on hand to get the quality required for a top performing consumer Web site," according to Sezer. Implementing Enterprise SOA provided Whirlpool with a way to reach a higher level of consistency and quality among the Web sites for the various brands.

Now, maintaining the Web sites is much more efficient because of the reusability of the enterprise business services used in the sites' development. IT works with the Master Data Management capabilities of NetWeaver to ensure that all the customer and product data across brands is available when needed. Sezer states that, as a result, "the consumer experience on the Whirlpool-branded Web sites is quite differentiated from competitors."

Efficiency is always a good thing, but Sezer points to other benefits that have come with the adoption of the Enterprise SOA platform. For example, Whirlpool has benefited greatly from the open architecture of the Enterprise SOA platform, which has made it increasingly easy for Whirlpool to include Web services from other platforms. But, if asked to point to the one major benefit they've experienced since the changeover, Sezer would settle on the benefits that come from moving from a complicated way of doing things to a simple way of doing things. Sure, the initial value of Enterprise SOA comes from operating cost reduction, but the real value comes when you see that you no longer need to maintain complicated technology in order to get things done. In the end, all this complicated technology gets replaced with a unified platform developed by SAP — and simplifying the infrastructure in this fashion frees up the resources you need to create new competing products.

Based on the work Whirlpool IT has done with Enterprise SOA, the business now recognizes the positive impact that IT has had on customer satisfaction. As a result, IT has been successful at getting approval for more expenditures. IT spending has doubled in the past two years, and the business is seeing the benefit in terms of competitive advantage. Sezer expects that, over time, IT operating costs will begin to decline, and Whirlpool will be able to focus on product offerings that make them stand out from the competition and become more efficient year after year.

Chapter 26

(J)Bossing SOA

*I*n telling you that JBoss is an open source platform for SOA, we're opening up a field of inquiry — the open source field — that we could conceivably plow for another 1,000 pages. That's our way of saying that the whole topic of open source deserves more space than we can give it in a book that's supposed to be about service oriented architecture. If pushed into a corner, though, we can radically oversimplify things and tell you that the open source movement leverages the work of an extended community to create (and better) the development of technologies for common use by the community. Open source software is commonly thought of as free, but under the cosmic law of "there's no such thing as a free lunch," distributing and maintaining open source software inevitably costs something. Open source, even when you pay for support, tends to cost less than similar products from proprietary vendors, and if you know enough to know what you're doing, you should certainly consider investing in open source software. That said, we'll return now to our previously scheduled program.

Who's da Boss?

JBoss is a division of Red Hat software, a company that offers a version of the Linux open source operating system. Like its parent company, JBoss's offerings are based on an open source model, which means that they add capabilities to the basic functions of their software and work with a community of developers who add even more value and content to the company's offerings, but that the company actually earns its money from servicing and supporting their products. The flagship of their product line is the JBoss Enterprise

Middleware Suite (JEMS), a collection of open source products for creating and deploying e-business applications within a SOA environment. Some of the products included in JEMS are the JBoss Application Server, the JBoss Portal, JBoss Rules, and JBoss Messaging. JBoss views SOA as the driving force behind its software and services offerings.

Marc Fleury founded JBoss in 1999, when he released the open source JBoss Application Server, which was based on the Java software development framework called the J2EE platform. The Application Server can work on many different platforms — as long as the platform supports Java. After JBoss was incorporated in 2004, the company added other products and is now an open source middleware vendor.

SOA for everyone

The JBoss middleware platform is an open source framework for SOA. One big goal for JBoss is to make SOA affordable, especially for companies trying to hold down IT costs. The license costs for the technology are free. The costs to the customer come from the maintenance, service, and support provided by JBoss.

The JBoss SOA framework is called JEMS, short for the JBoss Enterprise Middleware Suite. The suite integrates technologies and a variety of tools that JBoss has acquired over the past four years. JBoss supports federated architecture — a way for independent services and applications to be seamlessly connected to each other — and integrates components through the JBoss enterprise service bus. (We talk a lot about federation in Chapter 5, if you'd care to thumb back.)

JBoss has developed an extensive set of service offerings to support their open source technology — service offerings that end up representing pretty much their entire revenue stream, in a purely open source fashion. A significant part of their service involves sending developer teams to work alongside a customer's IT staff. Talk about personal service!

Looking at JEMS

The open source model is characterized by the donation of successful technology that has itself been developed by using open source software. The JBoss enterprise service bus (ESB) is the glue that brings all the components of JBoss Enterprise Middleware Suite (JEMS) together — and the JBoss ESB is a prime example of how such a donation works in practice.

JBoss actually got its ESB (playfully named "Rosetta") from Aviva Canada, one of the largest insurance companies in Canada. The company donated the ESB to JBoss, and then JBoss immediately made it available as open source technology. As evidence of the truth of the phrase "what goes around comes around," a JBoss technical support team was there for Aviva Canada every step of the way as Rosetta was put together — with the help of the JBoss Application Server and the JBoss Eclipse Integrated Development Environment (IDE), by the way — and the support team was also there to receive (and pass on) the fruits of their collaboration.

All in all, Aviva Canada spent four months developing their ESB by using JEMS, and they'd been using it for about three years when they made the donation to JBoss. So the technology had already been tested in a real-world environment by the time Aviva Canada donated it to JBoss and JBoss made it available for general use.

Aviva Canada created the ESB to help them share claims, product, and financial data across multiple disparate systems within their organization. (With over 2 million customers to deal with, that's a lot of sharing.) Their goal was to simplify the IT infrastructure and create a more cost-effective way of sharing information that was coming from their many legacy systems — goals shared by many enterprises looking at SOA solutions to their business and IT problems.

This is no bargain basement ESB. The JBoss enterprise service bus includes many of the features of pricier offerings, including a service registry and repository to aid in the governance of business services and support for multiple messaging services (such as JBoss MQ and the IBM MQSeries) to provide flexibility.

JBoss service offerings

Like other open source vendors, JBoss provides a spectrum of services, including the following:

- ✔ **A JBoss subscription:** Expert technical support for all stages of the application life cycle, certified downloads, and access to JBoss Operations Network (JBoss ON, an enterprise management platform for tracking application performance, provisioning new JEMS environments, and applying software updates and patches to single applications or across enterprise clusters).

- ✔ **Consulting services:** Consulting teams can come on-site to help customers design, develop, or deploy JEMS applications. Specialty consulting programs include a Migration Consulting program that assists

customers in migrating applications from other application servers to
the JBoss Application Server.

✔ **Training and Certification:** Parent company Red Hat provides training
for the JBoss Enterprise Middleware Suite (JEMS). Such training services
are designed for developers, architects, and administrators. Red Hat
delivers a wide range of JEMS training courses around the world.

The JBoss View

Figure 26-1 illustrates how JBoss lines things up when it comes to implementing its SOA architecture.

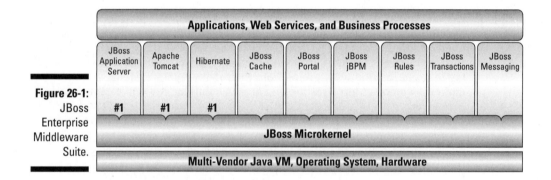

Figure 26-1:
JBoss
Enterprise
Middleware
Suite.

The complete JBoss Enterprise Middleware Suite includes the following
components:

✔ **The JBoss Application Server:** JBoss AS 4.0, a J2EE application server
(for running Java applications), was the first open source application
server to achieve J2EE 1.4 certification. It provides security, transaction
support, resource management, load balancing (where code residing on
different servers can be redistributed to make the system run more efficiently), and clustering (where different servers are loosely coupled
together so they can operate as one unified server).

✔ **Apache Tomcat:** Tomcat is the market's dominant open source Java
Servlet engine, which also happens to be the default Web container
within the JBoss Application Server.

✔ **Hibernate:** Hibernate is the persistence engine that popularized
object/relational mapping (ORM) for Java. (Persistence engines are software components that guarantee that data held in memory and used by

application components are stored (or *persist*) after use, in case you were curious about that.)

✔ **JBoss Cache:** This product was designed to cache frequently accessed Java objects in order to improve the application performance.

✔ **JBoss Portal:** Everyone needs a portal framework, and here's one based on Java.

✔ **JBoss jBPM:** As the BPM in the name makes clear, JBoss jBPM is a *business process management tool* — an embeddable workflow and orchestration engine that supports the most common workflow patterns, to be more precise. You can use JBoss jBPM for simple projects, or it can be scaled to work with more complex Java applications.

✔ **JBoss Rules:** The "Rules" in JBoss Rules refers to a standards-based business rules engine that supports access, change, and management of business policy.

✔ **JBoss Transactions:** Transactions make the (business) world go 'round; JBoss Transactions, a distributed transaction management engine that has been on the market for 20 years, makes that world go 'round a bit more easily.

✔ **JBoss Messaging:** This open source and standards-based messaging platform enables the development of portable, transaction-driven messaging applications (allowing all the components of a SOA environment to talk with each other).

✔ **JBoss Eclipse IDE:** The IDE here is short for *Integrated Development Environment,* a set of plug-ins that enable developers to build, test, and debug applications by using Eclipse, an open source development platform. These application components can then be deployed within the JBoss Application Server.

Polking around SOA

R. L. Polk is a privately held global firm based in Southfield, Michigan. They have operations in France, Germany, Spain, the Netherlands, the U.K., Japan, China, Australia, Canada, and the U.S. Their business is collecting global automotive market data, such as sales, registration, and auto-industry demographic statistics. They provide analysis and forecasts to automotive manufacturers, distributors, suppliers, and other companies with an interest in the automotive market — everything from sales and registrations by brand, vehicle class, and region, to vehicle customer loyalty.

R. L. Polk used SOA to increase the overall flexibility and efficiency of their business processes. The company implemented JBoss Application Server and Hibernate as the technology foundation for their SOA approach to the collection, analysis, and distribution of auto-industry market data. Previously, independent data stores required significant manual intervention to ensure accurate delivery of information to customers. Moving to SOA allowed the company to increase the timeliness, accuracy, and quality of information delivered to customers.

The business challenge

Anticipating that compliance regulations would continue to increase — a trend destined to add additional complexity to the utilization of auto-market data — R. L. Polk decided they needed a whole new approach to the way they collected and distributed data. The company provides automotive statistics and analysis to all the major manufacturers in the automotive industry, and it wanted to maintain its strong position in the industry by responding to customer demand for more timely high-quality data.

R. L. Polk's existing business processes included many manual steps for everything from loading data from different data sources to research for quality checks. In order to maintain its competitive advantage, the company wanted to

✔ Increase the timeliness and completeness of data delivered to customers.

✔ Automate the process by which they ensure data quality so that the quality of data would remain high and the data would be available faster.

✔ Add flexibility to the business process so that they could offer new data and services to customers quickly and easily.

The main business for R. L. Polk involves first collecting, reviewing, and analyzing automotive industry data and then delivering useful information about this data to their customers. They've been doing this for such a long time that their legacy information systems are well established and the number and variety of data sources have steadily increased. Even though they had long-established relationships with all the major automotive manufacturers, R. L. Polk felt that if a competitor figured out a faster and more efficient way to deliver the information, Polk could lose their competitive advantage.

The IT challenge

The data collected by R. L. Polk comes from a variety of state governments, as well as from numerous automotive manufacturers. That adds up to 240 different sources of data that need to be entered and checked for accuracy and completeness. Prior to the SOA implementation, these data were stored in various independent data stores in R. L. Polk's mainframe computers.

In pre-SOA days, the company used many manual steps to get the data into the right format, and they needed many hours to check for accuracy. In the legacy environment, data arrived at all hours of the day or sometimes in the middle of the night. Systems spent hours processing the data, prior to analysts checking for accuracy before it was ready for analytical applications.

The company knew that their manual processes were slowing down the delivery of quality information. For example, if data was received late at night, the processing step might not begin until the next day. IT decided to automate the manual tasks and move to a SOA environment to help them deliver the information faster.

R. L. Polk created a new subsidiary, RLPTechnologies, charged with the mission of implementing a SOA to collect, analyze, and distribute auto-industry data in a highly efficient and flexible way. They hired approximately 35 new IT staff so their group would have the necessary technology skills. (JBoss development skills were a must, for example.) They also moved some of their existing IT developers to this new subsidiary so they could maintain continuity of knowledge of internal systems and the industry. Polk wanted to complete this very large project within 13 months, so they supplemented their core team with consultants on a temporary basis, increasing the total number of team members on this project to as many as 130 people at the height of the project.. They also purchased new hardware and software that required hiring developers with a new skill set.

According to Norman Marks, VP of Sales and Marketing for RLPTechnologies, the company was "looking for a single source of the truth," and they didn't think they could reach this goal by continuing with any of their old methods. Making a decision to stop using their traditional software environment and create a completely new IT operation is a radical step for any company. Polk had a lot invested in their legacy technology systems, and many of the existing IT staff were highly skilled in maintaining the legacy code developed over the years. The company didn't want to tamper with what they had until they were ready with an alternative. Creating a separate operating division that would run in parallel to their legacy system allowed Polk to direct significant resources to the new system without putting the existing one at risk.

The move to SOA

Information about the data is at the center of the technical design. After looking at the capabilities of products in the market and their processing requirements, RLPTechnologies decided to develop their own propriety Web service orchestration engine, using JBoss. The JBoss Application Server and Hibernate are key components. This orchestration engine is designed to adapt to changing business conditions quickly by handling changes in data feeds, as well as the services applied to enhance this data.

The developers created a master dictionary, called a master XML tag library, to help organize and define the incoming data and the business services. All inbound data and all registered services must conform to this master dictionary. This information about data automatically creates interrelationships between inbound data sources and services, as well as between multiple services. Polk's proprietary orchestration engine uses the TIBCO Enterprise Message Service (EMS) as the primary transport of data. As set up, the engine feeds an Oracle 10g database grid containing 2½ billion vehicle transactions, representing ten years of vehicle ownership history that includes 500 million unique vehicles and 240 million households. (That's a lot of cars.) Joe LaFeir, RLPTechnologies VP of Product Development, stated that R. L. Polk now has a "state of the art data processing engine based on SOA that allows them to provide high quality information to their customers in the automotive industry and quickly respond to changes in their business."

A broad range of services, from data quality to data enrichment, is integrated into the Polk SOA solution. The services were delivered by integrating commercial off-the-shelf software with new custom development. JBoss provided consulting services to help integrate with commercial software products, such as ILOG and DataFlux.

Decoding a vehicle

Many of R. L. Polk's business applications require the information provided by a VIN (Vehicle Identification Number). A unique VIN is assigned to each vehicle when it's manufactured, and this number is used to identify the vehicle at the time of sale and registration.

The VIN is 17 characters in length. Important information about a vehicle is associated with this number, including the vehicle make, model, and year; the plant where the vehicle was manufactured; and the type of engine in the vehicle. The VIN decoder is an excellent example of a service. It takes in a bit of data (the VIN) and produces a very detailed description about a vehicle. The service doesn't care what transaction originated the VIN; its job is to always produce the same result — a full listing of the details of the vehicle.

The orchestration engine manages the association of services with the originating transaction, allowing a tremendous amount of reuse. In the Polk legacy environment, Polk used six to eight different VIN decoders for various purposes. Today, with their SOA architecture in place, they now use only one. This reduction in the number of decoders is a huge advantage because each VIN decoder had to maintain its own version of the millions of decoding rules for all vehicles manufactured since the early 1960s.

To minimize risk and disruption to current operations, the IT department set up a parallel system to run alongside the existing legacy system until they could be sure that everything was validated and working properly. Figure 26-2 provides a high-level process view of the R. L. Polk solution.

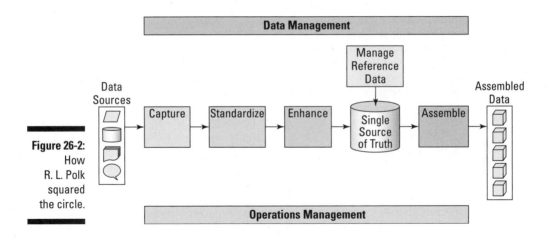

Figure 26-2: How R. L. Polk squared the circle.

The first step for Polk was to standardize the process of integrating 240 different data sources. The developers used SOA to help them take advantage of the similar elements found in many of the data sources. Polk began to make the integration process more efficient by referencing one common master tag library. The processes of capturing, standardizing, and enhancing the data are all leading to the creation of a "single source of truth" — data that is consistent regardless of the original source of the data. The process of integrating the automotive industry data from multiple sources was automated for delivery to Polk's 50+ analytical and operational applications.

The business impact

The improvements in data quality allowed the business analysts to spend more of their time focusing on data analysis so they could provide a quicker response to business issues. The SOA approach helped the company create a "hands off the data" environment. This means the business analysts are able to react to exceptions when they occur instead of waiting several hours or overnight for the data to be processed. The decoupled services provide information to the analyst as it occurs. Many automatic functions take the place of manual processes that used to require many hours of work. R. L. Polk plans to use what they've created to sell new products, and they expect to leverage their fast and efficient SOA operations as a way to add new services.

This implementation represents a huge organizational and operational change for R. L. Polk. The company has been able to shift many of the personnel from data operations to positions in product strategy and other areas of higher value to the business. By creating a parallel operating division, a team with the right skills was able to focus on this new implementation without having to be concerned about the old way of doing things.

Past experience showed how important this approach would be. Polk had tried re-engineering initiatives previously without creating a parallel operating division and they had failed. It was unreasonable to expect the IT staff to function in both the old way and the new way at the same time. Tackling the project and applying SOA increased the importance to have separation of duties. This time around, the developers in the new operating division (RLPTechnologies) were able to spend a lot of time at the beginning of the project reviewing all the business processes that were involved. The mainframe will operate in parallel until they're able to move off of it altogether, at which Polk will recognize the efficiencies of the grid computing platform, and the industry will benefit from timelier, high-quality data.

The use of open source technology allowed R. L. Polk to make very significant changes to their technical infrastructure and still keep costs in line. The services provided by JBoss were critical to Polk's success. According to LaFeir, "We would not have been able to use open source technology without the support provided by JBoss."

Part VI
The Part of Tens

The 5th Wave   By Rich Tennant

"We should cast a circle, invoke the elements, and direct the energy. If that doesn't work, we'll read the SOA manual."

In this part . . .

We found out early in our experiences writing *For Dummies* books that one shouldn't get too literal when it comes to the Part of Tens. In this part, we offer you a couple handfuls each of SOA resources, vendors, and caveats, but please don't count too carefully.

Chapter 27

Ten Swell SOA Resources

One cardinal rule for all would-be SOAjourners — don't go it alone! We've compiled a list of resources we hope you'll find useful.

Hurwitz & Associates

We here at Hurwitz & Associates are happy to help you with your questions about SOA. We can give a talk, provide SOA training, and help you find the right technology partners. We invite you to subscribe to our monthly newsletter and visit our site at www.hurwitz.com.

Finding OASIS

Standards are the linchpin for SOA success. Creating standards takes a lot of work — often volunteered, uncompensated (from a financial perspective) work by dedicated people determined to get things right. Sitting on standards committees deserves the undying gratitude of the rest of us. We thank you, standards committee members.

OASIS, the Organization for the Advancement of Structured Information Standards, is a global consortium focused on the creation and adoption of standards for electronic business. The consortium is a not-for-profit organization that relies on contributions from its member organizations.

OASIS creates topic-specific committees and has ten technical committees related to SOA. To check out the SOA committees, go to www.oasis-open. org/committees/tc_cat.php?cat=soa.

The Eclipse Foundation

The Eclipse Foundation is an open source community focused on providing a vendor-neutral open development platform and application frameworks for building software. It's not for profit and has widespread participation from developers and corporations around the globe. The Eclipse platform is written in Java and runs on most popular operating systems, including Linux, HP-UX, AIX, Solaris, QNX, Mac OS X, and Windows systems. Check out the Eclipse Foundation at www.eclipse.org.

soamodeling.org

If you want to watch a SOA project in action, check out www.soamodeling.org, where you'll see a model of SOA that many technical leaders are contributing to and one place to go for a listing of SOA standards and products. You're welcome to participate. You can find links to various OASIS documents, including the SOA reference architecture. The project under construction is the Global Response System for disaster relief. Live and breathe SOA even if you can't do it on your day job.

The SOA Institute

SOAInstitute.org is a peer-to-peer exchange for service oriented architecture professionals. The BrainStorm Group, an organization founded in 1997 that produces conferences on business process management and SOA, hosts it. The site provides a variety of articles, white papers, discussions, and events all about SOA. It includes contributions from various trade publications, industry analysts, and vendor technologists. Join and contribute your own SOA experiences at www.soainstitute.org.

Loosely Coupled

For a lot of folks, business process management and SOA go hand in hand. Loosely Coupled is a Web site built entirely from hosted components and online services. It provides articles, news feeds, and links to lots of business process automation info as well as links to lots of lively discussions about the benefits and trials of SOA implementation. Check it out at www.looselycoupled.com.

The SOA Pipeline

This site brings together articles from computer industry trade publisher CMP. The site provides lots of news, bunches of blogs, and articles about the latest happenings in the standards world. It also lets you search for products and gives you product reviews. Find it at www.webservicespipeline.com.

Manageability

Theory and practice, theory and practice. To truly succeed with SOA, you need to understand the philosophies of reuse and manageability — smart businesspeople and software architects alike value and pursue knowledge of such important informing principles. The Manageability site addresses such concerns within the context of software development in general, but it also has some specific SOA resources. Check out www.manageability.org/blog/stuff/ten-commandments-for-soa for some interesting points to ponder about SOA, including Carlos Perez's "Ten Commandments of SOA."

SOA Design Principles from Microsoft

For those most familiar with the world according to Microsoft, the folks in Redmond provide a series of SOA design principles along with an introduction to service oriented architecture. You can download them from

```
http://msdn.microsoft.com/library/default.asp?url=/
        library/en-us/dnbda/html/SOADesign.asp
```

ServiceOrientation.org

ServiceOrientation.org is the not-for-profit face of the consulting services of author/consultant Thomas Erl of SOA Systems, Inc. The site provides a lot of explanations about SOA issues, such as reuse, loose coupling, and abstraction.

Chapter 28

And That's Not All! Even More SOA Vendors

We hope that by now we've convinced you that SOA is a comprehensive way to move your business and IT organization forward. Although we highlight the strategies of the leading SOA infrastructure vendors back in Part V, we would be doing you a disservice if we didn't mention some of the vendors who are an important part of the overall ecosystem of SOA. None of the vendors we discuss in Part V exist alone. Each of them is increasingly partnering with a large number of important emerging vendors specializing in SOA. In this chapter, we divide these partner-oriented SOA players into five categories:

✔ SOA integration providers

✔ Business process management specialists

✔ SOA quality assurance and testing companies

✔ SOA governance

✔ Industry-specific SOA offerings

Read on to find out more about some important players in each of these categories.

Integration Providers

While some customers will buy their integration capabilities from the vendors we discuss in Part V, other key vendors offer independent integration capabilities. Here are some of the notable ones:

TIBCO Software

www.tibco.com

The company now known as TIBCO started life in 1985 as Teknekron Software Systems, Inc., with Vivek Ranadivé at the helm. The company's original product was called The Information Bus™ (TIB), which specialized in the integration and delivery of market data such as stock quotes, news, and other financial information to the trading rooms of large banks and financial services institutions. In January of 1997, TIBCO Software, Inc., was established as a separate entity to create and market software solutions for use in the integration of business information, processes, and applications across many business sectors.

For SOA, TIBCO offers an enterprise service bus and provides a number of software products focused on managing XML-based metadata.

IONA Technologies

www.iona.com

IONA was founded back in 1991 in Dublin, Ireland, and focuses on providing distributed (meaning software components sit on different systems but can talk to each other), standards-based solutions to IT organizations with heterogeneous (having stuff from different IT vendors mixed together) environments.

Initially, IONA built its products around a technology called CORBA, an early attempt to create a distributed infrastructure, but it now focuses on Web services and SOA.

IONA's flagship product is an enterprise service bus called Artix. In addition, the company offers Celtrix, an open source Java-based enterprise service bus. IONA has expanded to support a SOA environment by adding business process, data, and transaction capabilities in a heterogeneous environment. To support SOA, IONA's Artix product provides a Business Process Execution Language (BPEL) -based orchestration environment to coordinate services in a heterogeneous environment. The BPEL orchestration environment allows different business services to be linked together in a standard way to create a SOA solution. Artix also provides data services in order to enable customers to exchange data across sources.

Software AG

www.softwareag.com

Software AG, headquartered in Darmstadt, Germany, is a 25-year-old software company that started out in the database and application development arena. Over the past several years, the company has moved to provide products and services to support a service oriented architecture IT infrastructure.

Software AG has a product line called crossvision, a suite of offerings for SOA. The primary focus is the SOA repository called CentraSite, which was jointly developed with Fujitsu. Crossvision includes a metadata-driven central registry and repository that is intended to centrally store business policies. Working as partners, Software AG and Fujitsu intend to build a community of software providers to support the adoption of the product.

Sun Microsystems, Inc.

www.sun.com

Sun Microsystems was founded in 1982 as a technical workstation company with a focus on distributed computing infrastructure, in which lots of individual computers communicate with each other over a network to achieve a single objective. Over the years, the company expanded its offerings to include servers, storage, services, and software. Sun was the originator of the Java language that it has widely licensed to the industry.

While Sun offers a wide variety of hardware, software, and services, its primary offering for SOA is called the Java Composite Application Platform Suite (CAPS). CAPS provides an integrated set of components for use in the development, deployment, management, and monitoring of a SOA environment. The development platform sits on top of an enterprise service bus that was developed by a company called SeeBeyond that Sun Microsystems bought in 2005.

The CAPS offering includes the Sun Java B2B (business-to-business) suite for customers who need to connect their SOA implementations with partners.

SOA Quality Assurance Vendors

One key SOA requirement is that services work as designed. In other words, you need to test the software code before you put it into wide use. Companies that provide tools to test and ensure the quality of the Web services, business services, processes, and components are critical to SOA. Here are some of the companies that focus on SOA quality:

Parasoft Corporation

www.parasoft.com

Five graduates from the California Institute of Technology founded Parasoft in 1987. The company's earliest products were focused on software development tools for parallel processing and distributed computing. In the 1990s, the company transitioned to more general-purpose software development tools for software testing, specializing in Java, C, and C++. The company focuses on many aspects of testing, including code testing, unit testing, static analysis, and Web testing.

For the SOA market, Parasoft offers a product called SOAtest that focuses on Web service issues such as interoperability, security, change management, and scalability. Parasoft SOAtest automatically creates security penetration tests intended to protect Web services from threats such as unauthorized access to services.

Mindreef, Inc.

www.mindreef.com

The founders of testing software vendor, NuMega Technologies, founded Mindreef, Inc., in 2001. The goal was to focus on SOA and Web services testing. The company has more than 3,000 customers worldwide.

Mindreef SOAPscope Server provides testing and verifies the quality of service oriented architectures. It allows developers to easily read the contents of messages written in WSDL and SOAP for straightforward analysis. In addition, it offers the ability to test these services without writing code.

iTKO, Inc.

www.itko.com

iTKO, Inc., was founded in 1999 as a consulting firm focused on enterprise software quality. The company created the LISA Quality Platform for creating and executing SOA tests. iTKO also offers a set of SOA products that test Web services, SOAP, J2EE, .NET, Web applications, and databases. The company also offers load and performance testing products.

Registry/Repository/Governance Vendors

Registries, repositories, and governance rules are vital to SOA. Registries and repositories provide access to consistent definitions of data as well as the location of those definitions. Governance rules help organizations set in place the policies that are codified in SOA software implementations. Although some of the vendors discussed in Part V may have their own tools, many use the tools mentioned in this section.

Mercury Interactive (Systinet Division)

www.mercury.com

Systinet, a division of Mercury Interactive Corporation, provides a set of tools that are used to implement SOA governance and life cycle management.

Founded in 2000, Systinet's standards-based products include Systinet Registry and Systinet Policy Manager, both components of the Systinet 2 platform.

Systinet products are based on industry standards such as XML, SOAP, WSDL, and UDDI. A pioneer in SOA technology, Systinet led the development of important standards at the World Wide Web Consortium (W3C), OASIS, and elsewhere.

Infravio

www.infravio.com

Infravio, founded in 1999, was based on a research project at the Stanford University Department of Computer Science. The company's primary product is a SOA registry/repository called the X-Registry Platform. Infravio provides a number of development platform interfaces, including Java API for XML Registries (JAXR), UDDI version 2 and version 3, and OASIS ebRIM.

LogicLibrary, Inc.

www.logiclibrary.com

LogicLibrary, founded in 2000, provides a metadata repository and registry. The company offers a set of predesigned software models that are used in SOA implementations. LogicLibrary's main product, Logidex, includes a discovery engine and supports linking together repositories based in different locations.

SOA Software

www.soasoftware.com

SOA Software (formerly Digital Evolution) focuses broadly on SOA infrastructure design and management. The company has grown through acquisitions. In 2005, the company purchased SOLA Software, a mainframe XML Web services platform, from Merrill Lynch. In 2006, it purchased Blue Titan, a SOA system management platform. The company provides the following products: Service Manager, a UDDI-based registry that incorporates governance and security capabilities; Network Director, the company's SOA management platform that helps an organization make SOA components work together consistently; the Partner Manager, which helps companies share Web services interfaces securely; and SOLA, which helps organizations expose the mainframe applications as Web services.

SOA Systems and Application Management Vendors

After organizations begin to create their SOA environments, they need the ability to manage the interaction between services, the service bus, and the connections among all the moving parts. In addition to the vendors in Part V here are some independent vendors that provide management solutions.

AmberPoint

`www.amberpoint.com`

AmberPoint was founded in 2001 to focus on Web services and SOA management. AmberPoint provides a SOA management system that includes service network monitoring, the ability to determine how the network is responding; SOA runtime management, the ability to manage a collection of components to ensure that they are working efficiently; SOA security, the ability to determine whether the environment meets an organization's security requirements; and service-level management, the ability to test to see if the SOA environment is working in accordance with the company's performance needs.

AmberPoint's SOA Validation System validates services before putting them into production.

CA

`www.ca.com`

CA (formerly known as Computer Associates) was founded in 1976 and provides a collection of management and security products for SOA. These products are part of CA's Enterprise IT Management (EITM) platform, which supports SOA standards such as WSDM, WS-Management, WS-Security, and SAML. Capabilities include

- ✔ Automated discovery of IT assets and their configurations, relationships, and interdependencies
- ✔ IT governance tools, including portfolio management and BPM tools
- ✔ Compliance with industry standards for IT operations known as ITIL that focus on IT service management capabilities
- ✔ Health, availability, and performance monitoring for business processes and infrastructure components, including networks, servers and applications

Reactivity, Inc.

`www.reactivity.com`

Reactivity is a company that focuses on SOA-oriented, XML-enabled networking solutions through what it calls Adaptive Message Architecture. Its XML Accelerator is designed to optimize service performance and network throughput. Its XML Security Gateway inspects and secures XML messages, access control, and threat defense and mediates routing and acceleration tasks for XML. The company's XML Router accelerates the routing, authentication, authorization, and Web services security functions. It centralizes integration of XML management and helps enforce policies associated with XML deployment.

SOA Information Management Vendors

Without managing data, SOA won't work. Taking data from disparate information sources and allowing these sources to work together is essential for SOA. While some of the key information management vendors are associated with the vendors in Part V, we know some very important independent vendors. Here they are.

Informatica Corporation

www.informatica.com

Informatica focuses on the data integration life cycle. The company's products support data integration initiatives, including data warehousing, data migration and consolidation, data synchronization, data governance, master data management, and cross-enterprise data integration. The company's unified enterprise data integration platform is called Informatica PowerCenter.

Informatica's SOA strategy is called Universal Data Services (UDS). This architecture is designed to help customers eliminate data silos and simplify the integration of data across the enterprise. Informatica's solution for SOA is intended to provide consistent access to the data as needed by the business according to four key services: access services, integration services, metadata services, and infrastructure services.

Maintaining data quality is a high priority for companies developing data services for SOA environments. Informatica's data quality offerings expanded in 2006 when it acquired Similarity Systems and incorporated the company's software for data profiling, standardization, cleansing, matching, and monitoring into the PowerCenter data integration suite.

iWay Software

iWay Software, a subsidiary of Information Builders Inc. (IBI), has provided adapters of many different types and for varied software environments — over 300 types of adapters — since the company was founded in 2001. Adapters are used to create the interfaces needed to connect data, software, and infrastructure components to each other in different ways.

iWay's adapter framework has evolved to support custom SOA implementations. This led to the introduction in 2006 of the company's SOA middleware product called iWay SOA Middleware™. The suite includes four products: iWay Service Manager (an ESB for SOA that includes tools for publishing, monitoring, securing, and managing services), iWay Trading Manger (adds functionality to Service Manager to manage complex business-to-business environments), iWay Enterprise Index (combines Service Manager with the Google Search Appliance to enhance searching capabilities across the enterprise), and iWay Process Manager (a Business Process Management — BPM — tool to help customers build and simulate business processes).

MetaMatrix

MetaMatrix, a venture-backed company founded in 1998, provides data-management software designed to ensure that data is consistent and accurate when accessed from multiple sources across the enterprise. Their primary product, called MetaMatrix Enterprise, provides tools for creating, deploying, and managing data services — data that has been decoupled from its original application and made available for reuse in different situations. MetaMatrix Enterprise also includes a metadata repository to store data service reference data, such as definitions of the data services. The company introduced a new product in 2006, called MetaMatrix Dimension, to enable the design and execution of data services in SOA environments. This software is designed to help companies make data from existing relational and file-based databases available as XML schema-compliant Web services. The Web services and XML support technology of this new offering is also incorporated into MetaMatrix Enterprise.

Specialized SOA Business Services

Some SOA vendors are focused on particular industry segments, such as financial services and healthcare. The next sections highlight two specialized approaches.

SEEC

```
www.seec.com
```

SEEC provides service oriented software components for the insurance and financial services industries. The company's Service Oriented Business Applications (SOBAs) are based on industry-standard XML. SOBAs are a reusable collection of business services that customers can select and link together by using Web services interfaces to create customized SOA environments. A customer need only select the specific SEEC components they need, and these can be adapted or reused as business needs change. SEEC provides workspaces designed for specific functions in their customer base. Workspaces provided for the insurance industry include the following: Producer Workspace, Agency Workspace, Policy Service Center Workspace, and Customer Self-Service Workspace. SEEC includes some of the most commonly used capabilities in these workspaces and then provides a library of business services in the SEEC Advantage Library™ so that customers can customize their workspaces.

Webify

```
www.webifysolutions.com
```

Webify provides service oriented business software for specific industries. Its solutions for healthcare and insurance are well established, while solutions for the banking and telecommunications industries are under development. The products in each industry group include composite business services designed to automate functions common to organizations doing business in the particular industry. For example, Webify Healthcare composite business services automate industry-specific business processes such as insurance payer-provider interactions for heath claims processing and the management of high-deductible healthcare spending accounts. The prebuilt SOA components designed for the insurance industry include composite business services for business processes such as claims processing and policy origination. Another important aspect of each industry solution is the life cycle governance environment designed to enable the sourcing, assembly, delivery, and consistent use of the business services. This governance environment, called the Webify Industry fabric, is tailored to each vertical market and operates in multiple platforms.

Webify was acquired by IBM in August, 2006, and will be integrated into IBM Software Group under the WebSphere brand.

Chapter 29

Ten SOA No-Nos

....

....

*W*ith hundreds of pages in this book to show you what you can do, we thought we'd carve out a few caveats to warn you what *not* to do so you can benefit from the mistakes of others.

Don't Boil the Ocean

Make sure the SOA project you choose for your starting point is well defined and well confined. Prove SOA successful with something that is small, is achievable in a short time, and will have a significant impact — then build incrementally.

Don't Confuse SOA with an IT Initiative

If you relegate SOA to IT, we, the authors, have failed miserably. We throw up our hands. SOA must be a joint endeavor between business and IT. You have everything to gain — and everything to lose if you persist in such pigheadedness.

Don't Go It Alone

An entire industry is just waiting out there to help you. Don't ignore it. Beg, borrow, steal, but get help. Reinventing the world is definitely anti-SOA thinking.

Don't Think You're So Special

Stick to standards and standard interfaces. The proprietary software you build will be your own downfall. The sooner you part ways from evil temptations, the happier and healthier your software can be. (The happier and healthier your organization will be too, by the way.)

Don't Neglect Governance

SOA governance won't happen by itself. Address it early. SOA governance is as much about the way you work and the processes you put in place to create a SOA environment as it is about any technology issues. So, don't just go and buy a bucket full of tools labeled *SOA governance*. SOA governance is about leadership and thinking through how you are going to get from where you are today to a well-coordinated approach that conforms to your corporate goals and objectives.

Don't Forget about Security

In this brand new world of mixing and matching, it's easy to get caught up in the euphoria and forget about the nitty-gritty. Pay close attention to the security implications of exposing business services.

Don't Apply SOA to Everything

SOA makes a lot of sense for a lot of things, but not for everything. If you have an application that is so specialized that it is isolated from other aspects of the business and works just fine, leave it alone. At the same time, when you find the software that is appropriate for SOA, you need to prioritize, scrutinize, and make sure you're looking at the right level of granularity.

For example, if you make each service very small, you might end up with thousands of little pieces of code that are hard to find and hard to reuse. The bigger the reusable service, the easier it will be to find and reuse. And some things need never, ever be exposed as services. Really.

Don't Start from Scratch

Chances are, one of the SOA vendors has some sort of blueprint for a company just like yours. Take advantage of work already done. Look for a blueprint or model based on your industry first, such as insurance or financial services or banking — many already exist and more are being created every day.

Don't Postpone SOA

SOA is a long journey. The sooner you begin, the sooner you'll get somewhere.

Appendix A

Glossary

Access control: Determining who or what can go where, when, and how.

ACID: *A*tomicity, *C*onsistency, *I*solation, and *D*urability, the main requirements for proper transaction processing.

Adapter: A software module added to an application or system that allows access to its capabilities via a standards-compliant services interface.

AES: *A*dvanced *E*ncryption *S*tandard, an encryption algorithm developed in Belgium and adopted by the U.S. government as a standard to replace the older DES (*D*ata *E*ncryption *S*tandard). AES is the only published encryption algorithm that the United States government uses to protect Top Secret information.

AJAX: A hot new technology for producing highly interactive Web applications. AJAX stands for *A*synchronous *J*avaScript *a*nd *X*ML.

API: *A*pplication *P*rogramming *I*nterface, a collection of subroutine calls that allow computer programs to use a software system.

Architecture: In information processing, the design approach taken for developing a program or system.

Authentication: The process by which the identity of a person or computer process is verified.

B2B: *B*usiness *to* *B*usiness, typically used to refer to a kind of commerce (or trade). When a company sells primarily to other companies (businesses), its business is said to be B2B. IBM is a good example.

B2C: *B*usiness *to* *C*onsumer, typically used to refer to a kind of commerce (or trade). When a company sells primarily to consumers (ordinary people just shopping, you know) its business is said to be B2C. Amazon.com is a good example.

Basel II: Known more formally as the *International Convergence of Capital Measurement and Capital Standards — A Revised Framework,* Basel II is an internationally recognized set of rules for evaluating a bank's finances in light of various risks. It's also one of the big compliance regulations making organizations do things they wouldn't otherwise feel compelled to do. (Basel, by the way, is a very lovely city in Switzerland.)

Bean: In computing, a reusable software component.

Binding: Making the necessary connections between software components.

Biometrics: Using a person's unique physical characteristics to prove their identity to a computer — by employing a fingerprint scanner or voice analyzer, for example.

Black box: A component or device with an input and an output, whose inner workings need not be understood by or accessible to the user.

BPEL: *B*usiness *P*rocess *E*xecution *L*anguage, a computer language based on WSDL (the *W*eb *S*ervices *D*escription *L*anguage, an XML format for describing Web services) and designed for programming business services.

BPM: *B*usiness *P*rocess *M*anagement, a technology and methodology for controlling the activities — both automated and manual — needed to make a business function.

BPMN: *B*usiness *P*rocess *M*odeling *N*otation, the result of work done to standardize the way business processes are modeled to make it easy for any business analyst to understand.

Broker: In computer programming, a program that accepts requests from one software layer or component and translates them into a form that can be understood by another layer or component.

Browser: A program that lets you access information on the Internet. Browsers used to run on just personal computers, but now they are on cell phones and personal digital assistants and will soon appear on your refrigerator.

Bus: A technology that connects multiple components so they can all talk to each other.

Business process: The codification of rules and practices that constitute a business.

Business service: An individual function or activity that is directly useful to the business.

C#: C sharp, a relatively new programming language developed by Microsoft and designed around .NET. Some say it is intended as a Java killer.

Component: A piece of computer software that can be used as a building block in larger systems.

Container: In computer programming, a data structure or object used to manage collections of other objects in an organized way.

CORBA: *C*ommon *O*bject *R*equest *B*roker *A*rchitecture, the OMG's open, vendor-neutral architecture designed to help applications work together over a network.

CRM: *C*ustomer *R*elationship *M*anagement, software intended to help you run your sales force and customer support.

Database: A computer system intended to reliably store and conveniently access and search large amounts of information in an organized fashion.

Data federation: Data access to a variety of data stores, using consistent rules and definitions that enable all the data stores to be treated as a single resource.

Data profiling: The use of tools that help you to understand the content and structure of your data.

DES: *D*ata *E*ncryption *S*tandard, the first widely used computer encryption algorithm; it is now considered substandard, but a tripled-up version, **3DES**, is still considered strong and is widely used, though frequently being replaced by AES.

Distributed processing: Spreading the work of an information processing application among several computers.

Early binding: Making the necessary connections between software components when the software system is first put together, or "built," as opposed to *late binding*.

Eclipse: In computer programming, an open source integrated development environment (IDE) for the Java language, originally developed by IBM, that can be extended to other uses.

EDI: *E*lectronic *D*ata *I*nterchange, an older method for allowing computer systems at different organizations to exchange information.

Encryption: Transforming data in a way that makes it impossible to read but that can be reversed by someone in possession of a secret piece of information known as a "key."

ERP: *E*nterprise *R*esource *P*lanning, a packaged set of business applications that attempts to do pretty much everything for a business.

ESB: *E*nterprise *s*ervice *b*us, a distributed middleware software system that allows computer applications to talk amongst themselves in a standardized way.

ETL: *E*xtract — *T*ransform — *L*oad, tools for locating and accessing data from a data store (data extraction), changing the structure or format of the data so it can be used by the business application (data transformation), and sending the data to the business application (data load).

Extensible Stylesheet Language Transformations, or XSLT: A computer language, itself based on XML, that specifies how to change one XML document into another.

Federation: The act of bringing things together so they can act as one — as in the federated states, or federated data, or federated identity management — and making sure all the right rules apply, of course.

Framework: A support structure for developing software products.

GPL: GNU *G*eneral *P*ublic *L*icense, an open source copyright license created by Richard Stallman that, in its strictest form, requires programs built on code licensed under GPL to adopt the same license.

Grid computing: A step beyond distributed processing, grid computing involves large numbers of networked computers, often geographically dispersed and possibly of different types and capabilities, that are harnessed together to solve a common problem.

HIPAA: The *H*ealth *I*nsurance *P*ortability and *A*ccountability *A*ct of 1996 puts new demands on systems that have anything to do with healthcare. It's the reason you have to sign a statement every time you walk into a doctor's office. Regulations like HIPAA make software vendors dance with glee because they can sell more products to make everybody HIPAA compliant. Do you feel safer now?

HTML: *H*yper*T*ext *M*arkup *L*anguage, a data encoding scheme invented by Tim Berners-Lee in 1991 that is the basic way information is encoded over the World Wide Web.

HTTP: *H*yper*T*ext *T*ransport *P*rotocol is the basic way information is linked together and transmitted over the World Wide Web. HTTPS is a version of HTTP with encryption for security.

Hypertext: Documents that contain links to other documents and media; Web pages are an obvious example.

Identity management: Keeping track of a single user's (or asset's) identity throughout an engagement with a system or set of systems.

IMS: An *I*dentity *M*anagement *S*ystem keeps track of who users are and what they are allowed to do.

Infrastructure: The fundamental systems necessary for the ordinary operation of anything, be it a country or an IT department. Part of the infrastructure that we rely on includes roads, electrical wiring, and water systems. In IT, infrastructure includes basic computer hardware, networks, operating systems, and other software that applications run on top of.

Infrastructure services: Services provided by the infrastructure. In IT, these services include all the software needed to make devices talk to each other, for starters.

Internet: Computers from all over the world linked together so they can talk to each other with standard protocols (TCP/IP) and data formats (SMTP, HTML, XML).

IP: *I*nternet *p*rotocol (see TCP/IP), also can mean *i*ntellectual *p*roperty (patents, trademarks, copyrights, and trade secrets).

ISO9000: An international standard for quality management that includes a certification procedure.

ITIL: *I*nformation *T*echnology *I*nfrastructure *L*ibrary, a framework for IT governance based on best practices.

Java: A computer programming language developed by Sun; has proven to be popular for enterprise applications. See also *C#*.

JavaEE: Java Platform, Enterprise Edition, a Java-based platform for distributed, multitier, client-server applications.

JavaScript: A scripting language, somewhat modeled after Java, that is built into almost all browsers, hence popular for delivering Web-based applications.

JBoss: An open source application server written in Java.

JCA: *J2EE Connector Architecture*, a technology that enables Java programs to talk to other software, such as databases and legacy applications.

Kerberos: An authentication system for distributed computing developed at MIT.

LAMP: An increasingly popular open source approach to building Web applications, consisting of the *Linux* operating system, *Apache* Web server, *My*SQL database, and a scripting language such as *P*HP, Perl, or *P*ython.

Late binding: Deferring the necessary connections between applications to when the connection is first needed. Late binding allows more flexibility for changes than *early binding* does, but it imposes some cost in processing time.

Legacy application: Any application that is more than a few years old. When applications cannot easily be disposed of and replaced, they become legacy applications. The good news is that they are doing something useful. The bad news is that they were built for software environments of the past.

Loose coupling: An approach to distributed software applications in which components interact by passing data and requests to other components in a standardized way that minimizes dependencies between components. The emphasis is on simplicity and autonomy. Each component offers a small range of simple services to other components.

Malware: The general term for computer software that intentionally does ill, such as viruses, Trojans, worms, and spyware.

Markup language: A way of encoding information that uses plain text containing special tags often delimited by angle brackets ("<" and ">"). Specific markup languages are often created, based on XML, to standardize the interchange of information between different computer systems and services.

Mash-up: A Web site that combines content from more than one source, for example, Google Maps and a real-estate listing service.

Metadata: The definitions, mappings, and other characteristics used to describe how to find, access, and use the company's data and software components.

Metadata repository: A container of consistent definitions of business data and rules for mapping data to their actual physical location in the system.

Middleware: Multipurpose software that lives at a layer between the operating system and application in distributed computing environments.

MOM: *M*essage *O*riented *M*iddleware, a precursor to the enterprise service bus. (See *ESB*.)

MySQL: An open source option to SQL that is making some people very, very happy and some vendors notably less so.

.NET: ("dot-net") The latest and greatest Microsoft programming framework, with heavy emphasis on Web services.

OASIS: *O*rganization for the *A*dvancement of *S*tructured *I*nformation *S*tandards, a consortium promoting e-business and Web service standards.

Object oriented: An approach to computer programming that ties together data and the methods needed to manipulate that data into units called objects.

OMG: *O*bject *M*anagement *G*roup, a consortium that sets standards for distributed systems and modeling, including CORBA, UML, and the BPMN business modeling language.

Open source: A movement in the software industry that makes programs available along with the source code used to create them so others can inspect and modify how programs work.

P2P: *P*eer *to* *P*eer, a networking system in which nodes in a network exchange data directly instead of going through a central server.

Password/passphrase: String of text that is entered into a computer to help authenticate a user. Passphrases are typically longer than passwords and are used in situations in which more security is required, such as when an encryption key is directly formed from the entry.

Password cracking: The process of trying to obtain a password without the cooperation of the password's owner, usually by using software to assist. It typically involves trying large numbers of commonly used passwords or simply trying every possibility. It can become very sophisticated, with password guesses being encrypted and then compared to the encrypted version that is often made available as part of authentication challenges.

Perl: *P*ractical *E*xtraction and *R*eport *L*anguage, a powerful scripting language in widespread use in system administration, Web development, and more.

PHP: *P*HP *H*ypertext *P*rocessor, an open source scripting language (originally designed in Perl) used especially for producing dynamic Web pages.

PKI: Public Key Infrastructure, a way to keep track of and certify all the public keys needed in a large organization. People have dreamed of a universal Public Key Infrastructure, but it hasn't happened yet.

Plumbing: The underlying pipe structure that transports water to and from the places in a building where it is needed and used, such as washrooms, bathrooms, and kitchens. In this book, plumbing is used as a metaphor to refer to a SOA's *infrastructure services.*

Portal: In computing, a window that contains a means of access, often a menu, to all the applications throughout the whole network that the user is able to run. Often the window is segmented into a number of smaller windows, or *portlets,* that provide direct access to some applications, such as stock market price feeds or e-mail.

Programming in the large: An approach to developing business software that focuses on the various tasks or business processes needed to make the business function — processing an order, for example, or checking product availability — as opposed to more low-level technical tasks like opening a file.

Protocol: A set of rules that computers use to establish and maintain communication amongst themselves.

Provisioning: Making resources available to users and software. A provisioning system makes applications available to users and makes server resources available to applications.

Public key cryptography: An encryption technique that uses pairs of keys, one that is kept secret by its owner and is used for decoding and signing information, and a second, public key that can be used to encode data and verify signatures.

RC4: A simple encryption algorithm invented by Ron Rivist that is widely used on the Internet. RC4 is very strong if used properly, but there have been several security problems resulting from its misuse.

Real-time event processing: A class of applications that demand timely response to actions that take place out in the world. Typical examples include automated stock trading and RFID.

Registry: A single source for all the metadata needed to gain access to a Web service or software component.

Repository: A database for software and components, with an emphasis on revision control and configuration management. Where they keep the good stuff, in other words.

RFID: *R*adio *F*requency *ID*entification is a technology that uses small, inexpensive chips attached to products (or even animals) that then transmit a unique identification number over a short distance when interrogated by a special radio transmitter/receiver. RFID systems produce vast amounts of real-time data that can be difficult to interpret properly.

RPC: *R*emote *P*rocedure *C*all is a way for a program running on one computer to run a subprogram on another computer.

SaaS: *S*oftware *as a S*ervice involves the delivery of computer applications over the Internet.

Sarbanes-Oxley: The Public Company Accounting Reform and Investor Protection Act of 2002, a U.S. law enhancing standards for all U.S. public company Boards of Directors, resulting in substantial new requirements for corporate IT.

Scripting language: A computer programming language that is interpreted and has access to all or most operating system facilities. Common examples include Perl, Python, Ruby, and JavaScript. It is often easier to program in a scripting language, but the resulting programs generally run more slowly than compiled languages, such as C and C++.

Security token: A small device that an individual can carry that provides a secure way of proving the individual's identity to a computer system, such as displaying a unique number to type in based on the time of day.

Semantics: In computer programming, what the data means, as opposed to formatting rules (syntax).

Server farm: A room filled with computer servers, often needed to run large Internet sites.

Service broker: Software in a SOA framework that brings components together by using the rules associated with each component.

Servlet: A program that runs on a Web server in response to an action taken by the user via a browser. Contrasts with an Applet, a program that runs on the user's computer in similar circumstances.

Silo: A long cylinder used to store grain or intercontinental missiles. In IT, *silo* is used to refer to an application with a single, narrow focus — for example, human resource management or inventory control — with no intention or preparation for use by others.

Six sigma: A statistical term meaning six standard deviations from the norm; used as the name for a quality improvement program that aims at reducing errors to one in a million.

SLA: A *Service-Level Agreement* is a document that captures the understanding between a service user and a service provider as to quality and timeliness.

SMTP: *Simple Mail Transfer Protocol*, the basic method used to transmit electronic mail (e-mail) over the Internet.

SOA: *Service Oriented Architecture*, an approach to building applications that implements business processes or services by using a set of loosely coupled black-box components orchestrated to deliver a well-defined level of service.

SOAP: *Simple Object Access Protocol*, a protocol based on XML, used to exchange messages between Web services.

SOA supervisor: Software that orchestrates the entire collection of computers, network resources, and software in a SOA framework so that they can run continuously at an appropriate level of service.

SQL: *Structured Query Language*, the most popular computer language for accessing and manipulating databases; sometimes pronounced "sequel."

SSL/TLS: *Secure Sockets Layer*, a popular method for making secure connections over the Internet, first introduced by Netscape. In its latest versions, it has been renamed TLS, short for *Transport Layer Security*. It is ubiquitous in electronic commerce but has been adapted for other applications as well.

Structured programming: An early "magic bullet" for improving software based on eliminating go to statements in programs.

Subroutine: A piece of computer code that can easily be used ("called") by many other programs, as long as they are on the same computer and (usually) are written in the same programming language.

TCP/IP: *Transmission Control Protocol/Internet Protocol*, the complex stack of communications protocols that underlies the Internet. All data is broken down into small packets that are sent independently over the network and reassembled at the final destination.

TLS: *Transport Layer Security*, a newer name for *SSL*.

TQM: *T*otal *Q*uality *M*anagement, another popular quality improvement program.

Transaction: A computer action that represents a business event, such as debiting an account. When a transaction starts, it must either complete or not happen at all.

Trojan: A computer program that pretends to do one thing, but actually does something else, usually nefarious. Named after the Trojan horse of Greek mythology.

Two-factor authentication: An approach to verifying the identity of an individual that requires two separate forms of proof, such as a password and a security token or a password and some form of biometric.

UDDI: *U*niversal *D*escription, *D*iscovery, and *I*ntegration is a platform-independent, XML-based services registry, sponsored by the Organization for the Advancement of Structured Information Standards (OASIS).

UML: *U*nified *M*odeling Language, a standardized graphical notation used to create abstract models of IT systems. Think of it as flowcharts on super-mega-steroids.

Virus: A computer program that spreads from computer to computer without permission. Much like biological viruses, they often evolve to get past defenses intended to stop them, and some cause more damage than others.

W3C: A handy way of referring to the World Wide Web Consortium, an organization that coordinates standards for the World Wide Web.

Web services: A software system that supports machine-to-machine interaction over a network.

Workflow: The sequence of steps needed to carry out a business process.

World Wide Web: Better known as WWW, the World Wide Web is a system built on top of the Internet that displays hyperlinked pages of information that can contain a wide variety of data formats, including multimedia.

WSDL: *W*eb *S*ervices *D*escription *L*anguage, an XML format for describing Web services.

WSRP: *W*eb *S*ervices for *R*emote *P*ortlets, a protocol that allows portlets to communicate by using standard Web service interfaces.

XML: e*X*tensible *M*arkup *L*anguage, a way of presenting data as plaintext files that has become the *lingua franca* of SOA. In XML, as in HTML, data is delimited in tags that are enclosed in angle brackets ("<" and ">"), although the tags in XML can have many more meanings.

XSD: *X*ML *S*chema *D*efinition describes what can be in an XML document.

XSLT: See *Extensible Stylesheet Language Transformations.*

Index

• X •

Notes

BUSINESS, CAREERS & PERSONAL FINANCE

0-7645-9847-3   0-7645-2431-3

Also available:

Business Plans Kit For Dummies
0-7645-9794-9

Economics For Dummies
0-7645-5726-2

Grant Writing For Dummies
0-7645-8416-2

Home Buying For Dummies
0-7645-5331-3

Managing For Dummies
0-7645-1771-6

Marketing For Dummies
0-7645-5600-2

Personal Finance For Dummies
0-7645-2590-5*

Resumes For Dummies
0-7645-5471-9

Selling For Dummies
0-7645-5363-1

Six Sigma For Dummies
0-7645-6798-5

Small Business Kit For Dummies
0-7645-5984-2

Starting an eBay Business For Dummies
0-7645-6924-4

Your Dream Career For Dummies
0-7645-9795-7

HOME & BUSINESS COMPUTER BASICS

0-470-05432-8   0-471-75421-8

Also available:

Cleaning Windows Vista For Dummies
0-471-78293-9

Excel 2007 For Dummies
0-470-03737-7

Mac OS X Tiger For Dummies
0-7645-7675-5

MacBook For Dummies
0-470-04859-X

Macs For Dummies
0-470-04849-2

Office 2007 For Dummies
0-470-00923-3

Outlook 2007 For Dummies
0-470-03830-6

PCs For Dummies
0-7645-8958-X

Salesforce.com For Dummies
0-470-04893-X

Upgrading & Fixing Laptops For Dummies
0-7645-8959-8

Word 2007 For Dummies
0-470-03658-3

Quicken 2007 For Dummies
0-470-04600-7

FOOD, HOME, GARDEN, HOBBIES, MUSIC & PETS

0-7645-8404-9   0-7645-9904-6

Also available:

Candy Making For Dummies
0-7645-9734-5

Card Games For Dummies
0-7645-9910-0

Crocheting For Dummies
0-7645-4151-X

Dog Training For Dummies
0-7645-8418-9

Healthy Carb Cookbook For Dummies
0-7645-8476-6

Home Maintenance For Dummies
0-7645-5215-5

Horses For Dummies
0-7645-9797-3

Jewelry Making & Beading For Dummies
0-7645-2571-9

Orchids For Dummies
0-7645-6759-4

Puppies For Dummies
0-7645-5255-4

Rock Guitar For Dummies
0-7645-5356-9

Sewing For Dummies
0-7645-6847-7

Singing For Dummies
0-7645-2475-5

INTERNET & DIGITAL MEDIA

0-470-04529-9   0-470-04894-8

Also available:

Blogging For Dummies
0-471-77084-1

Digital Photography For Dummies
0-7645-9802-3

Digital Photography All-in-One Desk Reference For Dummies
0-470-03743-1

Digital SLR Cameras and Photography For Dummies
0-7645-9803-1

eBay Business All-in-One Desk Reference For Dummies
0-7645-8438-3

HDTV For Dummies
0-470-09673-X

Home Entertainment PCs For Dummies
0-470-05523-5

MySpace For Dummies
0-470-09529-6

Search Engine Optimization For Dummies
0-471-97998-8

Skype For Dummies
0-470-04891-3

The Internet For Dummies
0-7645-8996-2

Wiring Your Digital Home For Dummies
0-471-91830-X

* Separate Canadian edition also available
† Separate U.K. edition also available

Available wherever books are sold. For more information or to order direct: U.S. customers visit www.dummies.com or call 1-877-762-2974.
U.K. customers visit www.wileyeurope.com or call 0800 243407. Canadian customers visit www.wiley.ca or call 1-800-567-4797.

SPORTS, FITNESS, PARENTING, RELIGION & SPIRITUALITY

0-471-76871-5   0-7645-7841-3

Also available:

⊯Catholicism For Dummies
0-7645-5391-7

⊯Exercise Balls For Dummies
0-7645-5623-1

⊯Fitness For Dummies
0-7645-7851-0

⊯Football For Dummies
0-7645-3936-1

⊯Judaism For Dummies
0-7645-5299-6

⊯Potty Training For Dummies
0-7645-5417-4

⊯Buddhism For Dummies
0-7645-5359-3

⊯Pregnancy For Dummies
0-7645-4483-7 †

⊯Ten Minute Tone-Ups For Dummies
0-7645-7207-5

⊯NASCAR For Dummies
0-7645-7681-X

⊯Religion For Dummies
0-7645-5264-3

⊯Soccer For Dummies
0-7645-5229-5

⊯Women in the Bible For Dummies
0-7645-8475-8

TRAVEL

0-7645-7749-2   0-7645-6945-7

Also available:

⊯Alaska For Dummies
0-7645-7746-8

⊯Cruise Vacations For Dummies
0-7645-6941-4

⊯England For Dummies
0-7645-4276-1

⊯Europe For Dummies
0-7645-7529-5

⊯Germany For Dummies
0-7645-7823-5

⊯Hawaii For Dummies
0-7645-7402-7

⊯Italy For Dummies
0-7645-7386-1

⊯Las Vegas For Dummies
0-7645-7382-9

⊯London For Dummies
0-7645-4277-X

⊯Paris For Dummies
0-7645-7630-5

⊯RV Vacations For Dummies
0-7645-4442-X

⊯Walt Disney World & Orlando
For Dummies
0-7645-9660-8

GRAPHICS, DESIGN & WEB DEVELOPMENT

0-7645-8815-X   0-7645-9571-7

Also available:

⊯3D Game Animation For Dummies
0-7645-8789-7

⊯AutoCAD 2006 For Dummies
0-7645-8925-3

⊯Building a Web Site For Dummies
0-7645-7144-3

⊯Creating Web Pages For Dummies
0-470-08030-2

⊯Creating Web Pages All-in-One Desk
Reference For Dummies
0-7645-4345-8

⊯Dreamweaver 8 For Dummies
0-7645-9649-7

⊯InDesign CS2 For Dummies
0-7645-9572-5

⊯Macromedia Flash 8 For Dummies
0-7645-9691-8

⊯Photoshop CS2 and Digital
Photography For Dummies
0-7645-9580-6

⊯Photoshop Elements 4 For Dummies
0-471-77483-9

⊯Syndicating Web Sites with RSS Feeds
For Dummies
0-7645-8848-6

⊯Yahoo! SiteBuilder For Dummies
0-7645-9800-7

NETWORKING, SECURITY, PROGRAMMING & DATABASES

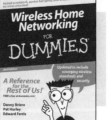

0-7645-7728-X   0-471-74940-0

Also available:

⊯Access 2007 For Dummies
0-470-04612-0

⊯ASP.NET 2 For Dummies
0-7645-7907-X

⊯C# 2005 For Dummies
0-7645-9704-3

⊯Hacking For Dummies
0-470-05235-X

⊯Hacking Wireless Networks
For Dummies
0-7645-9730-2

⊯Java For Dummies
0-470-08716-1

⊯Microsoft SQL Server 2005 For Dummies
0-7645-7755-7

⊯Networking All-in-One Desk Reference
For Dummies
0-7645-9939-9

⊯Preventing Identity Theft For Dummies
0-7645-7336-5

⊯Telecom For Dummies
0-471-77085-X

⊯Visual Studio 2005 All-in-One Desk
Reference For Dummies
0-7645-9775-2

⊯XML For Dummies
0-7645-8845-1

HEALTH & SELF-HELP

0-7645-8450-2   0-7645-4149-8

Also available:

- Bipolar Disorder For Dummies
  0-7645-8451-0
- Chemotherapy and Radiation
  For Dummies
  0-7645-7832-4
- Controlling Cholesterol For Dummies
  0-7645-5440-9
- Diabetes For Dummies
  0-7645-6820-5* †
- Divorce For Dummies
  0-7645-8417-0 †

- Fibromyalgia For Dummies
  0-7645-5441-7
- Low-Calorie Dieting For Dummies
  0-7645-9905-4
- Meditation For Dummies
  0-471-77774-9
- Osteoporosis For Dummies
  0-7645-7621-6
- Overcoming Anxiety For Dummies
  0-7645-5447-6
- Reiki For Dummies
  0-7645-9907-0
- Stress Management For Dummies
  0-7645-5144-2

EDUCATION, HISTORY, REFERENCE & TEST PREPARATION

0-7645-8381-6   0-7645-9554-7

Also available:

- The ACT For Dummies
  0-7645-9652-7
- Algebra For Dummies
  0-7645-5325-9
- Algebra Workbook For Dummies
  0-7645-8467-7
- Astronomy For Dummies
  0-7645-8465-0
- Calculus For Dummies
  0-7645-2498-4
- Chemistry For Dummies
  0-7645-5430-1
- Forensics For Dummies
  0-7645-5580-4

- Freemasons For Dummies
  0-7645-9796-5
- French For Dummies
  0-7645-5193-0
- Geometry For Dummies
  0-7645-5324-0
- Organic Chemistry I For Dummies
  0-7645-6902-3
- The SAT I For Dummies
  0-7645-7193-1
- Spanish For Dummies
  0-7645-5194-9
- Statistics For Dummies
  0-7645-5423-9

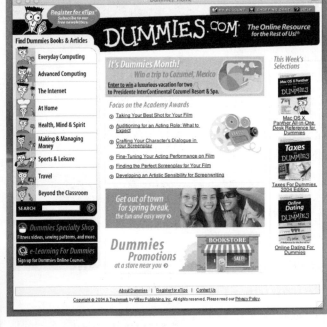

Get smart @ dummies.com®

- **Find a full list of Dummies titles**
- **Look into loads of FREE on-site articles**
- **Sign up for FREE eTips e-mailed to you weekly**
- **See what other products carry the Dummies name**
- **Shop directly from the Dummies bookstore**
- **Enter to win new prizes every month!**

* Separate Canadian edition also available
† Separate U.K. edition also available

Available wherever books are sold. For more information or to order direct: U.S. customers visit www.dummies.com or call 1-877-762-2974.
U.K. customers visit www.wileyeurope.com or call 0800 243407. Canadian customers visit www.wiley.ca or call 1-800-567-4797.

Do More with Dummies

Tickle my ribs!

Grilling FOR DUMMIES

Scrapbooking Basics FOR DUMMIES
12" x 12" kit

Quilting Notions FOR DUMMIES

Sewing Patterns FOR DUMMIES

Cocktail Kit FOR DUMMIES

Poker FOR DUMMIES

Golf FOR DUMMIES

Pilates Workout FOR DUMMIES

'80s Pop Music FOR DUMMIES

'70s Soul Music FOR DUMMIES

Wall & Ceiling Repair Kit FOR DUMMIES

Tarot Deck & Book Set FOR DUMMIES
Tarot for the Rest of Us!

Sudoku FOR DUMMIES The Game

Texas Hold 'em FOR DUMMIES
A Card Game for the Rest of Us!

Instructional DVDs • Music Compilations
Games & Novelties • Culinary Kits
Crafts & Sewing Patterns
Home Improvement/DIY Kits • and more!

Check out the Dummies Specialty Shop at www.dummies.com for more information!

WILEY